Pandemic culture

Manchester University Press

Pandemic culture

The impacts of COVID-19 on the UK cultural sector and implications for the future

Edited by

Abigail Gilmore, Dave O'Brien
and Ben Walmsley

MANCHESTER UNIVERSITY PRESS

Published by Manchester University Press
Oxford Road, Manchester, M13 9PL

www.manchesteruniversitypress.co.uk

British Library Cataloguing-in-Publication Data
A catalogue record for this book is available from the British
Library

ISBN 978 1 5261 6834 4 hardback
ISBN 978 1 5261 6835 1 paperback

First published 2024

Typeset by Newgen Publishing UK

Contents

Figures

Tables

Abbreviations

ACE	Arts Council England
ACN	Arts Collaboration Network
ACNI	Arts Council of Northern Ireland
AHRC	Arts and Humanities Research Council
BICS	Business Impact of COVID-19 Survey
CRF	Culture Recovery Fund
DCAL	Department for Culture, Arts and Leisure
DCMS	Department for Digital, Culture, Media and Sport
DfC	Department for Communities
ERF	Economic Resilience Fund
GM	Greater Manchester
GMCA	Greater Manchester Combined Authority
HETV	high-end TV
LFS	Labour Force Survey
MCC	Manchester City Council
MIF	Manchester International Festival
MIMA	Middlesbrough Institute of Modern Art
NI	Northern Ireland
NPOs	National Portfolio Organisations
NT	National Theatre
ONS	Office for National Statistics
PSB	Public Service Broadcaster
RFO	Regular Funded Organisation
SCPP	Salford Culture and Place Partnership
SCVO	Scottish Council for Voluntary Organisations
SEISS	Self-Employed Income Support Scheme
SG	Scottish Government

SMEs   Small and Medium Enterprises
UBI   Universal Basic Income
UKRI   UK Research and Innovation
WFH   Working from Home
WHO   World Health Organization

Contributors

Orian Brook is Chancellor's Fellow in Social Policy at the University of Edinburgh. She researches social and spatial inequalities, particularly in the creative economy, and has a special interest in the use of administrative and linked data. She has a PhD from the University of St Andrews, and previously worked as a researcher within the cultural sector.

Danielle Child is Senior Lecturer in Art History at Manchester Metropolitan University. Her research explores the relationship between contemporary art and capitalism through the lens of labour and work. Her book *Working Aesthetics: Labour, Art and Capitalism* was published in January 2019 with Bloomsbury Academic, and she is currently working, as editor, on *The Routledge Companion to Art and Capitalism*.

Ben Dunn is Lecturer in Performance and Creative Practice at the University of Leeds and co-principal editor of *Performing Ethos: International Journal of Ethics in Theatre and Performance*. Informed by a background as a performance practitioner in contemporary and applied settings, his research incorporates theatre, place and cultural policy, with a focus on the social and political dynamics of performance in social contexts.

Tal Feder is a post-doctoral fellow at the Faculty of Architecture and Town Planning at the Technion – Israel Institute of Technology. Prior to this, he was a post-doctoral fellow at Indiana University and the University of Sheffield. He is a sociologist with interests in cultural policy, sociology of art and culture, inequality, consumption and quantitative research methods. His current research studies cultural justice and cultural inequality from a spatial perspective.

Ali FitzGibbon is Senior Lecturer in Creative and Cultural Industries Management at Queen's University Belfast. She researches and publishes on decision-making, ethics, leadership and labour in contemporary cultural production. She has over twenty-five years' experience as a multi-arts producer, programmer and consultant. She continues to pursue collaborative, useful and practice-informed research and is regularly called upon as an advisor, particularly supporting arts and cultural policy bodies, festivals and working with cultural companies to develop strategies and change management.

Rebecca Florisson is Principal Analyst at the Work Foundation, at Lancaster University, where she leads the Insecure Work research programme. Alongside this, she is a part-time PhD candidate at Queen Mary, University of London, conducting an ESRC-funded study on the impact of precarious work during the early career on life course employment trajectories.

Abigail Gilmore is Senior Lecturer in Arts Management and Cultural Policy at the University of Manchester. Her research concerns cultural policy, participation and place, and she has published articles and books on local cultural policy, devolved industrial strategies and the municipal public park. She is an Affiliate of the AHRC Creative Industries Policy and Evidence Centre; she is also the lead for culture on the ESRC Strategic Coordination Hub for Local Policy Innovation Partnerships.

Karen Gray is a Senior Research Associate in the School for Policy Studies at the University of Bristol. Karen's research interests centre around the role played by arts and culture in society and the intersection there between policy and practice.

Sue Hayton is a creative industries professional with a career that spans visual and performing arts, publishing and heritage. Heading the Cultural Institute at the University of Leeds, Sue developed Leeds Creative Labs as a tool for collaboration between creative practitioners and academic researchers. She was Associate Director of Policy Engagement at the Centre for Cultural Value, at which she is now a consultant. Her interests include creative knowledge exchange, exploring the role of artists as researchers and as catalysts for innovation.

Rachel Johnson is Lecturer in Film Studies at the University of Leeds. She researches cultural institutions and transnational flows of culture, specialising in film festivals and policy-making. Rachel is also co-founder of the DIY film club Leeds Cineforum.

Jenny Kidd is Reader in the School of Journalism, Media and Culture at Cardiff University. She has published widely on new media, cultural institutions and digital heritage. She is a Managing Editor of *Museum and Society*, and a Series Editor for *Bloomsbury Studies in Digital Cultures*.

Trevor MacFarlane is Founding Director of Culture Commons, a policy design and advocacy organisation supporting the UK's creative and cultural ecosystem, and a Fellow of the Royal Society of Arts. Trevor is a former policy and political advisor to senior parliamentarians, including the Vice President of the Culture and Education Committee in the European Parliament, the Deputy Leader of the Labour Party (UK) and the Shadow Secretary of State for Digital, Culture, Media and Sport.

Oliver Mantell is Director of Evidence and Insight at The Audience Agency, where he has worked in a variety of audience research and consultancy roles since 2012. His areas of focus include audience analysis and segmentation, collaborative benchmarking and the national cultural behaviour and attitudes survey, the Cultural Participation Monitor.

Siobhan McAndrew is Senior Lecturer in Politics, Philosophy and Economics at Sheffield Methods Institute, University of Sheffield. Her research interests are in the quantitative study of culture, perceptions, moral values and pluralism. She is currently examining cultural and moral responses to crises, both historically and during the COVID-19 pandemic.

Eva Nieto McAvoy teaches and researches digital cultures and media at the School of Journalism, Media and Culture, Cardiff University. Recent work includes the 'pivot to digital' in museums and galleries during COVID-19 and algorithmic memory.

Dave O'Brien is Professor of Cultural and Creative Industries at the University of Manchester. He is the co-author of *Culture is Bad for You* and the *Creative Majority* report, as well as numerous papers on the creative sector. He is currently co-investigator on the AHRC-funded Creative Industries Policy and Evidence Centre, as well as working on projects about class in the television industry, diversifying creative higher education and taste in contemporary Britain.

Ania Ostrowska is a Research Manager at the British Film Institute, supporting its activities as an Independent Research Organisation, including building and maintaining partnerships with UK-based academics and universities and managing Collaborative Doctoral Awards. Building on her experience of researching British filmmakers (culminating in her doctoral thesis defended at the University of Southampton) and UK film and TV industries (working with Cardiff University and the Centre for Cultural Value at the University of Leeds, among others), she also helps commission and supervises external research projects into all aspects of British film, TV and gaming industries.

Gwilym Owen is a researcher who uses statistics and data to better understand the causes and consequences of social inequalities. He has particular interests in health, culture, environment and housing and has worked at the Universities of Liverpool, Sheffield and Bristol. He worked in the first few months of the COVID-19 project tracking trends in the numbers of workers in cultural and creative occupations with the UK Labour Force Survey.

Mark Taylor is Senior Lecturer in Quantitative Methods (Sociology) at the Sheffield Methods Institute, University of Sheffield. His research interests are in the sociology of culture: in consumption, production and education and its relationship to inequality, as well as in quantitative methods, particularly data visualisation. He leads research on the Arts, Culture and Heritage sectors for the Creative Industries Policy and Evidence Centre.

Anne Torreggiani is founding CEO of The Audience Agency – a UK charity for research and development in cultural participation – and Co-Director of the Centre for Cultural Value at the University of Leeds. She is a specialist in audience research, data and trends with particular interest in human-centred design and organisational change. She works as a facilitator and adviser.

Ben Walmsley is Dean of Cultural Engagement at the University of Leeds (UK) and Director of the national Centre for Cultural Value. He is an Expert Advisor for the UK Government's Department for Digital, Culture, Media and Sport (DCMS). Prior to his academic career, Ben worked as an arts manager for ten years, most recently as Producer at the National Theatre of Scotland. Ben has published widely on arts marketing, arts management, cultural policy and cultural value.

Harry Weeks is Lecturer and Head of Art History at Newcastle University. His research focuses on socially engaged art practices and labour and contemporary art. His work has been published in the *Third Text* journal, and he co-edited a special issue of this journal on art and anti-fascism in 2019.

John Wright is a research associate with the Centre for Cultural Value, University of Leeds. He has previously worked as a visiting lecturer at Leeds Arts University on the BA Fine Art programme and as a module leader on the MA Critical Studies programme at Bradford College. In his professional life before academia, he co-founded the artist-led collective The Retro Bar at the End of the Universe and developed a curatorial background in museums, galleries and in artist-led activity.

Preface

This book is part documentary, part analysis, part catharsis and part provocation. Back in 2020, when we began the research project that the book draws from, we were already aware of the likelihood that the UK's, and the world's, cultural and creative sectors would never be the same. This idea stayed with us, even when we observed their ongoing resilience and the agility of their responses to the pandemic's impact.

As we describe in the Introduction that follows, the motivation to assemble a team, devise a project methodology and undertake the research was instinctual and undertaken with sympathy. It was also done with empathy: as academic researchers who are also lecturers, tutors and supervisors, we were also physically divorced from our audiences and partners, our students and work colleagues. We were quickly learning to adapt to remote delivery and digital content creation to keep the business of higher education afloat. This gave the reflections of our research participants the quality of shared experiences and frustrations in common, as we met on our home office screens.

Our Introduction also reflects on the lack of time available for theorisation and critical reflection during the research. This was caused by the sheer pace and intensity of the pandemic; the nature of in-depth, mixed-method research undertaken with engaged partners and participants; and the desire for almost-real-time analysis. This jarred with the sense emerging from the sector that COVID-19 had unwittingly opened up a space for reflection, a potential strategic pause that might address issues and inequalities in creative and cultural production, participation and values.

This desire to regroup and reset was noted across the sector, even when the space to do so was limited. It was also an aim of our research project. We were able, through workshops, conferences and reference groups, to consider the broader implications of our findings for policy and investment models, sector strategy and operations. Yet it is through the process of writing that the analysis and synthesis of theory and empirical findings have been possible. We are grateful for the opportunity to undertake some of this critical thinking here in this volume.

Our research happened in a maelstrom during which we had to rely heavily on new and existing partnerships and collaborations. This large-scale consortium approach to research was new to many of us; but it was perhaps typical of much of the academic research and cultural activity that took place during the pandemic in its generous and highly collaborative nature. Just as we all hoped to see a better and more equitable cultural sector emerge from the pandemic, so do we hope that projects such as ours might herald a new era of more collaborative and engaged research, between academics themselves and between scholars and cultural organisations and practitioners.

Acknowledgements

There are so many people to thank for making this book possible that it is difficult to know where to begin. But without the agility and confidence of our funders, this research would simply not have taken place, so we would like to thank the Arts and Humanities Research Council (AHRC) and UK Research and Innovation (UKRI) for their generous funding of this research. We extend these thanks to the core funders of the Centre for Cultural Value (AHRC, Arts Council England and Paul Hamlyn Foundation) and our colleagues at the University of Leeds for their ongoing support for the Centre. We would also like to thank our Policy Reference Group and all those who participated in our Covid research conference in November 2021. Heartfelt thanks go to our dedicated Advisory Group, who provided expert support and guidance over the course of the project: Geoffrey Crossick, Alastair Evans, Sharon Heal, Sarie Mairs-Slee, Harman Sagger, Jose Seisdedos, Liz Thompson and Michelle Wright.

We are very grateful to those organisations who generously agreed to host one of our policy placements: Creative Scotland, Department for Communities (Northern Ireland), Department for Culture, Media and Sport (UK), Greater Manchester Combined Authority, Leeds City Council and the Welsh Government's Department for Culture, Heritage, Sport & Tourism. We benefitted hugely from the generosity and time of research partners Salford Culture and Place Partnership and Manchester City Council. Most importantly, we would like to thank all of our research participants who generously gave their time in what for many were very challenging personal and professional circumstances. Over the course of the project we interviewed over 238 cultural sector professionals, ranging from freelancers and general managers of micro-organisations to representatives of large regional and national cultural organisations, funders and policy-makers. Along the journey we interviewed employees from a wide range of cultural organisations, and we'd like to thank them for providing us with such a privileged insight into their worlds as they shifted over the course of the pandemic in 2020–2021.

We would personally like to thank our project partners – The Audience Agency, the Creative Industries Policy and Evidence Centre, and Culture Commons, as well as the core team at the Centre for Cultural Value (Tamsin Curror, Liz Harrop and Alex Lancastle) and all of our colleagues in the wider project team (Maria Barrett, Bruce Davenport, John Davies, Rachel Johnson, Fanny Martin, Tammi Murphy, Alice Nightingale, Ceri Pitches, Bethany Rowley and Richard Turpin), many of whom worked above and beyond their allocated hours to produce what we believe to be one of the most meticulous and comprehensive studies of the impact of COVID-19 on the cultural sector that has been undertaken anywhere in the world. This book is testament to their diligent and sensitive work and also to the dedication of everyone who has kept the cultural sector alive during its darkest hours.

Introduction: framing mixed-methods analyses of the impact of COVID-19 on the cultural sector

Ben Walmsley, Abigail Gilmore and Dave O'Brien

Reflections on the impact of the COVID-19 pandemic on the arts, cultural and creative sectors have been ongoing since the implications of public health and safety restrictions and impositions of lockdowns emerged globally in the first quarter of 2020. Arts audiences, creative producers and culture scholars alike have observed the particular shifts and 'pivots' required to sustain the mixed economies and often precarious business models of activities that rely on physical co-presence, state intervention and freedom of movement to survive. As the months, and now years, have passed, the shock and scale of these impacts and the calls from the cultural sector advocating for a 'new normal' have subsided, despite the fact that the memories of this extraordinary period, the sector-specific stresses and the wider societal trauma it caused, continue.

In the UK, the mobilisation of government funds targeted at the arts and cultural industries, many of which were already in receipt of grant funding, prevented a far more significant erosion of artists, creative workers and cultural managers' livelihoods than would have been the case without intervention. Organisational strategies were put on pause, however, as audiences and performers were locked out bar digital participation, with many taking the time to reflect on social missions and visions, while constantly rescoping programming and budget lines as conditions frequently changed. The motivation to document these turbulent times through empirical research, and to consider through analysis potential pathways to resilience and recovery for cultural organisations and those who work in and with them, was therefore obvious. This book is an outcome of such a motivation, one of a number of outputs from the eighteen-month UKRI-funded research that took place in England, Scotland, Northern Ireland and Wales between September 2020 and November 2021.[1]

This introductory chapter sets out the rationale and context for this wide-ranging research. It outlines its aims and objectives, describing and justifying the mixed-methods methodology and the sampling mechanisms deployed by the research and outlining the areas of synergy between the different strands of the study so as to draw out common objectives and themes between the chapters that follow. Its core aim, therefore, is to set the scene for the rest of the book. It does this by providing a brief analysis of the structural challenges and issues facing the UK's cultural industries prior to the pandemic that hampered the cultural sector and became exacerbated as the COVID-19 pandemic hit and progressed. The chapter goes on to contextualise and introduce the forthcoming chapters and offer readers a narrative arc to guide them through the book.

Study context and aims

This book presents findings from one of the most comprehensive studies of the impacts of COVID-19 on the cultural sector undertaken anywhere in the world. This national research project was led by the Centre for Cultural Value and conducted by twenty-four researchers from twelve research institutions and four national partners: the Centre for Cultural Value, The Audience Agency, the AHRC Creative Industries Policy and Evidence Centre, and Culture Commons. This consortium approach meant that the study benefitted from policy and artform experts embedded in different nations and regions of the UK. Those experts represented universities, research centres, cultural agencies and consultants. The study brought together statisticians, quantitative sociologists, art historians and audience researchers with interdisciplinary scholars from the fields of media studies, performance studies, arts management and cultural policy studies.

Based on the findings of this extensive research project, this book offers a comprehensive overview of the impacts of COVID-19 on the UK's cultural sector and highlights the implications for the sector's future direction. Over the course of eleven chapters, the book provides a summary of the local, regional and national policy responses to the crisis; a statistical analysis of the impacts of these policy responses and of the pandemic itself on the UK's cultural workforce; and a mixed-methods analysis of audiences' responses to the pandemic. These insights are nuanced and illustrated via detailed case studies of a number of key sub-sectors of the cultural industries (theatre, museums and galleries, screen industries, libraries and festivals), via interviews with emerging cultural leaders and via taking an ecosystem approach to the case study of the Greater Manchester city region.

The book identifies the core, recurrent themes that have emerged from the research. It offers a robust analysis of the short, medium and longer-term impacts of COVID-19 on the cultural sector and its audiences, and highlights the implications for cultural practitioners, organisations, funders and policy-makers as we continue to move into the endemic stage of the pandemic. The unique contribution of the book lies in its presentation of research findings coordinated to highlight the challenges faced by cultural practitioners, organisations and audiences from different backgrounds, regions and art forms. Using lenses which focus on both macro and micro levels, the book provides fresh insights into the implications for policy and research on, with and around the cultural sector, highlighting possible future directions for arts management, audience research and cultural policy studies.

The pandemic has impacted the creative and cultural industries more globally and traumatically than any other crisis in living memory (Sargent, 2021). It has wrought a seismic shock across the arts and cultural sector in particular. But as Sargent also argues, 'as always, amongst the loss and damage there has been invaluable learning of new kinds of thinking, new ways of doing things. We need to identify all those new learnings around the world, then build on those new foundations rather than just reassembling the broken pieces from the past' (Sargent, 2021). It is in this spirit of fostering positive change that we have researched and written this book.

The research presented in the book is based on the following strands of activity:

1. Policy analysis: review of fiscal and strategic support and relief interventions across the UK at local, regional and national levels, supported by an international review of policy measures related to social security for cultural practitioners.
2. Workforce analysis: scoping, synthesising and appraising existing and emerging data – bringing together a fragmented approach through a meta-analysis to understand the impacts of COVID-19 on the cultural workforce.
3. Organisational analysis: case studies of different cohorts and sub-sectors providing a detailed exploration of the impacts on specific organisations and practitioners and analysis of representative case studies drawn from the following sub-sectors: theatre in England, museums and galleries in northern England, festivals in Scotland, media and screen industries in Wales, and emerging cultural leaders in Northern Ireland.
4. Audience research: longitudinal tracking study of cultural consumption and attitudes towards cultural engagement over the course of the pandemic.
5. Social media analysis: quantitative analysis of 9,000 tweets and qualitative analysis of 450 tweets under the Twitter hashtags #CultureInQuarantine and #MuseumAtHome to explore how cultural organisations and audiences engaged and interacted on social media.
6. Ecosystem analysis of Greater Manchester: place-based research with key stakeholders in the city region including local government and regional authority policy actors, cultural freelancers and organisations, and emerging cultural practitioners.
7. Policy engagement: meetings, discussions, interviews, presentations and placements with funders and policy-makers, including the four UK arts councils and governmental teams with responsibility for culture.

The strands of activity were designed to address the following research questions:

1. What were the short, medium and longer-term impacts of COVID-19 across different sub-sectors of the UK's cultural industries?
2. To what extent did the COVID-19 crisis perpetuate, exacerbate or temper existing inequalities relating to cultural production and consumption? How will this change how the cultural

industries engage with audiences in the short, medium and longer term?

3. How and to what extent has cultural consumption and consumer behaviour changed in the short, medium and longer term as a result of social distancing measures and the closure of cultural spaces?

4. What were the drivers and effects of the immediate policy responses to mitigate the impact of COVID-19 crisis on the cultural industries? How will the crisis impact policy-making as the sector emerges from the pandemic? What are the implications of COVID-19 for future cultural policy-making and the broader creative economy?

Research context

To situate the findings of the research in a meaningful context, here we note briefly the underlying structural conditions that characterised the cultural sector prior to the pandemic. The impacts of the pandemic did not occur in a vacuum: many were prefigured by the policy and management contexts that, to some extent, determined them. For example, a poor understanding of the complex ecosystem within which the sector operates and scant knowledge of the relationships between different parts of cultural production from a ground-up perspective meant that decisions regarding how to best target relief funding were initially delayed. These delays added to the sector's existing uncertainty when the pandemic hit and exacerbated the impact on less protected cultural workers.

When we developed our research questions and design, we were almost certain that the existing inequalities that have long characterised the cultural sector would only magnify the impacts of the pandemic on the sector. These inequalities include the extractive overreliance on freelance workers engaged on precarious contracts and an evident lack of diversity among cultural workers.

Cultural policy scholars (e.g. Brook, O'Brien and Taylor, 2018, 2020) were highlighting these problems to government in the UK even before the pandemic hit, for example through parliamentary groups such as the Creative Diversity All Party Parliamentary Group (APPG). In this sense, the sector went into the pandemic in a poor state of readiness and with its eyes tightly shut. This situation was exacerbated by outmoded and highly risky business models.

These structures sat alongside deeply flawed interpretations of personal and organisational 'resilience', which extolled earned income, corporate sponsorship and private giving over peer collaboration and the public good (O'Connor, 2020). To make matters worse, and highly significantly in the context of the COVID-19 pandemic, the cultural workforce suffered from long-standing underinvestment and skills gaps in HR and digital production and distribution. Thus, the pandemic acted as a long-overdue wake-up call for the sector and its funders to get their house in order.

The supply side was not the only problem. Pre-pandemic, report after report, study after study, for example the influential Warwick Commission Report (Neelands *et al.*, 2015; Taylor, 2016), evidenced the stark lack of representation of all socio-economic groups and forms of cultural diversity within audiences for the arts in the UK, calling for urgent change. Decades of generally well-intentioned and expensive so-called 'audience development' initiatives and related policy interventions had seemingly failed to diversify who engaged with publicly funded arts and culture and to address pressing notions such as the deficit treatment of everyday participation and cultural value (Miles and Gibson, 2016), cultural democracy (Hadley, 2021), and the politics of participation and 'non-participation' in culture (Stevenson, 2019).

At the same time, relationships between cultural organisations and audiences were becoming increasingly superficial and transactional within policy and practice, hampered by an overreliance of product-led marketing and a poor understanding of evolving modes of engagement (Walmsley, 2019). Beyond the walls of cultural institutions, the sector suffered from a patchy and arguably disingenuous approach to civic engagement, driven by outcomes-led funding which often brought its core purpose and social relevance into question. These issues inevitably arise in each chapter of the book. We return to them in a more summative and future-focused way in the final chapter, where we highlight the myriad implications for policy, for the cultural sector and for research.

Methodology

Given the immediacy of the context, the research project was inevitably both highly empirical and reactive in nature. Designed over an intense period at the start of the pandemic, it responded to a specific urgent call from UK Research and Innovation (UKRI) to investigate the phenomenon of COVID-19 across society. As such and given that the research context we found ourselves in was unprecedented, there was limited time to embark on an extensive literature review (there was of course in any case very little literature published on culture in a pandemic).

Over the course of the project, cultural funders and policy-makers urged us to share our findings in real time so that they could react and respond as quickly as possible. This was not a usual or comfortable place to find ourselves in as academic researchers: the pandemic certainly opened doors with policy-makers and forced academics to work at a different pace. While this made us feel vulnerable and exposed at times, it also provided momentum and the impetus to identify the most pertinent research questions that would engage as many relevant stakeholders as possible in the limited time we had.

Informed by the structural issues facing the sector, our core research question was to explore the extent to which the pandemic might replicate, exacerbate or perhaps even temper existing inequalities in the cultural sector. We hypothesised that, like most crises, COVID-19 would highlight existing problems and speed up changes and evolutions that were already taking place, such as the digital distribution of creative content, for example. Although the focus of this study was not theoretical, the time between the end of the empirical research and the drafting of the book has enabled us to reflect on our findings and to situate and theorise them within the context in which they unfolded. Hindsight has also enabled us to reflect on the broader implications of what occurred in the sector for the fields of arts management and cultural policy studies. In particular, there are important lessons for the future of collaborative and engaged research within these disciplines.

The twenty-four researchers who contributed to this study collectively formed a cohesive multidisciplinary team that provided expertise in a rare and rich mix of complementary research methods, including statistical analysis, social media analysis, ecosystem analysis, case studies, population surveys, semi-structured depth interviews, and policy analysis and engagement. Early on in the research design process we decided to deploy a mixed-methods approach to properly evaluate the variety of impacts of the pandemic on the cultural sector. This approach also enabled us to capture the strategic and emotional implications for cultural work-ers and audiences dealing with the crisis on a daily basis in both qualitative and quantitative detail and from macro and micro perspectives. However, other methodological considerations also needed to be addressed. The most prominent of these was the need and determination to capture the impacts of the pandemic across the UK from a representative range of different art forms and sub-sectors of the cultural industries, and to represent a diverse range of sector voices and organisations.

Difficult choices had to be made with regard to the sampling of art forms and sub-sectors. In order to narrow the parameters of the research to make it as cohesive and feasible as possible, we decided to focus on the arts and cultural industries rather than the broader crea-tive industries. Some of our statistical analysis does include compari-son with sectors such as advertising, architecture, publishing and IT, but the core of the analysis is focused on the arts and cultural sector.

We hypothesised that the impacts of the pandemic would be more comparable across the cultural sector than across the creative indus-tries, given that some of the latter, notably IT software and computer services, may have benefitted from the explosion of online activity and thus fare in a fundamentally different way from sub-sectors largely reliant on live audiences. We were also aware that resources would not allow for qualitative work with every sub-sector of the cultural industries and that sectors such as live music were being studied else-where. In the end we opted for four of the largest sub-sectors: festi-vals; media and screen; museums and galleries; and theatre.

In the flurry of sector concern as the impact of the pandemic unfolded, a proliferation of surveys circulated in the spring and summer of 2020 with the aim of establishing priorities for action and mitigation. Many of these were poorly designed and sampled, producing at best a very fragmented and at worst a wholly invalid set of results. The importance of accessing comprehensive, stand-ardised and robust data on the impact on creative and cultural work was clear and pressing. As a result, we prioritised analysis of the Office for National Statistics' Labour Force Survey, representa-tive of the UK workforce, to investigate the impacts on the cultural sector's workforce and its different sub-sectors. The findings of this analysis are provided in Chapter 2.

We were also aware that most of the emerging studies of cultural consumption focused on existing audiences, and hence were failing to capture how the population at large was engaging with and thinking about culture during the pandemic. In light of recent policy interventions to develop and diversify audiences, we were particularly interested to explore whether the 'pivot' to digital culture might attract new cultural audiences and even democratise cultural consumption. We therefore opted for a large-scale population survey and contracted The Audience Agency to deliver the Cultural Participation Monitor. This was delivered in six waves across 2020–2022 with samples of up to 6,057 UK residents.[2] An analysis of the findings and a full discussion of their implications is offered in Chapter 3.

To understand how the pandemic impacted psychologically on cultural workers and in order to fully appreciate the implications for organisations and their respective art forms or sub-sectors, we undertook a large series of professional or 'expert' interviews. Our interviews were modelled to elicit guided introspection from participants (Wallendorf and Brucks, 1993) to produce the kind of context-dependent analysis (Rubin and Rubin, 2005) and thick description (cf. Geertz, 1973) that we knew we needed to capture the nuances of cultural workers' lived experiences of the pandemic. In total we conducted 238 semi-structured depth interviews of forty-five to sixty minutes with a diverse sample of cultural sector professionals ranging from freelance technicians to CEOs of national companies. Our organisational interviews were sampled to account for size, scale, model and location. For example, in our study of theatre organisations in England, we interviewed staff from small touring companies, a range of regional venues and the National Theatre. For each of our four sub-sectors we developed a series of organisational case studies which are presented and discussed below in their respective chapters. Case study analysis is a tried-and-tested method for retaining a 'holistic and real-world perspective' (Yin, 2018, p.5), especially, as in our study, when the focus is on a contemporary phenomenon within a real-life context (Yin, 2018, p.15). The case studies offer readers a holistic view of how the pandemic looked and felt within very different types of cultural organisation.

One particular aspect of organisational activity that we were particularly keen to explore was how organisations engaged and interacted with their audiences and communities on social media. Social media generates an abundance of what Zappavigna (2011) refers to as the 'searchable talk' of social networks. Analysis of such public discourse can enable more dynamic and meaningful forms of cultural participation and foster a more productive relational and ethical trajectory for the institutions which engage with it (Kidd, Nieto McAvoy and Ostrowska, 2022). Our study involved analysing data collected from Twitter from the hashtags #CultureInQuarantine and #MuseumAtHome during the first six weeks of the UK lockdown (March–April 2020). These two hashtags were used by museums and galleries during this timeframe as key connective devices and produced 9,000 tweets which were analysed quantitatively by the team using Twitter's metadata to draw out recurrent themes, before a random 5 per cent sample of 450 tweets was qualitatively analysed using NVivo. The emerging sentiments and themes shed light on how audiences were using culture to navigate the pandemic, as is presented alongside the population study in Chapter 3.

In addition to the imperative to engage with sector policy-makers and the potential to inform their critical interventions through empirical data and analysis, the study offered a unique view of how the activities of the cultural sector are valued, protected, promoted and regulated by cultural policy. The pandemic presented an opportunity to understand the sector's perceived value to policy in the unprecedented context of its survival, acting almost like a contingent valuation exercise, where a proxy of the value of public good can be derived from the costs of saving and sustaining it. We therefore knew we needed channels with which to consult with policy-makers as well as to undertake research with and on them, and to this end we formed a policy reference group and worked closely with local and national policy bodies, including the Department for Culture, Media and Sport (DCMS), Creative Scotland, culture officers from the Welsh Government and Northern Ireland's Department for Communities, and representatives from local councils including Leeds and Salford. The group met three times and further engagement opportunities were also provided by regular workshops with DCMS, providing the chance for dialogue and reflective practice, and a series of policy placements at regional and national level towards the end of the study, which embedded researchers within various policy contexts. A narrative account of the timeline and evolution of policy responses over 2020 and 2021 comparing the devolved nations of the UK is presented in Chapter 1.

The research was augmented by the inclusion of a case study of Greater Manchester's cultural ecosystem, which began in November 2020, working in consultation with Greater Manchester Combined Authority, Manchester City Council and Salford Culture and Place Partnership to develop a programme of interviews and action research with policy actors, cultural leaders, and practitioners across the city region in the north-west of England. The resulting two waves of qualitative interviews (fifty in total) provided unique insights from a creative and cultural ecosystems perspective, which offered a lens on the intersection of local networks, initiatives and strategic priorities with the efficacy (or otherwise) of national policy responses.

Creative and cultural ecosystems analysis recognises the complex and interconnected matrix of actors involved within creative and cultural ecologies to consider relationships between different nodes of networks, made up of individual actors and institutions (Barker, 2019). The term's appearance in UK policy discourse is concurrent with John Holden's promotion of 'cultural ecology' as a model for the 'intensively interlinked' (Arts and Humanities Research Council, 2015, p.2), cyclical, generative characteristics of cultural and creative production. It aims to avoid a linear production chain model that focuses solely on connections between inputs and outputs, distinguishing between values-driven policy approaches and those that seek to generate values as an outcome. In this way, it encompasses a spectrum of interdependent qualities across and between public and private spheres, formal and informal strategy, and amateur and professional practice. Although not bound to geography, ecosystems approaches provide useful frameworks for local cultural policy analysis. They make visible the processes through which capitals are mobilised, taken up and generated across networks and relationships. By doing so, they show that places are not simply sites that policies affect, but rather that places have their own effects on policies as situated practices (Durrer, Gilmore and Stevenson, 2019), which require the negotiation of boundaries and capabilities that are attached to place (Gross and Wilson, 2020). We discuss key findings from the cultural ecosystem case study in Chapter 9.

The ethical context

Planning this significant body of engaged research in the context of a global health pandemic inevitably raised significant ethical issues that the research team had to address and navigate. The most obvious of these, perhaps, was the risk of causing further psychological harm to cultural practitioners by asking them to reflect in online, depersonalised interviews on what had clearly been traumatic lived experiences. Although informed consent was always secured well in advance and interviews were conducted with the utmost sensitivity by sector specialists, our approach at times felt extractive and some participants understandably broke down in the course of their interviews. The experience of conducting interviews was deeply humbling, and although mitigation of ethical issues also extended to the researchers themselves, who occasionally found themselves in the role of the quasi therapist, overall the interviewers felt a heightened sense of privilege to bear witness first-hand to participants' personal journeys through the pandemic.

As a research team we shared a sense of responsibility to tell our interviewees' stories accurately and authentically, and to capture the reality of their lived experiences in a way that might eventually effect positive change. We can only hope that we have achieved this; but ultimately, the only valid judges of this will be them as participants in our research and you as readers of this book.

Structure and overview of the book

The structure of the book is intended to let the research findings breathe a little and to offer a tailored route for individual reader interests through the different chapters, which are organised by work strand or art form/sub-sector.[3] The exceptions to this are this introductory chapter, and the final chapter, where we summarise the core findings and highlight the implications for future research, policy development and cultural sector practice as we emerge from the pandemic.

Chapter 1 traces the key developments in cultural policy across the four UK nations since the start of the COVID-19 pandemic. It provides an overview of policy responses and interventions at regional and national levels, charting the national policy landscape over the timescale of the pandemic and highlighting the implications for cultural sector recovery. The chapter draws on desk-based policy analysis at a national and regional level, consultation with key policy stakeholders, and interviews with policy-makers, cultural workers and freelancers representing perspectives from music, museums, festivals and theatre across the four UK nations. It finds that while there are commonalities between their national government responses, even as the turmoil and changing conditions of the pandemic disrupted the ordinary process of policy decision-making, there were also differences guided by the distinctive organising logics or 'policy assemblages' (Prince, 2010).

Chapter 2 explores the cultural sector through the lens of longer-term trends in the workforce, primarily focused on the long-standing and structural inequalities characteristic of culture in the UK. The chapter shows the impact of lockdown, and the subsequent attempts to arrest the spread of the virus, on differing parts of the cultural industries, noting the distinct patterns in publishing, film and television and the performing arts. The analysis reveals how each sub-sector experienced different consequences, for example increased demand for working from home in publishing compared to significant losses of employment in the performing arts, with different dilemmas for the organisations, businesses and workers who constitute these sectors.

Chapter 3 investigates how audiences and the wider UK population have engaged with cultural content during the pandemic, in both live and digital spaces. It presents, contextualises and discusses the findings of the Cultural Participation Monitor, a bespoke longitudinal tracking survey of the UK population that analyses changing digital engagement habits and attitudes towards re-engagement in live events. The chapter also offers an analysis of Twitter data shared across two hashtags, #CultureInQuarantine and #MuseumAtHome, in order to explore the parameters of engagement between cultural institutions and members of the public over the pandemic. It explores the popularity of content through a thematic lens, as well as by tone, before exploring how the sample connects with other debates at the time. This research is significant because it reveals what seemed to work, and what worked less well, as strategies for engagement during the pandemic. It tells a story about the kinds of content and interaction users found valuable and unpacks how we can understand and articulate that value during a time of crisis. It also suggests how cultural interaction may have shifted during the pandemic in ways that could be meaningful in the longer term if institutions have the capacity to build on those developments. The chapter concludes by assessing longer-term trends in audience behaviour and engagement and by exploring the implications of these trends for artists, cultural organisations, funders and policy-makers.

Chapter 4 investigates how England's theatre sector fared over the course of the pandemic. During the COVID-19 crisis, the sector was forced into making and accelerating changes to the strategies and modes it uses to make work and to engage with its audiences. This unsurprisingly involved a strong focus on digital distribution and adaptation, which, alongside the enforced and repeated closure of buildings, challenged organisations of all scales to make radical decisions about their business models and to tackle issues of productivity, quality, capacity and skills that will have significant implications for policy, management and training.

Lockdown experiences of making and consuming theatre have raised important questions around the role of physical spaces, of shared or synchronous experience and definitions of authenticity, and regarding audience perceptions of the relative value of digital and live performance. They have drawn closer attention to inequalities of access of all kinds. Some organisations have 'leant into' their learning and participation functions with the aim of maintaining and sometimes deepening audience relationships that otherwise may have been fractured during the crisis. This activity reflects the intensified attention that has been paid towards the social and civic role of theatre. Chapter 4 examines this evolution, highlighting some of the convergences and divergences within the theatre sector and between it and other cultural sectors. In so doing, it builds on research engaging with the concept of cultural value and the public role of arts and culture, and with the 'relational turn' in audience engagement (Walmsley, 2019).

Chapter 5 traces the impact of COVID-19 on cultural festivals in Scotland. It is based primarily on a series of interviews and conversations carried out in 2020 and 2021 with festival producers, directors and organisers. The chapter presents findings that illuminate the different responses that festivals implemented during the pandemic from moving to hybrid models of live and digital content to fundraising for local foodbanks. These shifts in working practices have fundamentally brought into question the role of festivals within their communities and this chapter considers how digital and hybridised programming, performing and gathering have changed festivals' approaches to future planning, strategy and audience engagement.

Chapter 6 traces the impact of COVID-19 on arts and cultural activity in Northern Ireland through the lens of emerging and collaborative approaches to leadership. It draws principally from a series of practitioner interviews and discussions carried out in 2020 and 2021, combining the knowledge of a range of organisational leaders with that of creative freelancers and policy-makers. The authors examine the role and nature of what constitutes leadership within the Northern Irish cultural economy. Although exacerbated by the crisis, the tensions of how cultural leadership is recognised and defined pre-date the pandemic and are intrinsically linked to concerns of representation and consideration in regional, national and subnational policy structures and within the systems of arts and cultural practices. By pointing to where leadership has emerged in new or more strident forms, the chapter equally points to where it has been absent, excluded or ignored. Through analysing these emergent forms of collaborative leadership, the authors suggest ways in which these practices could shape the future direction of cultural policy-making in Northern Ireland.

Chapter 7 investigates the effect that the pandemic, lockdown and the subsequent support measures had on the screen sector in Wales. It does so by focusing on the challenges facing the workforce, including the impact of COVID-19 on people's working practices, financial situations and mental health. The chapter also analyses different organisational approaches to lockdown, the emergency funding made available to film and TV professionals in Wales, and the emerging signs of polarisation in the sector.

Chapter 8 builds on and contributes fresh empirical research to the existing discourse on cultural value by examining the heightened civic responsibility identified in arts institutions in the north-east and north-west of England in response to the pandemic. The north of England was hit particularly hard by the pandemic, experiencing extended lockdowns and high-tier restrictions. From interviews with over thirty gallery, museum and arts workers in these regions, including freelancers and artist-led organisations, the authors identify an increase in community engagement and outreach from galleries and museums in the north of England during periods of lockdown. The chapter examines the community engagement and outreach activities provided by these institutions and asks: How do galleries and museums provide support during unprecedented times? Whom do galleries and museums serve? Who benefits from this provision, and can it be sustained in the long term? What are the implications for the workforce, management and business models of galleries and museums? How do these practices inform new narratives of 'levelling up' and post-pandemic recovery within areas already highlighted for investment? In responding to these fundamental questions about the civic responsibility of arts institutions in times of crisis, the chapter undertakes a close analysis of three case studies. These include a large gallery, a group of museums and a small interdisciplinary arts organisation, all based in the north of England.

Chapter 9 considers the impact of COVID-19 on the arts and cultural industries from a place-based perspective, focusing on a specific geography, the city region of Greater Manchester, and the social and political relationships that comprise its cultural ecology and policy infrastructure. Following a cultural ecosystems approach, which recognises the complex and interconnected matrix of actors involved within creative and cultural ecologies, the authors explore how the pandemic has affected the delivery of local cultural strategies within the first devolved English city region, and how national policy responses, such as Culture Recovery Funds, have been received and operationalised locally.

The chapter focuses on three intersections of policy, culture and place to interrogate further the political, socio-economic, spatial and locational dimensions that underpin the response and recovery plans of local governance. These 'mini case studies' concern: (a) models of cultural leadership and coordination within the local sector to support freelancers; (b) policy-led responses to support creativity within social care and voluntary settings, through creative care kits; and (c) site-specific cultural recovery planning and cultural programming, including the development of Creative Improvement Districts in Greater Manchester district towns.

The concluding chapter draws together the core themes emerging from the analyses presented in the previous chapters. It offers a critical overview of emerging findings; highlights notable areas of synergy and divergence between different sectors, art forms, sizes, scales and locations of cultural organisation; and identifies the implications for cultural management and policy. Reflecting on the broader socio-political context, the chapter reviews the global context of the pandemic and discusses the extent to which the UK context and experience might be said to be exceptional. It investigates aspects of divergence and convergence between different art forms and how these relate to instances of continuity and change, for example by highlighting the continuity of inequality in the sector and noting that the pandemic has not changed the seemingly entrenched economic rationalism of cultural policy.

The final chapter also reflects back on the key findings of the research, including the sector's pivot to civic engagement and digital distribution, and draws out the implications of such phenomena for policy, management and future research – not least for cultural data and leadership. Finally, it discusses how the sector might become more relevant, representative, equitable and 'regenerative' (Walmsley *et al.*, 2022).

Notes

1 COVID-19: Impacts on the cultural industries and implications for policy (Reference AH/V00994X/1).

2 The Audience Agency received additional funding to enable it to continue the survey beyond the lifetime of our funded research.

3 Readers who would also like a chronological summary overview of the research might like to read the *Culture in Crisis* report (Walmsley *et al.*, 2022), available at: www.culturehive.co.uk/CVIresources/culture-in-crisis-impacts-of-covid-19/

References

Arts and Humanities Research Council. 2015. *The ecology of culture.* Swindon: Arts and Humanities Research Council.

Barker, V. 2019. The democratic development potential of a cultural ecosystem approach. *Journal of Law, Social Justice and Global Development* (Special Issue: Democracy, Development and Culture, eds. John Clammer and Jonathan Vickery). 24, pp.86–99. https://doi.org/10.31273/LGD.2019.2405

Brook, O., O'Brien, D. and Taylor, M. 2018. *Panic! Social class, taste and inequalities in the creative industries.* London: Create London.

Brook, O., O'Brien, D. and Taylor, M. 2020. *Culture is bad for you: inequality in the cultural and creative industries.* Manchester: Manchester University Press.

Durrer, V., Gilmore, A. and Stevenson, D. 2019. Arts councils, policy-making and 'the local'. *Cultural Trends.* 28(4), pp.317–331.

Geertz, C. 1973. *The interpretation of cultures: selected essays.* New York: Basic Books.

Gross, J. and Wilson, N. 2020. Cultural democracy: an ecological and capabilities approach. *International Journal of Cultural Policy.* 26(3), pp.328–343.

Hadley, S. 2021. *Audience development and cultural policy.* London: Palgrave Macmillan.

Kidd, J., Nieto McAvoy, E. and Ostrowska, A. 2022. Negotiating hybridity, inequality, and hyper-visibility: museums and galleries' social media response to the COVID-19 pandemic. *Cultural Trends.* https://doi.org/10.1080/09548963.2022.2122701

Miles, A. and Gibson, L. 2016. Everyday participation and cultural value. *Cultural Trends.* 25(3), pp.151–157.

Neelands, J., Belfiore, E., Firth, C. and Hart, N. 2015. *Enriching Britain: culture, creativity and growth* (report of the Warwick Commission on the Future of Cultural Value). Coventry: University of Warwick.

O'Connor, J. 2020. Art and culture after Covid-19. 9 April. Wake in Fright. [Online]. [Accessed 27 January 2023]. Available from: https://wakeinalarm.blog/2020/04/09/art-and-culture-after-covid-19/

Prince, R. 2010. Policy transfer as policy assemblage: making policy for the creative industries in New Zealand. *Environment and Planning A: Economy and Space.* 42(1), pp.169–186.

Rubin, H.J. and Rubin, I. 2005. *Qualitative interviewing: the art of hearing data.* London: Sage.

Sargent, A. 2021. *COVID-19 and the global cultural and creative sector: what have we learned so far?* Leeds: Centre for Cultural Value.

Stevenson, D. 2019. The cultural non-participant: critical logics and discursive subject identities. *Arts and the Market.* 9(1), pp.50–64.

Taylor, M. 2016. Nonparticipation or different styles of participation? Alternative interpretations from Taking Part. *Cultural Trends*. 25(3), pp.169–181.

Wallendorf, M. and Brucks, M. 1993. Introspection in consumer research: implementation and implications. *Journal of Consumer Research*. 20(3), pp.339–359.

Walmsley, B. 2019. *Audience engagement in the performing arts: a critical analysis*. London: Palgrave Macmillan.

Walmsley, B., Gilmore, A., O'Brien, D. and Torreggiani, A. (eds.). 2022. *Culture in crisis: impacts of Covid-19 on the UK cultural sector and where we go from here*. Leeds: Centre for Cultural Value.

Yin, R. 2018. *Case study research: design and methods*. 6th ed. London: Sage.

Zappavigna, M. 2011. Ambient affiliation: a linguistic perspective on Twitter. *New Media & Society*. 13, pp.788–806.

1

Cultural policy and the pandemic: response and recovery in the United Kingdom

Abigail Gilmore, Sue Hayton, Trevor MacFarlane,
John Wright, Ben Dunn and Rachel Johnson

Introduction

This chapter explores the efforts to mitigate the impact and effects of the coronavirus pandemic on the cultural sector in the UK, using a narrative account of policy responses by the national governments and associated arm's-length bodies within the UK. We consider these responses in relation to two propositions: firstly, that they act as evidence of the values and significance attached to the functions of creative and cultural production in society, and the role of the nation-state within these dynamics. Secondly, they provide an indication of the distinctive relations which are informed by the networks of policy actors within and between different regional geographies in the UK's overlapping cultural policy territories. The structure of this chapter is as follows. Firstly, we present a timeline of the main phases of government intervention and recovery funding in the UK, before presenting narrative accounts of key similarities and differences between the four nations of Scotland, Wales, Northern Ireland and England. We finish by considering the implications of these accounts for the values and rationales for future cultural policy.

With increasing distance from the pandemic, it is easy to assume a smooth journey through the policy landscape, from venue closure and lockdown to emergency funding and recovery plans. However, the reality between March 2020 and the end of 2021 across the four UK nations was a divergence of approaches, mixed messages and measures, with delayed and contradictory announcements.

This made decisions for organisations, as well as individual artists and creative practitioners, incredibly challenging. It also discouraged some audience groups from returning to in-person participation (Audience Agency, 2021). To simplify the chronology, we set out three main phases of emergency and mitigation measures below and in Tables 1.1, 1.2 and 1.3 with examples of cross-regional interventions designed to support the creative and cultural sectors.

Phase One: locking down

The World Health Organization (WHO) declared a pandemic on 11 March 2020. On 16 March the UK Prime Minister advised against all non-essential travel, urging the population to avoid gatherings and crowded places, such as pubs, clubs and theatres but did not announce any policy support for affected sectors (Prime Minister's Office, 2020). By 23 March 2020, the UK Government announced the first formal lockdown, outlawing all social and public gatherings, restricting non-emergency travel and closing schools and other educational establishments with instructions to work from home where possible. This initial three-week lockdown was extended for a further three weeks in April 2020, when the UK Government also announced a series of unprecedented economy-wide financial support packages, including the Coronavirus Business Interruption Loan Scheme, the Coronavirus Job Retention Scheme ('furlough') and the Self-Employed Income Support Scheme (SEISS). In July 2020, a temporary cut in value added tax (VAT) rates (Cabinet Office, 2020) was subsequently replaced with a 12.5 per cent rate from September 2021 through to March 2022 (Seely, 2022). Each UK nation introduced a business rates relief scheme which gave additional support to retail, hospitality and leisure businesses; in England, these businesses received a discretionary 100 per cent rates holiday for the duration of the 2020–2021 tax year (HM Revenue and Customs, 2021). However, as discussed in Chapter 2, many freelance, self-employed workers were left unable to access state support. Meanwhile, the response of the national grant-giving and arm's-length bodies was to quickly reprofile funding streams to target artists organisations, with the Arts Council England alone

Table 1.1 Policy interventions, March to Autumn 2020

2020	England	Northern Ireland	Scotland	Wales
March UK wide	11 March 2020: WHO declares pandemic 11 March 2020: £30bn package of business relief and loans announced by UK Treasury as part of Chancellor's budget **20 March 2020: Theatres, cinemas, gyms, leisure centres, cafés, restaurants, pubs and bars closed** 20 March 2020: Job Retention (Furlough) Scheme announced **23 March 2020: UK-wide lockdown #1 announced** 25 March 2020: Coronavirus Act 2020 granted Royal Assent 26 March 2020: Support for self-employed (SEISS) announced			
March			27 March: Creative Scotland Bridging Bursary Fund, £2m for freelancers Screen Scotland Bridging Bursary Fund, £1.5m Open Fund: Sustaining Creative Development, £7.5m; Open Fund for Individuals £5m	
April UK wide	7 April 2020: DCMS Select Committee inquiry into impact of COVID-19 on DCMS sectors launches **10 April 2020: Five-tier alert levels implemented by UK Government** 10 April 2020: Four nations 'stay at home' policy approach diverges between England, Scotland, Wales and Northern Ireland (NI) **16 April 2020: Lockdown #1 extended for at least three weeks**			
	9 April: Arts CouncilEngland's (ACE) Emergency Fund opens Round 1 of the Emergency Response Fund for creative practitioners in England	27 April: Arts Council of Northern Ireland (ACNI) launches £500k Artists Emergency Programme (AEP)	13 April: Scottish CouncilforVoluntary Organisations (SCVO) launches Wellbeing Fund of £50m 15 April: Scottish Government (SG) £34m Newly Self-Employed Hardship Fund, £20m Creative, Tourism and Hospitality Enterprises Hardship Fund, £45m Pivotal	1 April: Welsh Government announces Arts Resilience Fund, reallocating money from existing budgets to create an urgent response fund of £7m managed by Arts Council Wales

Table 1.1 (Cont.)

2020	England	Northern Ireland	Scotland	Wales
			Enterprise Resilience Fund 21 April: SG £50m Wellbeing Fund	
May **UK wide**	**11 May 2020: Those who cannot work from home return to workplaces; UK Government launches 'Our Plan to Rebuild'; cultural venues cited as partially reopening at Stage 3** 12 May 2020: Furlough Scheme extended until end of October 2020 13 May 2020: SEISS opens for Round 1 applications			
	12 May: ACE launches £90m financial support for NPOs and Creative People and Places organisations	6 May: ACNI launches £25k Deaf/Disabled Artist Support Fund	4 May: SG launches Caring Communities campaign 7 May: SG launches £5m Connecting Scotland, digital poverty funds **21 May: SG publishes the 'Route Map' for staged reopening**	
June			10 June: SG Scottish Recovery Tourism Taskforce launched SG distributes £257.6m to local councils to support local services 29 June: Edinburgh Fringe Society £1m interest-free loan	
July **UK wide**	**Significant easing of lockdown this month** 5 July 2020: DCMS launches £1.57bn Culture Recovery Fund (CRF) 8 July 2020: UK Government 'mini budget' including Job Retention Bonus scheme 23 July 2020: DCMS Select Committee publishes first report on impact of COVID-19 on DCMS sectors.			
	4 July: First local lockdown followed by 30 July tiered restrictions	3July:NIExecutive reopens museums, galleries and heritage sites with social distancing measures	3 July: Creative Scotland launches Performing Arts Venues Relief Fund of £12.5m	

(continued)

Table 1.1 (Cont.)

2020	England	Northern Ireland	Scotland	Wales
		NI receives £33m CRF: £29m Arts, Culture and Heritage. £4m emergency	15 July: Phase 3 route map reopens some museums, galleries, cinemas and libraries with social distancing measures	
August UK wide	Eat Out to Help Out scheme announced: Subsidies of up to 50 per cent for people to eat in pubs and restaurants – 3 August to 1 September 2020			
August	10 August: CRF Round 1 opens 14 August: Indoor cultural venues allowed to open 21 August: CRF Round 2 opens		16 August: £3.8m for National Trust Scotland 26 August: £2.2m GrassrootsMusicVenues Stabilisation Fund 28 August: £59m emergency funding package for culture and heritage, distributed through Creative Scotland	

Table 1.2 Policy interventions, Autumn 2020 to Summer 2021

	England	Northern Ireland	Scotland	Wales
September 2020 UK wide	15 September: 'Working safely through COVID-19: seven inclusive principles for arts & cultural organisations' guidance is published 24 September: UK Government launches the 'Winter Economy Plan' with new Job Support Scheme and SEISS extension			
	14 September: Additional restrictions implemented (including 'rule of six') 24 September: 10pm curfew begins and home working	10 September: Localised restrictions in some postcode areas for two weeks minimum 18 September: Art galleries reopen	10 September: Restrictions on social gatherings introduced; theatres and live venues remain closed	

Table 1.2 (Cont.)

	England	Northern Ireland	Scotland	Wales
October	12 October: Three-tier local tiering system introduced	16 October: Northern Ireland (NI) Executive announces four-week tighter restrictions	23 October: SG announces five-tier local system	
November UK wide	5 November: UK Government extends Furlough second round to end of March 2021 and SEISS confirmed at 80 per cent of trading profits to end of March 2021			
	5 November: Lockdown #2 in England begins	9 November: NI Executive announces £1.5m for arts, culture and heritage renewal 16 November: NI Executive increases self-isolation grant 19 November: Four-week circuit breaker closing venues	3 November: Local lockdown rules to combat second wave 5 November: Creative Scotland launches £6m Culture Collective Fund for creative infrastructure development with local authorities 26 November: Creative Scotland launches the Youth Arts Fund package of £3m 30 November: SG £11.8m fund for digital businesses to invest in digital	
December	2 December: Lockdown #2 ends tiers return 19 December: Tier 4 leaves 18m people in regional lockdowns	26 December: Rule of 6 social distancing imposed for Tier 4	14 December: First vaccinations take place 19 December: Restrictions tightened	20 December: Tier 4 lockdown reintroduced

(*continued*)

Table 1.2 (Cont.)

	England	Northern Ireland	Scotland	Wales
January 2021	6 January: Lockdown introduced 6 January: CRF Round 2 opens for applications		4 January: Lockdown announced 17 January: SG announces emergency support of £3m for three major arts organisations 22 January: National Partnership for Culture announced	
February	23 February: ACE publishes roadmap for easing of restrictions for arts and culture	24 February: NI Executive introduces £6.9m to support individual artists as part of Individual Emergency Resilience Programme	17 February: Hardship Fund for Creative Freelancers and Screen Hardship Fund £9m 17 February: Extension of Pivotal Event Business Fund/ Events Industry Support Fund £8.5m 23 February: SG publishes Strategy Framework Update for reopening	17 February: Arts Council Wales opens Connect and Flourish 2 £2.7m (of £5m) 10 February: Freelancer Fund extended by £8.9m 19 February: Restrictions eased
March UK wide	3 March: UK Government present the 2021 Budget with SEISS rounds 4 and 5 22 March: CRF Round 2 extension announced for support up to September 2021			
April				6 April: Arts Council Wales Fund for organisations opens
April UK wide	17 April: DCMS launches Events Research Programme with pilot event at World Snooker Championships			
May UK wide	10 May: The four Chief Medical Officers of the UK agree to reduce the UK COVID-19 alert level from 4 to alert level 3			
May	15 May: Events Research Programme pilot event at FA Cup Final	18 May: Taskforce and cultural strategy announced	17 May: Most of Scotland is level 2, allowing live venue opening	10 May: Welsh Government announce events pilot series

Table 1.2 (Cont.)

	England	Northern Ireland	Scotland	Wales
June	21 June: DCMS Events Research Programme first report published		17 June: Creative Scotland Culture Organisations & Venue Recovery Fund Round 2, £25m	25 June: NHS Covid passes introduced

Table 1.3 Culture Recovery Fund revenue funding for DCMS sectors showing distribution by arm's length body (England only)

Arm's-length body	Funding pot	Sub-sectors targeted	Amount (£m)
Arts Council England	Culture Recovery Fund (Grants)	National Portfolio Organisations (NPOs[1]) – organisations that recieve substantial funding from ACE	118
		Non-National Portfolio Organisations	209
		ACE-accredited museums and museums working towards accreditation[2]	137
		Music venues – independent grassroots music venues, including indoor arenas and concert halls	36
Arts Council England total			500
Historic England and the National Lottery Heritage Fund	Heritage Restart and Rescue Grants (CRF for Heritage)	Heritage sites, venues or attractions in England, and organisations managing culturally significant assets or collections (including non-accredited museums)	92[3]
British Film Institute	Independent Cinema Grants	Independent cinemas that provide a year-round programme	30
Total available in phase 1 for England			622
Contingency			258
Revenue grants total			880

[1] The arts organisations, museums and libraries, ranging in size and location, in which Arts Council England (ACE) invests.

[2] Museum accreditation is the benchmark for a well-run museum. Accreditation is made by ACE. There are about 1,700 accredited museums in England. Accredited museums and those working towards accreditation had to apply for CRF through ACE. All other museums could apply to the CRF for Heritage.

[3] £2m of this was for the Architectural Heritage Fund and up to £2m was for digital support and business support programmes.

Source: National Audit Office analysis of the Department for Digital, Culture, Media & Sport's documentation.

providing over £100m in Emergency Funding to nearly a thousand applicants in Spring 2020, including 7,484 individual creative practitioners and 2,374 organisations) (SQW, 2022, p.1).

Phase Two: attempting recovery

The UK Government eased some restrictions in May 2020 in England as part of a pandemic recovery strategy (Cabinet Office, 2020), however, these were quickly reversed to avoid a potential 'second wave' (Home Office, 2020a). Although 'Cultural Renewal Taskforce' led by Lord Mendoza was established by the Department for Digital, Culture, Media and Sport (DCMS) Secretary of State (DCMS, 2020a) national support did not fully emerge until July 2020, when the £1.57bn Culture Recovery Fund (CRF) was announced, the single largest investment in the creative and cultural sectors ever made in the UK (DCMS, 2020b). Until then, the high degree of uncertainty led to a considerable number of open letters and campaigns by sector advocates which continued to hold the UK governments to account throughout the pandemic period (see, for example, Equity, 2020; The Stage, 2020). The CRF was created in response to evidence of the severity of the impact of the pandemic on the sector, with DCMS estimating that the cultural sector had seen commercial income fall by 95 per cent since March 2020, provisionally aiming to ensure survival of a target 75 per cent of those organisations at risk of falling off the 'cliff-edge' of financial failure by September 2020 (NAO, 2021, p.5). Overseen by a new Culture Recovery Board, with revenue and capital grants and repayable loans distributed via the arm's-length bodies within the four nations, CRF calculations were based on a worst-case scenario assumption that social distancing might remain in place until March 2021. The criteria for shaping funding decisions were established broadly according to two principles: firstly, cultural value and significance, such as organisations recognised as excellent by their peers or assets that are deemed nationally important or irreplaceable and, secondly, by their significance to place, for example, by providing access for participation to audiences or contribution to creative economies and/or local policy agendas (NAO, 2021, p.13). Although the loan scheme remained undersubscribed, the grant schemes were heavily oversubscribed. By February 2021, around £495m had been paid out to recipients, of the total of £830m awarded to the DCMS sectors, which included £622m revenue funding and £120m capital awards, plus a further £100m provided to the arm's-length bodies as grant in aid (NAO, 2021, p.20); see Table 1.3.

The timing and policies for reopening cultural venues differed across England, Scotland, Wales and Northern Ireland, primarily driven by monitoring of localised case rates, with venues in Northern Ireland and Scotland reopening in July 2020, while those in England were delayed from reopening until mid-August 2020. By September 2020, as new variants of the virus emerged, national and localised restrictions were reintroduced, lasting throughout the winter into 2021, and despite attempts by the four nations to harmonise regulation over Christmas (Welsh Government, 2020a) there remained distinctive approaches across the UK. A 10pm curfew for pubs and restaurants, the 'rule of six' (Home Office, 2020b) and the Eat Out to Help Out scheme (Hutton, 2020) were introduced in England in quick succession, creating further confusion, and in some cases further spikes in cases. On 31 October 2020, the UK Prime Minister announced a new England-wide lockdown, Wales moved in and out of localised lockdowns (Welsh Government, 2020b), while Northern Ireland saw restrictions introduced for a four-week 'circuit breaker' which forced cultural venues to close on 19 November 2020 (Executive Office of Northern Ireland, 2020). In Scotland, restrictions on social gatherings were reintroduced with local lockdowns from November 2020 which, coupled with a national lockdown coming into force over the new year, encouraged the launch of specific funds targeting Scottish cultural venues (Creative Scotland, 2020).

At this time, it remained unclear when the furlough scheme would end, and there was continued lack of guidance on how venues might reopen safely. Reopening with reduced capacity but a full staff complement placed a huge financial strain on cultural organisations that were already facing further loss of income at a traditionally busy time of year. The furlough scheme was eventually extended in November 2020 through to March 2021, with calls to extend and plug the ongoing gaps in the SEISS left unheeded despite growing lobbying from pressure groups, workforce

Table 1.4 Policy interventions, Summer to November 2021

	England	Northern Ireland	Scotland	Wales
July 2021	19 July: 'Freedom Day' ending of Covid restrictions – English cultural venues reopen	27 July: Phased reopening of venues and removal of restrictions	13 July: Self-isolation grants of £500 for low income 19 July: Scotland moves to alert level 0	
August	16 August: CRF opens Continuity Support for Rounds 1 and 2 recipients		23 August: £750k Scottish Government (SG) Touring Fund for live music	5 August: Wales moves to alert level 0
September		16 September: Northern Ireland (NI_ Executive transfers £500k to Arts and Business NI	7 September: Strategic vision and policy review for culture announced 10 September: SG launch Public Libraries COVID recovery Fund	
October		13 October: Arts Council of Northern Ireland (ACNI) launches £750k Health & Safety Capital Programme	1 October: SG Covid certification of vaccination for venue access	11 October: NHS Covid Passes for large events, nightclubs
November UK wide	27 November: Omicron variant detected in UK			
	29 November: CRF Round 2 rolling programme		16 November: SG update Scotland's Strategy Framework 29 November: Omicron detected in Scotland	15 November: NHS Covid Pass for cinema, theatres and concert halls

networks, arm's length bodies, funders and cultural organisations (Bectu, 2020). Attempts to support workforce development were hindered by these turbulent conditions; for example, the launch of the UK Government's 'Kickstart' scheme which encouraged young people to take up apprenticeships, including in the creative and cultural sectors, yielded mixed results (Powell, 2022). Meanwhile, financial support through grants and loan schemes continued, with the opening of CRF Round 2 in January 2021 (Arts Council England, n.d.).

Phase Three: continuing uncertainty

In February 2021, a further roadmap out of the lockdowns was published by the Prime Minister's Office (2021), with sector-specific guidance added by the DCMS (Woodhouse and Hutton, 2021). The government budget statement in March confirmed an extension to the SEISS and an uplift in funding for the culture department (DCMS, 2021a). A research programme was launched in April 2021 to test the impact of holding large-scale events under certain conditions, and underpinned further guidance as new variants were beginning to take hold in the UK (DCMS, 2021b). By May 2021, Wales and most of Scotland had moved into Level 2 restrictions, allowing theatres, cinemas and live venues to re-open (Welsh Government, 2021). However, full reopening across the whole of the UK was not permitted until the summer, when the so-called 'Freedom Day' on 19 July 2021 saw the removal of all Covid-related restrictions in England against a backdrop of increased transmission rates and a prime minister in quarantine (James, 2021). This apparent change in logic was tempered politically by a broadly successful rollout of the vaccination programme, and a high uptake of 'booster jabs' reducing the risk of serious illness and hospitalisation. It also provided the means to propose safer venue opening, with vaccination certification schemes trialled in Scotland and Wales in 'high-risk venues' such as theatres, cinemas and music venues (Morris, 2021).

The third round of the CRF opened in August 2021 and saw a further £100m in continuity and recovery grants. The autumn budget in October 2021 included funding to boost culture in local communities and on the high street. It also confirmed temporary extensions of tax reliefs for theatres, orchestras, museums and galleries, plus further support for creative industries through schemes such as the Live Events Reinsurance Scheme and the Film & TV Production Restart Scheme, which were successful in reinstating cultural production (RSM, 2022) despite the initial delays in their inception. However, after eighteen months of turmoil, in November 2021, the first cases of the Omicron variant were detected in the UK, and transmission rates soared back up. Despite the substantial injection of public funds, evolving models for safe return to cultural venues, and growing understanding of the specific issues caused and revealed by the pandemic concerning workforce and business model precarity, the uncertainties for arts and cultural producers and consumers, as well as the challenges for policy-makers, were set to continue.

In the next section we examine further the variety of policy responses, beginning with the distinctive challenges in Scotland, Wales and Northern Ireland, before considering the significant and central role of Westminster in setting policy (and rhetoric) not just for England but across the UK. We then turn briefly to discuss the implications of these responses for understanding cultural policy in the UK context.

Tailoring interventions in Scotland

The Scottish Government's ambitions for culture prior to the pandemic were laid out in a new cultural strategy, published on 28 February 2020. The result of lengthy sector stakeholder consultation lasting several years (Scottish Government, 2020), the policy articulated a nuanced vision for culture that is responsive to the diverse histories, geographies, cultures and communities of the national population (Scottish Government, 2020, p.3). Although derived before the beginning of the pandemic, the policy provided a template of stated aims and action planning, and principles of place, inclusion and cultural democracy, which were used to guide the national response.

Much of this was delivered through the national arm's-length body for culture Creative Scotland, who distributed £85.3m in emergency funding on behalf of the national government between 2020 and 2021 (EKOS, 2022). As with Arts Council England in England, Creative Scotland was able to act ahead of national legislative policy, relaxing delivery restrictions for their portfolio of Regular Funded Organisations (RFOs) and redirecting existing funds to provide emergency support for the sector, with £11m of funding announced on 27 March. However, where analysis of emergency funding in England has confirmed that 'relief flowed disproportionately to institutions' (de Peuter, Oakley and Trusolino, 2022, p.8), Scotland's initial emergency response prioritised support for individuals, with further funding decisions detailing significant distinctions across the devolved national responses within the UK.

Predominantly funded by £97m released to Scotland through the Barnett formula following the announcement of the Culture Recovery Fund,[1] the period after July 2020 saw a programme of eight rolling funds targeted at different areas of the sector. Some outcomes of these interventions are unsurprising. Glasgow and Edinburgh, the two largest cities in the country with the highest concentration of RFOs and the largest creative workforce, benefitted from the most funding, receiving over 50 per cent of the total amount distributed across all funds with the two highest levels of inward investment per person (see Figure 1.1). Beyond these headline figures, however, the picture is more varied. While Glasgow and Edinburgh dominated general funds, such as the £28m Cultural Organisations and Venues Recovery Fund which was open to commercial and publicly funded organisations, targeted funds, such as the £24.5m Performing Arts Venue Relief Fund for publicly funded theatres and performance venues or the £5.9m Culture Collective Fund for local creative networks, reached different areas of the sector, with a higher proportion of funds going to a wider range of local authorities. Direct support for freelancers also continued, with two in-parallel hardship funds, totalling £17m, replacing the emergency support established in the first month of the pandemic. Delivered in partnership with sector bodies such as Craft Scotland and Help Musicians Scotland, these programmes offered support for freelancers until the end of March 2021, accounting for 17 per cent of the total spend across all funds (EKOS, 2022, p.33).

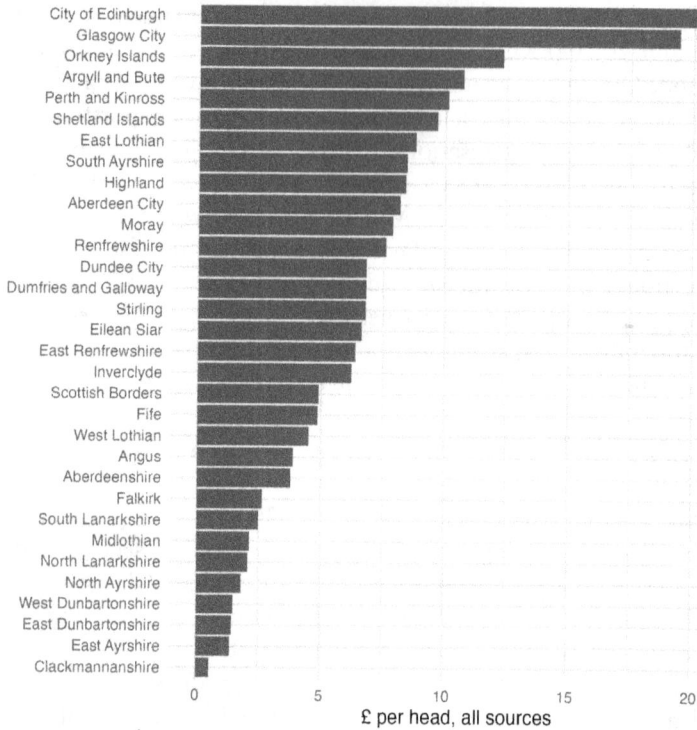

Figure 1.1 Distribution of emergency cultural recovery funding per head across Scottish local authority areas, analysis by Mark Taylor
Source: Creative Scotland

A number of these programmes ringfenced grants for non-RFO organisations, reaching beyond existing funding patterns to protect local cultural infrastructures alongside the nation's flagship assets. Alongside this expansion, there was notable recognition of cross-sector support through the establishment of the Scottish Tourism Emergency Response Group (STERG) with a £25m fund to support the recovery of the tourism industry (STERG, 2021). Projects that impacted culture and heritage through this fund were primarily concerned with enticing audiences through days out schemes and holiday vouchers. However, the group was also concerned about longer term infrastructure and capacity building around sustainable travel to the more remote areas of the highland and islands particularly for festival attendance.

The delivery of these policies and the efficiency with which they were able to achieve their aims was significantly affected by networks, knowledges and individual and organisational capacities as they existed before the pandemic. Primary research into how festivals in Scotland fared throughout 2020 helps illustrate these dynamics, discussed below.

The restrictions on social gatherings had particularly acute impacts for festivals. Additionally, while other areas were served with bespoke funding programmes, there was no targeted support for festivals, leaving many organisations feeling overlooked and under supported. Many of the interviewees from festivals expressed frustration at a lack of coherent messaging from the Scottish Government, particularly in relation to eligibility and to changing health and safety guidance, leading to concerns that the Scottish Government did not understand how the festival sector operated. In the absence of policy leadership, networks of rural and smaller festivals resorted to pooling resources and knowledge, disseminating advice from other festivals and individuals that had managed to receive guidance from civil servants.

One of the major communication issues concerned the eligibility criteria for emergency funding and the employment of freelancers. For many festivals, the collapse of box office income meant that they were applying for and receiving more public funding than before the pandemic. One effect of this influx was that organisations were working with unfamiliar financial restrictions, and festivals found themselves having to seek clarification from the government and funders, with irregular working patterns and portfolio work of creative and cultural freelancers proving a particular challenge (Tsioulakis and FitzGibbon, 2020; Jones, 2022). This caused major delays for some festivals and logistical problems when it came to hiring seasonal workers, whose numbers were already depleted due to restrictions on movement and travel. Eligibility criteria also differed between emergency funding programmes without explanation, leading to frustration for festival organisations desperate to receive funding to stop them from going under.

Of course, these experiences are not universal. Throughout the pandemic, local authorities acted as a proxy for national

government, and several festivals reported that they received substantial support and advice, linking these experiences with long-
term relationships with local authority departments and officers.
Where present, established relationships with local authorities
helped mitigate the tensions and challenges associated with the
delivery of these policies; however, they also relied on resources
and capacities that not all festivals possess, and on a local
authority that values culture. A consultancy report published
just prior to the pandemic (EKOS, 2020) observed that 'com-
paratively small services such as culture can end up in very large
portfolios where they have low visibility' (p.17), noting also that
'Creative Scotland (2020) has a diminished visibility with many
local authorities' (p.72), highlighting long-standing challenges
and uneven capacities that disadvantaged some festivals during
the pandemic.

Ahead of their 2022–2023 annual budget, the Scottish
Parliament opened a public consultation, inviting responses from
sector stakeholders on how investment should be prioritised and
managed to best support the sector, and whether a more substantial rethink of the relationship between national government and
the sector might be required in light of the pandemic (Scottish
Parliament, 2021). This openness to consultation and critical
reflection on the possibilities raised by emergency responses to the
pandemic is striking and signals further commitment to collaborative policy-making that seeks to incorporate sector knowledge into
national decision-making. As our research partners observed, the
pandemic has also underlined the need to strengthen and rebalance relationships with local authorities. A new programme called
Culture Collective was designed to address these issues and inform
an internal review of relationship management between Creative
Scotland and local government. Finally, the pandemic brought
new urgency to long-standing discussions around the economic
conditions of work in the cultural sector and, as Doustaly and
Roy observe (2022), increased support for Scottish Government
intervention, potentially through a Universal Basic Income (UBI)
for culture. However, as they note, early experiments in UBI have
been frustrated by the conditions of the devolution agreement
(2022, p. 13), and further investigation would require leadership
from Westminster.

Future-proofing in Wales

As with elsewhere in the UK, policy statements pre-pandemic for the devolved Welsh Government characterised the creative industries as important because of their rapid growth, potential contribution to national economy and importance to 'brand'; a new sector development agency, Creative Wales, launched in January 2020 with a focus on music, film and TV, digital and publishing sectors, and connecting policy approaches to theatre, festivals and grassroots music activities (Elis-Thomas, 2020). Creative industries and cultural sectors were calculated to contribute around £1.5bn and 85,000 jobs annually to the Welsh economy, based on the DCMS Sectors Economic Estimates in 2019, with an estimated £100m financial impact caused by the pandemic, particularly affecting micro-businesses and the self-employed (Parkinson *et al.*, 2022, p.13). At the height of lockdown, survey data from the Film & TV Charity suggested that 93 per cent freelancers in the creative industries were not working, with a staggering 74 per cent ineligible for SEISS and the Coronavirus Job Retention Scheme (CJRS) (Welsh Parliament, 2020).

As with Scotland, emergency funds were made available to the sector most rapidly by the devolved government when, in April 2020, the Welsh Government announced an £18m rescue fund. The Arts Council of Wales administered £7m of the package via an Arts Resilience Fund, with approximately £1.5m allocated to individuals and £5.5m for organisations (Arts Council of Wales, 2020). Both funds were further divided into two types of grant: 'Urgent Response' and 'Stabilisation', offering immediate hardship support and funding continuation of work. The rescue package included a targeted £1m fund for grassroots music venues which was separately administered by Creative Wales, a £1m 'Cultural Resilience Fund' for museums, galleries, archives and libraries, and a further £750,000 fund to support the smallest and most vulnerable independent sport, museum and heritage organisations (Welsh Government, 2022).

Wales received £59m of the UK-wide £1.57bn Culture Recovery Fund announced in July 2020 and was able to allocate the second highest per capita figure of £18.71, after England's £25.37 per capita (Wright, 2020). The first tranche received in July 2020 led to an announcement of £53m funding for arts and culture in Wales, distributed by Welsh Government (£18.5m) and administered by Business Wales; £27.5m via the Arts Council of Wales, and £7m targeting individual freelancers, which was administered by local authorities. In November 2020, the Welsh Government contributed a further £10.7m due to high demand, taking the total to £63.7m, and in January 2022 a further £15.4m was released as part of the CRF round 3 (Welsh Government, 2022). Evaluation of the CRF rounds 1 and 2 suggests the approach in Wales, informed by its smaller-scale and close relationship with local authorities, permitted targeted interventions to the micro-businesses and freelancers identified as most vulnerable. Of the £71.6m awarded, 90 per cent of funds were awarded to 'micro-businesses' and £10.39m to the 3,783 freelancers supported across both rounds (Welsh Government, 2022), contrasting with England's initial prioritisation of 'crown jewels'.

The vulnerability of the freelancers who make up half of the cultural workforce in Wales, many of whom were working full-time equivalent prior to the pandemic, was noted by an in-depth report which surveyed a cross-section of the sector (Donnelly and Komorowski, 2022). The report found that the negative impact of the pandemic on the wellbeing of freelancers had worsened between 2020 and 2021, and that, as detailed in Chapter 2, freelancers with protected characteristics and/or who had caring responsibilities in 2021 had less access to support and were at greater risk of leaving the industry. It also found the Welsh Government-run Freelancers funding was the most successful in terms of eligibility, access and satisfaction, followed by Universal Credit and SEISS, supporting the recommendation for a Welsh Government UBI pilot scheme, which targeted theatre and performance freelancers, following the call from a new role in Wales, the Future Wellbeing Commissioner (Howe, 2020; Donnelly and Komorowski, 2022).

In contrast to other nations, Wales embedded its distribution of recovery funding in its sustainable development legislation, the Wellbeing of Future Generations Act (2015), described as a 'possible roadmap to future-proofing the sector' post-COVID-19 (Wright, 2020, p.12). The legislation lists 'thriving culture' as a wellbeing goal, identifying participation in arts, culture and heritage as a national indicator, vital to achieving the other wellbeing goals such as prosperity, resilience, health, equality and cohesive community

(Welsh Government, 2015). Followed by the Prosperity for All – Economic Action Plan (Welsh Government, 2019) which threaded culture through its policy aims and justifications, the Wellbeing of Future Generations legislation asks those in public service to collectively consider the longer-term impacts of their decision-making in relation to societal challenges. It aims to pre-empt future outcomes for Welsh people through convening 'big' and 'simple' change projects, led by a Future Wellbeing Commissioner.

This fundamental shift in policy planning can be seen in both the rhetoric and administration of funds during COVID-19. On the practical level, the receipt of Culture Recovery Funds required participating organisations to commit to a 'Cultural Contract' as part of their application. An extension of the 'Economic Contract' (proposed in the Prosperity for All plan) and accompanied by a corresponding 'Freelancer's Pledge', the Cultural Contract required an evidenced commitment to a series of principles. These included the promotion of diversity, health (with a special emphasis on mental health) and workplace skills training, progress in clean growth, climate resilience and reduced carbon footprint, and encouragement for retained staff to take part in broader public service, for example, contact tracing to support COVID-19 case tracking and social prescribing to promote and support health and arts initiatives (Business Wales, 2020). These essentially non-economic policy measures were also reiterated in the Arts Council Wales *Re-setting the Dial* report, which articulated similar principles, extolling the importance of systems change for a fairer, more just sector, and celebrating both the particularity of the Welsh language and the creativity of the individual artist over the arts institution (Arts Council Wales, n.d.). As discussed above, the Future Generations commission was an early advocate for a UBI for artists and creatives on the basis that artists can help support recovery by bringing creative skills to societal problem-solving and should be valued as exceptional since they cannot be replaced by automation (Howe, 2020). However, the eventual UBI pilot, launched in 2022, focused not on creatives but on young care leavers, and has been dogged by central government rules which mean that participants may lose some benefits as their allocation is not devolved (Morris, 2022).

Networks and power in Northern Ireland

Northern Ireland received £33m of the UK-wide £1.57bn Culture Recovery Fund. Of this funding the Executive allocated £29m for arts, languages, heritage and culture in September 2020. The remaining £4m had already been allocated as part of emergency funding by the Executive in July 2020 (DfC, 2020). The Arts Council of Northern Ireland (ACNI) and the Department for Communities (DfC) also committed an extra £1.5m to the initial £4m emergency fund to help support organisations and individual artists. Notable among initial emergency funds was the Deaf/Disabled Artist Support Fund, which was the first of its kind in response to the pandemic in the UK (ACNI, 2020).

Policy responses within Northern Ireland can be characterised as a series of interventions at different levels of government, driven both by necessity and by a growing sense of collaboration across the cultural sector. These policy decisions were not uniform or cohesive, taking different strategic approaches and models at various stages, revealing tensions between policy-makers, stakeholders and cultural sub-sectors which are deeply rooted in entrenched power structures. They were not triggered solely in response to the impact of the pandemic, but rather recognised a publicly funded sector in Northern Ireland already suffering underinvestment, with a 40 per cent decrease from the ACNI's exchequer budget for arts and culture in Northern Ireland over the last ten years (ACNI, 2022, p.4). The lack of public funding is highlighted by comparison with the Welsh and Scottish arts and culture budgets, which were found in 2017 to be over twice those of Northern Ireland's budget when expressed as per capita figures (FactCheckNI, 2019). This is partly due to the value of grant in aid determined by the Barnett formula, which is calculated against what is spent by the UK Government per capita (Cheung, 2020).

Interestingly, in terms of cultural spend the Northern Ireland Executive has marginally more control than Scotland or Wales. However, since culture sits under the DfC there was also real fear that the initial COVID-19 recovery package for culture would not fully filter through to the sector and instead be used for housing or other areas. Against this context, the mobilisation of networks of influence became vital from the initial response to the lockdown measures and some perceived ACNI's response was far too slow. Indeed, one interviewee stated that 'the uncertainty that it's caused has really made planning impossible'. Coupled with fears about the direction of the CRF and a decision-making vacuum, this became a strong mitigating factor in the galvanisation of several networks of influence from the culture sector itself. Some of these networks existed prior to the pandemic but others developed as a direct result. However, what is significant in policy terms is that they became lobby groups directly feeding evidence and recommendations into the DfC.[2]

The shift in relationship between the cultural sector and policy was also noticeable in some local authorities. Significantly, Belfast City Council changed their policy direction, bringing in a directly funded bursary scheme for artists which was not based on project outcomes. Instead, the Creative Practitioners Bursary scheme offered a £10,000 grant to ten individual artists for one year to support their practice (Journal of Music, 2021). The initial grant was oversubscribed, and was eventually distributed to five musicians and five creative practitioners across various art forms. While the direct state funding of artists without specific output requirements is not new, it is increasingly rare within arm's length bodies in the UK (Jackson and Devlin, 2005; Jones, 2019). The DfC has taken on elements of the model for national rollout through the ACNI after consultation with Belfast City Council, although specific conditions relating to output remain for national schemes (ACNI, 2022).

The pandemic brought closer consultation and collaboration between policy-makers and the cultural sector in Northern Ireland, characterised by the development of a cultural taskforce. The Arts Collaboration Network (ABNI) had been lobbying during the early stages of the pandemic for this form of action (ABNI, 2020). In summer 2021, the taskforce was formed by the DfC, comprising sector representatives of organisations and freelancer communities, and with the goals of formulating recommendations for opening up the cultural and heritage sectors in the short term and the production of a cultural strategy for Northern Ireland in the medium to long term (DfC, 2021a). Through an intensive consultation period with various organisations, institutions, networks and individuals, the taskforce published a report with nine evidence-based recommendations for policy (DfC, 2021b) The main focus of this report highlighted the interconnections between freelance creative practitioners and the health of the wider cultural ecology in Northern

Ireland. As a result, its recommendations are practitioner focused and deal with long-standing issues around inaccessible and inflexible funding (p.18). This approach was notably different to that of the DCMS but had similarities with the general consensus in both the Welsh and Scottish Governments' commitments to freelancers and individuals through more collaborative policy-making. This closer engagement with decision-makers and successful lobbying for more experimental and risk-taking investment has led to schemes such as the £4.7m Future Screens Northern Ireland Art Works programme, which aims to increase the attraction and retention of creative workers in local arts organisations by creating three-year posts (Moore, 2022).

Policy, rhetoric and Westminster

The timeline and accounts of the devolved nations above recognise the dominant role of government in Westminster. It sets levels of budgets and direction of travel for policy approaches and fiscal interventions which were distributed by the devolved and local governments and arm's-length bodies. It also offered guidance from newly established bodies such as the Cultural Renewal Taskforce, with some variations in the timing of restrictions and in the distribution and allocation of funds. While at the time of writing the efficacy of both process and outcome for the arts and cultural sector is still being evaluated, within the moment these interventions received intense scrutiny and prompted debates on social media and within sector publications, which we argue are indicative not only of policy rationale but of rhetoric. Amid the eddies of uncertainty and continual pressure of funding applications for stabilisation and recovery funding from national and local sources, certain discursive moments rose to the surface which revealed prevailing attitudes and tensions concerning the value of arts, creativity and culture within national public life. These were articulations of crisis, but like the outcries and movements coalescing around the contemporaneous activism of Black Lives Matter, following the murder of George Floyd, and the toppling statuary and culture battles pitched against the National Trust (see, for example, Henley, 2020; Aaronovitch, 2021; The Guardian, 2021; Adesina, 2022), these mediated moments punctured any sense of coherent and consensual national policy for the arts and cultural sector in England, despite the vital importance and magnitude of the CRF and other public funds.

For example, the Arts Council England's Emergency Fund scheme, rapidly established within weeks after the first lockdown, included the earmarking of £90m out of £160m for its national portfolio, the organisations who are in receipt of regular funding from the arm's-length body. This provoked debates about the fairness of the funding formula and eligibility criteria, and accusations that these favoured trickle-down economics which neglected organisations and places outside of the regular funding ringfence (Hill, 2020). Similarly, the announcement of the CRF scheme was accompanied by a mis-stepped statement of commitment by the UK Secretary of State to prioritise the (predominantly London-based) institutions who were 'the crown jewels of our national life' (Evans, 2020). Such utterances opened old wounds about the metropolitan bias of arts funding, but also represented concerns for the precarious position of creative freelancer ecologies who were perceived to be doubly neglected by general fiscal policy and targeted sector funds (Thompson, 2020). This concern seemed justified as the pandemic wore on, when those responsible for these policies appeared to undermine the case for sector support further. In October 2020, a poorly considered campaign to encourage people to retrain in digital technologies featured an image of a ballet dancer with the caption 'Fatima's next job could be in cyber', causing acute embarrassment to Secretary of State Oliver Dowden (Bakare, 2020) and the then Chancellor of the Exchequer, Rishi Sunak, to back-track on comments about adaptation for survival (Snow, 2020). Meanwhile, those who received CRF funding were required to share assets across their social media channels, publicly thanking the government for support through a #HereForCulture hashtag, and tagging arm's-length bodies, the Treasury and the DCMS (Arts Council England, n.d.).

Responses from within arts commentary showed the exasperation of a sector who was watching its business model slip through its fingers. At times those with leadership roles seemed to simply misunderstand how creative production works, for example, underestimating the lead time for 'opening up' required for theatres and performing arts in recovery roadmaps (Billington, 2020), or providing cripplingly delayed and inadequate policy levers to help festivals and events with cancellation insurance (Jowett, 2022). The importance of arm's-length bodies in providing expertise and relationship management at a local level, in partnership with local government arts officers, anchor institutions and local networks, was underlined by the frustration with centralised policy, as discussed in Chapter 5.

As the pandemic progressed, Westminster turned to policies for regeneration and economic recovery, which aimed to address geographical inequalities in productivity under the banner of the idea of levelling up (DLUHC, 2022). A cluster of funds for capital projects and infrastructure investment was brought together under this agenda, organised by place-based eligibility criteria and prioritising projects with culture and heritage themes. The rationale for allocation of funding shifted from the need to stabilise a critically undermined arts and cultural sector to the leverage that arts and culture can provide in aiding place recovery:

> Investment in cultural assets can rejuvenate places, leading to positive economic and social outcomes at a local level. It can help to retain and grow a highly skilled workforce, attract tourists to bolster local business, and provide opportunities to grow people and communities' connections with places. (HM Treasury, 2021, p.12)

Furthermore, the renewed focus on place, signalled also in the criteria of CRF allocation, was identified in the Levelling Up White Paper as a requirement for delivery by Arts Council England, who were compelled to increase the number of sites for targeted investment in their Priority Places scheme, from the fifty-four identified by their Delivery Plan to 109 local authority areas, all outside of Greater London (ACE, 2022; DLUHC, 2022). While addressing long-standing issues of place inequality in arts investment in 'left behind' places, this was a clear example of centralised government intervention with ramifications for the sanctity of the arm's-length decision-making of Arts Council England.

Implications and conclusion

As outlined above, the unfolding timeline of the pandemic shows the unevenness and fragmentation of decision-making and policy interventions across the UK, at times rapid and timely but often frustratingly delayed. The waves and spikes of coronavirus cases driven by new variants were interwoven with shifting public health restrictions and fiscal policies, in attempts to control the spread of the virus and mitigate its impacts on the nations' economies. For creative workers, organisations and arts leaders this meant successive appraisal and reappraisal of business models, audience confidence, operational structures and value propositions, plus continuous lobbying and bidding for emergency funding. For policy-makers this meant decisions on the borrowing and distribution of public spending, making calls on what levels of attrition were palatable among the hardest-hit sectors and the forms of mitigation that would protect both publics and economic futures. It also repositioned the role of expertise and evidence, within a climate of suspicion of the former and cynicism about the latter, following the clamouring rise of 'fake news' and 'culture wars' in post-EU-referendum UK.

The policy responses that emerged over the course of the pandemic demonstrate different approaches and capabilities within statecraft at national, regional and local levels. They reveal dissonance between public health strategies, economic policy and the mitigation of the impact of these strategies on the arts and cultural sector. However, commonalities between the four nations' responses can be characterised broadly within the following categories:

- Unprecedented injections of funds to secure the survival of the sector through emergency and recovery funding primarily at the national level, but also locally.
- Relaxed criteria for eligibility and use of funds, although with anomalies and controversy for freelancers and for prioritising places.
- Policy interventions to support innovation and experimentation with new business models – e.g. hybrid delivery, commercialisation of streaming and other assets.
- Ad hoc strategies repurposing arts and cultural activities and spaces to cater for new needs and values revealed by the pandemic – e.g. Cultural Care Kits, food banks and 'Nightingale Courts' in theatres.
- Policies that continue to instrumentalise the value of culture and attach it to other policy objectives – e.g. levelling up, creative improvement districts, local high street recovery plans.

There were variations however, which we argue reflect the distinct policy assemblages (Prince, 2010) which advocate and mediate specific rationales for decision-making, and which have direct and indirect consequences for cultural and creative industries. At different moments in the pandemic these rationales were drawn on and instantiated within policy guidance, such as the levelling up prospectus, and interacted with local recovery plans which highlighted the role of cultural and creative industries in attracting inward investment and agglomeration. The turmoil of the pandemic has also brought together, or perhaps more aptly collapsed the boundaries between, discrete rationales for cultural policy-making. For example, the aspirations of the devolved nations for UBI for artists prioritise particular rationales for policy interventions within creative and cultural industries that were embedded in their policy assemblages, even when frustrated by the centralised control from Westminster. Ultimately, COVID-19 proved to be a device for revealing the divergence of cultural governance across the regions and nations of the United Kingdom, as well as the unequal capacity of different places to support strategies for recovery.

Notes

1 The Barnett formula, named after Chief Secretary to the Treasury Joel Barnett, who introduced it in 1979, provides a mechanism for setting the budgets for public monies from Westminster to the devolved governments of Scotland, Wales and Northern Ireland. The calculation is based on the previous year's figures by budget line combined with comparable per capita spending in England; devolved budgets are not ringfenced, allowing flexibility in the decision over their allocation. For arts and cultural devolved spending, the proportion of Culture, Media and Sport funding which is devolved for allocation is between 68 per cent and 70 per cent. However, during the coronavirus pandemic the method for allocating funds was changed to allow additional money to be released with guaranteed amounts for the devolved nations, avoiding delays in decision-making at Westminster (Institute for Government, 2020).
2 See Chapter 6 for further discussion of the Northern Irish context.

References

Aaronovitch, D. 2021. Hardly anyone cares about the culture wars. *The Times*. [Online]. 26 May. [Accessed 27 January 2023]. Available from: www.thetimes.co.uk/article/hardly-anyone-cares-about-the-culture-wars-blw6jbv3s

Adesina, P. 2022. In the UK, public art shifts toward Black experiences. *The New York Times*. [Online]. 28 October. [Accessed 27 January 2023]. Available from: www.nytimes.com/2022/10/28/arts/design/public-art-black-britain.html

Arts and Business Northern Ireland (ABNI). 2020. *Statement from the Arts Collaboration Network*. [Online]. [Accessed 27 January 2023]. Available from: www.artsandbusinessni.org.uk/news/2020/may/statement-from-the-arts-collaboration-network-12-may-2020

Arts Council England (ACE). 2022. *Let's Create Delivery Plan 2021–2024*. [Online]. [Accessed 27 January 2023]. Available from: www.artscouncil.org.uk/lets-create/delivery-plan-2021-2024/delivery-plan-2021-24

Arts Council England (ACE). n.d. *Emergency Resource Support round two*. [Online]. [Accessed 27 January 2023]. Available from: www.artscouncil.org.uk/culture-recovery-fund/culture-recovery-fund-emergency-resource-support-round-two

Arts Council of Northern Ireland (ACNI). 2020. *Deaf/Disabled Artist Support Fund announced by Arts Council and University of Atypical*. [Online]. [Accessed 15 November 2022]. Available from: http://artscouncil-ni.org/news/deaf-disabled-artist-support-fund-announced-by-arts-council-and-university

Arts Council of Wales. 2020. *Arts Council of Wales announces Resilience Fund for the arts in Wales*. [Online]. [Accessed 27 January 2023]. Available from: https://arts.wales/news-jobs-opportunities/arts-council-wales-announces-resilience-fund-for-arts-wales

Arts Council of Wales. n.d. *Re-setting the dial: responding to Covid-19*. [Online]. [Accessed 10 January 2024]. Available from: https://arts.wales/resources/thought-piece-resetting-dial

Arts Council of Northern Ireland (ACNI). 2022. *Funding for individuals*. [Online]. [Accessed 27 January 2023]. Available from: http://artscouncil-ni.org/funding/funding-for-individuals

Audience Agency. 2021. *Winter 2021*. [Online]. [Accessed 27 January 2023]. Available from: www.theaudienceagency.org/evidence/covid-19-cultural-participation-monitor/recent-key-insights/winter-2021

Bakare, L. 2020. Government scraps ballet dancer reskilling ad criticised as 'crass'. *The Guardian*. 22 October. [no pagination].

Bectu. 2020. *Unions, business groups and campaigners write to the Chancellor, urging him to fix the gaps in support*. [Online]. [Accessed 27 January 2023]. Available from: https://bectu.org.uk/news/unions-business-groups-and-campaigners-write-to-the-chancellor-urging-him-to-fix-the-gaps-in-support

Billington, M. 2020. Dear Oliver Dowden, have you even begun to grasp the scale of our arts crisis? *The Guardian*. 3 July. [no pagination].

Business Wales. 2020. *Wales Cultural Recovery Fund FAQs*. [Online]. [Accessed 27 January 2023]. Available from: https://businesswales.gov.wales/sites/business-wales/files/Wales%20Cultural%20Recovery%20Fund%20FAQs%20English.pdf

Cabinet Office. 2020. *Our plan to rebuild: the UK Government's COVID-19 recovery strategy*. [Online]. London: Cabinet Office. [Accessed 27 January 2023]. Available from: www.gov.uk/government/publications/our-plan-to-rebuild-the-uk-governments-covid-19-recovery-strategy#full-publication-update-history

Cheung, A. 2020. *Barnett formula*. [Online]. [Accessed 27 January 2023]. Available from: www.instituteforgovernment.org.uk/article/explainer/barnett-formula

Creative Scotland. 2020. *Culture Organisations and Venues Recovery Fund launches*. [Online]. [Accessed 27 January 2023]. Available from: www.creativescotland.com/what-we-do/latest-news/archive/2020/09/culture-recovery-fund-launches

de Peuter, G., Oakley, K. and Trusolino, M. 2022. The pandemic politics of cultural work: collective responses to the COVID-19 crisis. *International Journal of Cultural Policy*. https://doi.org/10.1080/10286632.2022.2064459

Department for Communities (DfC). 2020. *Minister announces reopening of the Creative Support Fund, 23 July 2020*. [Online]. [Accessed 10 January 2024]. Available from: www.communities-ni.gov.uk/news/minister-announces-reopening-creative-support-fund

Department for Communities (DfC). 2021a. *Culture, Arts and Heritage Recovery Taskforce*. [Online]. [Accessed 2 February 2023]. Available from: www.communities-ni.gov.uk/articles/culture-arts-and-heritage-recovery-taskforce

Department for Communities (DfC). 2021b. *The art of recovery - survive: stabilise: strengthen. The report of the Culture, Arts and Heritage Recovery Taskforce*. [Online]. London: The National Archives. [Accessed 27 January 2023]. Available from: www.communities-ni.gov.uk/

Department for Digital, Culture, Media and Sport (DCMS). 2020a. *Culture Secretary announces Cultural Renewal Taskforce*. [Press release]. [Online]. [Accessed 27 January 2023]. Available from: www.gov.uk/government/news/culture-secretary-announces-cultural-renewal-taskforce

Department for Digital, Culture, Media and Sport (DCMS). 2020b. *Culture Recovery Fund*. [Online]. London: The National Archives. [Accessed 27 January 2023]. Available from: www.gov.uk/government/groups/culture-recovery-board

Department for Digital, Culture, Media and Sport (DCMS). 2021a. *Main estimate memorandum (2022 – 23)*. [Online]. London: The National Archives. [Accessed 27 January 2023]. Available from: https://committees.parliament.uk/publications/22317/documents/165015/default/

Department for Digital, Culture, Media and Sport (DCMS). 2021b. *Events Research Programme: Phase 1 findings, policy paper*. [Online]. London: The National Archives. [Accessed 27 January 2023]. Available from: www.gov.uk/government/publications/events-research-programme-phase-i-findings/events-research-programme-phase-i-findings

Department for Levelling Up, Housing and Communities (DLUHC). 2022. *Levelling up the United Kingdom*. [Online]. [Accessed 27 January 2023]. Available from: www.gov.uk/government/publications/levelling-up-the-united-kingdom

Donnelly, S. and Komorowski, M. 2022. *Road to recovery? Cultural Freelancers Wales Report*. [Online]. [Accessed 27 January 2023]. Available from: https://cfw.wales/recovery

Doustaly, C. and Roy, V. 2022. A comparative analysis of the economic sustainability of cultural work in the UK since the COVID-19 pandemic and examination of Universal Basic Income as a solution for cultural workers. *Journal of Risk and Financial Management*. 15(5), pp.1–17.

EKOS. 2020. *Local government support to arts, culture and creative industries in Scotland. Final report to Creative Scotland. February 2020*. Glasgow: EKOS Limited.

Elis-Thomas, D. 2020. *Written statement: creative industries*. [Online]. [Accessed 27 January 2023]. Available from: https://gov.wales/written-statement-creative-industries

Equity. 2020. *Take action, share your experience and urge the Chancellor to support the creative workforce*. [Online]. [Accessed 27 January 2023]. Available from: www.facebook.com/EquityUK/posts/10158377454917394/

Equity. 2021. *DCMS summary of roadmap details for performing arts*. [Online]. [Accessed 27 January 2023]. Available from: www.equity.org.uk/news/2021/february/dcms-summary-of-roadmap-details-for-performing-arts/

Evans, R. 2020. Arts bailout: Oliver Dowden says £1.57bn of government support will start with 'crown jewels' such as Royal Albert Hall. *iNews*. [Online]. 6 July. [Accessed 27 January 2023]. Available from: https://inews.co.uk/news/arts-bailout-oliver-dowden-says-1-57bn-of-government-support-will-start-with-crown-jewels-like-royal-albert-hall-483790

Executive Office of Northern Ireland. 2020. *Executive tightens restrictions to curb Covid-19*. [Online]. [Accessed 8 August 2022]. Available from: www.executiveoffice-ni.gov.uk/news/executive-tightens-restrictions-curb-covid-19

FactCheckNI. 2019. *Do Northern Ireland arts need a 660per cent uplift in government funding?* [Online]. [Accessed 10 October 2022]. Available from: https://factcheckni.org/topics/economy/do-northern-ireland-arts-need-a-660-uplift-in-government-funding/

Henley, D. 2020. Black Lives Matter. 5 June. *Arts Council England blog*. [Online]. [Accessed 27 January 2023]. Available from: www.artscouncil.org.uk/blog/black-lives-matter

Hill, L. 2020. *'Trickle-down funding for artists doesn't work', and Arts Council England knows it*. [Online]. [Accessed 9 August 2022]. Available from: www.artsprofessional.co.uk/news/trickle-down-funding-artists-doesnt-work-and-arts-council-england-knows-it/

HM Revenue & Customs. 2021. *VAT: reduced rate for hospitality, holiday accommodation and attractions*. [Online]. [Accessed 14 December 2022].

Available from: www.gov.uk/guidance/vat-reduced-rate-for-hospitality-holiday-accommodation-and-attractions

HM Treasury. 2021. *Levelling Up Fund: prospectus.* Published 3 March. [Online]. [Accessed 1 February 2023]. Available from: www.gov.uk/government/publications/levelling-up-fund-prospectus

Home Office. 2020a. *Home Secretary announces new public health measures for all UK arrivals.* [Online]. [Accessed 27 January 2023]. Available from: www.gov.uk/government/news/home-secretary-announces-new-public-health-measures-for-all-uk-arrivals

Home Office. 2020b. *Rule of six comes into effect to tackle coronavirus.* [Online]. [Accessed 27 January 2023]. Available from: www.gov.uk/government/news/rule-of-six-comes-into-effect-to-tackle-coronavirus

Howe, S. 2020. *Future Generations Commissioner calls for a basic income pilot for creatives.* [Online]. [Accessed 30 August 2022]. Available from: www.futuregenerations.wales/news/future-generations-commissioner-calls-for-a-universal-basic-income-pilot-for-creatives/

Hutton, G. 2020. *Eat Out to Help Out Scheme* (Briefing Paper Number CBP 8978). [Online]. London: House of Commons Library. [Accessed 10 January 2024]. Available from: https://researchbriefings.files.parliament.uk/documents/CBP-8978/CBP-8978.pdf

Institute for Government. 2020. Barnett formula. [Online]. [Accessed 9 January 2024]. Available from: www.instituteforgovernment.org.uk/article/explainer/barnett-formula.

Jackson, A. and Devlin, G. 2005. *Grants for the arts: evaluation of the first year, Research Report 40.* London: Arts Council England.

James, W. 2021. England's 'freedom day' marred by soaring cases and isolation chaos. *Reuters.* [Online]. 19 July. [Accessed 9 August 2022]. Available from: www.reuters.com/world/uk/pm-johnson-pleads-caution-freedom-day-arrives-england-2021-07-18/

Jones, S. 2019. *The chance to dream: why fund individual artists?* [Online]. [Accessed 27 January 2023]. Available from: https://padwickjonesarts.co.uk/the-chance-to-dream-why-fund-individual-artists

Jones, S. 2022. Artists' precarity is not just about pay. *Arts Professional.* [Online]. [Accessed 7 June 2022]. Available from: www.artsprofessional.co.uk/magazine/article/artists-precarity-not-just-about-pay

Journal of Music. 2021. Creative Practitioner Bursary Programme. [Online]. [Accessed 10 January 2024]. Available from: https://journalofmusic.com/listing/09-03-21/creative-practitioner-bursary-programme

Jowett, P. 2022. Low uptake of live events insurance scheme by festivals. *Arts Professional.* [Online]. 23 June. [Accessed 8 August 2022]. Available from: www.artsprofessional.co.uk/news/low-uptake-live-events-insurance-scheme-festivals

Moore, P. 2022. *How a placed-based employment programme is bringing creative workers back to Northern Ireland.* [Online]. [Accessed 22 January 2023]. Available from: https://pec.ac.uk/blog/how-a-placed-based-employment-programme-is-bringing-creative-workers-back-to-northern-ireland

Morris, S. 2021. Wales to require NHS Covid passes to attend night-clubs and events. *The Guardian.* [Online]. 17 September. [Accessed 23 January 2023]. Available from: www.theguardian.com/uk-news/2021/sep/17/wales-to-require-nhs-covid-passes-to-attend-nightclubs-and-events

Morris, S. 2022. Basic income pilot scheme for care leavers to be tri-alled in Wales. *The Guardian.* [Online]. 15 February. [Accessed 30 August 2022]. Available from: www.theguardian.com/society/2022/feb/15/basic-income-pilot-scheme-for-care-leavers-to-be-trialled-in-wales

National Audit Office (NAO). 2021. *Investigation into the Culture Recovery Fund, Department for Digital, Culture, Media & Sport.* London: National Audit Office.

Parkinson, A., Turner, D., Gallagher, P., Usher, S., Grunhut, S. and Heath, O. 2022. *Evaluation of the Wales Cultural Recovery Fund 2020–2021* (GSR report number 44/2022). [Online]. Cardiff: Welsh Government. [Accessed 10 January 2024]. Available from: https://gov.wales/evaluation-wales-cultural-recovery-fund-2020-2021

Powell, A. 2022. *Coronavirus: getting people back into work* (CPB 8965). [Online]. London: House of Commons Library. [Accessed 10 January 2024]. Available from: https://commonslibrary.parliament.uk/research-briefings/cbp-8965/

Prime Minister's Office. 2020. *Prime Minister's statement on coronavirus (COVID-19): 16 March 2020.* [Online]. [Accessed 27 January 2023]. Available from: www.gov.uk/government/speeches/pm-statement-on-coronavirus-16-march-2020

Prime Minister's Office. 2021. *Prime Minister sets out roadmap to cau-tiously ease lockdown restrictions.* [Press release]. [Online]. 22 February. [Accessed 27 January 2023]. Available from: www.gov.uk/government/news/prime-minister-sets-out-roadmap-to-cautiously-ease-lockdown-restrictions

Prince, R. 2010. Policy transfer as policy assemblage: making policy for the creative industries in New Zealand. *Environment and Planning A: Economy and Space.* 42(1), pp.169–186.

RSM UK Consulting LLP. 2022. *Process evaluation of the Film and TV Production Restart Scheme. Final evaluation report.* [Online]. [Accessed 27 January 2023]. Available from: https://assets.publishing.service.gov.uk/government/uploads/system/uploads/attachment_data/file/1051224/Film_and_TV_Production_Restart_Scheme_-_Final_Report_2601.pdf

Scottish Government. 2020. *A culture strategy for Scotland.* [Online]. [Accessed 27 January 2023]. Available from: www.gov.scot/policies/arts-culture-heritage/culture-strategy-for-scotland/

Scottish Parliament. 2021. *Scotland's public finances in 2022–23 and the impact of Covid-19.* [Online]. [Accessed 1 February 2023]. Available from: www.audit-scotland.gov.uk/uploads/docs/um/ags_210813_fpac_consultation_response.pdf

Scottish Tourism Emergency Response Group (STERG). 2021. *COVID-19 tourism recovery programme.* [Online]. [Accessed 27 January 2023].

Available from: www.visitscotland.org/supporting-your-business/advice/coronavirus/sterg/tourism-recovery-programme

Seely, A. 2022. *VAT on tourism (number 6812)*. [Online]. London: House of Commons Library. [Accessed 10 January 2024]. Available from: https://researchbriefings.files.parliament.uk/documents/SN06812/SN06812.pdf

Snow, G. 2020. Rishi Sunak: creative sectors must adapt to survive Covid crisis. *The Stage*. 6 October. [no pagination].

SQW. 2022. *Evaluation of Arts Council England's Emergency Response Fund (ERF), report for Arts Council England*. Stockport: SQW.

The Guardian. 2021. The Guardian view on the National Trust: battleground for a culture war. Editorial. *The Guardian*. [Online]. 14 October. [Accessed 31 January 2023]. Available from: www.theguardian.com/commentisfree/2021/oct/14/the-guardian-view-on-the-national-trust-battleground-for-a-culture-war

The Stage. 2020. *Theatre bosses urge government to halt 'obliteration' of sector*. [Online]. 27 May. [Accessed 27 January 2023]. Available from: www.thestage.co.uk/news/theatre-bosses-urge-government-to-halt-obliteration-of-sector

Thompson, T. 2020. The real 'crown jewels' of the arts? An unprotected freelance workforce. *The Guardian*. 22 July. [no pagination].

Tsioulakis, I. and FitzGibbon, A. 2020. *Performing artists in the age of COVID-19: a moment of urgent action and potential change*. [Online]. [Accessed 7 June 2022]. Available from: http://qpol.qub.ac.uk/performing-artists-in-the-age-of-covid-19/

Welsh Government. 2015. *Wellbeing of Future Generations (Wales) Act 2015 Essentials Guide*. [Online]. Cardiff: Welsh Government. [Accessed 10 January 2024]. Available from: https://gov.wales/sites/default/files/publications/2021-10/well-being-future-generations-wales-act-2015-the-essentials-2021.pdf

Welsh Government. 2019. *Prosperity for All: economic action plan*. [Online]. Cardiff: Welsh Government. [Accessed 10 January 2024]. Available from: https://gov.wales/prosperity-all-economic-action-plan

Welsh Government. 2020a. *Four UK nations agree new rules for the festive period*. [Online]. [Accessed 27 January 2023]. Available from: https://gov.wales/four-uk-nations-agree-new-rules-festive-period

Welsh Government. 2020b. *Written statement: local coronavirus restrictions update, Vaughan Gething MS, Minister for Health and Social Services*. [Online]. [Accessed 27 January 2023]. Available from: https://gov.wales/written-statement-local-coronavirus-restrictions-update

Welsh Government. 2021. *Coronavirus restrictions relaxations confirmed*. [Press release]. [Online]. [Accessed 27 January 2023]. Available from: https://gov.wales/coronavirus-restrictions-relaxations-confirmed

Welsh Government. 2022. *Evaluation of the Wales Cultural Recovery Fund: 2020 to 2021 (summary)*. [Online]. [Accessed 27 January 2023]. Available from: https://gov.wales/sites/default/files/pdf-versions/2022/6/4/1655967612/evaluation-wales-cultural-recovery-fund-2020-2021-summary.pdf

Welsh Parliament. 2020. *Impact of the COVID-19 outbreak on the creative industries*. [Online]. Cardiff: Welsh Parliament. [Accessed 27 January 2023]. Available from: https://senedd.wales/media/poibdvyl/cr-ld13352-e.pdf

Woodhouse, J. and Hutton, G. 2021. *Covid-19 and the arts and culture sectors* (Briefing Paper Number CBP 9018), 25 February 2021. [Online]. London: House of Commons Library. [Accessed 10 January 2024]. Available from: http://researchbriefings.files.parliament.uk/documents/CBP-9018/CBP-9018.pdf

Wright, J. 2020. *Policy review: cultural policy responses to COVID-19 in the UK*. Version 1, October 2020. Leeds: Centre for Cultural Value.

2

What happened to the workers? Understanding the impact of the pandemic on jobs and working hours in the cultural sector

*Tal Feder, Orian Brook, Rebecca Florisson,
Siobhan McAndrew, Dave O'Brien, Gwilym Owen
and Mark Taylor*

The pandemic in 2020, alongside the necessary public health response, created considerable challenges for the cultural sector. This chapter offers a broad overview of what happened to jobs and working hours during that year. In doing so, it tells a story of the uneven impact of the pandemic on working life in the cultural sector. It also helps to contextualise the policy responses detailed in Chapter 1, demonstrating the scale of interventions that were needed.

For some workers in Britain's cultural industries, 2020 was a disaster. They lost jobs, income and contact with their art forms. Others witnessed new possibilities, as changing working practices and increased demand saw growth in employment opportunities. As is common to almost all general analysis of cultural employment, the uneven impact was differentiated by key demographic characteristics. Those groups already marginalised from the cultural sector were more likely to face further exclusions. The lessons from debates over the need for a more open and equitable cultural sector were given a forceful illustration in 2020. Sadly, it seems that the rush to return to 'business as usual' means a return to an already exclusionary and exploitative model of cultural and creative work.

The opening parts of this chapter tell the story of 2020 itself, using nationally representative data on the UK labour force. The chapter then moves to look at 2020 through to 2022, to show that even where there has been a recovery for jobs and hours worked, this has not been shared across all art forms and all workers.

The chapter concludes by linking this analysis to the literature, suggesting that working practices in our cultural industries needed major reforms before the impact of the pandemic, reforms which have only become even more pressing since much of the sector reopened in 2021.

What happened to jobs and working hours in 2020?

In spring 2020, live performance venues and museums and galleries across the UK closed their doors for long periods; films and television programmes put a halt on production; and self-employed creatives experienced immense job instability. However, given the pace of change, and limited data availability, it was difficult for policy-makers and industry to understand the exact scale of the pandemic's impact on employment within the sector.

In order to paint a clearer picture, our analysis uses Labour Force Survey (LFS) data from the Office for National Statistics (ONS). This source gives a nationally representative picture of the entire British workforce, including the sub-sectors constituting the cultural and creative industries.

In the six months following the beginning of lockdown, the UK witnessed:

- a collapse in working hours across the creative industries;
- 60,000 job losses (a 30 per cent decline) in music, performing and visual arts;
- significantly higher than average numbers of people leaving creative occupations compared to previous years (Figure 2.1).

This is clear evidence of the existence, and the scale, of a jobs crisis. We look at job losses for creative occupations, the creative industries as a whole and then specifically for the cultural sector. We also examine the impact that lockdown has had on the number of hours worked by those who continued in the sector.

Creative occupations include a wide range of job roles across the creative industries, for example writers, film-makers and game designers. They also include people doing creative roles in other industries, such as designers working in manufacturing companies.

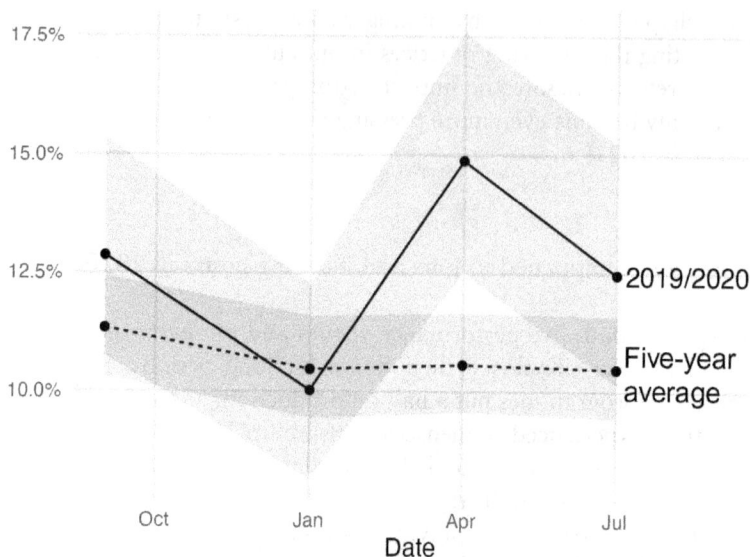

Figure 2.1 Percentage of workers leaving creative occupations, per quarter

The figure shows two things: the five-year average proportion of people leaving creative occupations in each quarter; and the proportion leaving in each quarter between Q4 (October–December) 2019 and Q3 (July–September) 2020. The comparison allows us to see how unusual the 2020 employment patterns were.

Using the ONS data set, Figure 2.1 shows that 15 per cent of people who worked in creative occupations in January–March in 2020 were no longer working in creative occupations in April–June.[1] This is significantly greater than between the same period in the previous five years, where on average we saw around 10.5 per cent of creatives leave the sector.[2]

We also found that the percentage of workers who left creative occupations between April and September 2020 was higher than normal, at 12.5 per cent compared with 10.5 per cent – although in this case the difference is not statistically significant. Of those who reported having left creative occupations between Quarter 1 (Q1) (January–March) and Quarter 2 (Q2) (April–June), around two-thirds (69 per cent) were now working in other occupations, while 10 per cent of those who left creative occupations were classified as unemployed.[3]

Creative industries

We also used the ONS data to analyse the impact of the pandemic on the creative industries as a sector, as distinct from creative occupations. The 'creative industries' includes those who work in what are termed 'non-creative occupations' within the wider sector, for example hospitality staff working in museums, but does not include those working in creative roles in other sectors (Brook, O'Brien and Taylor, 2020). For workers in the creative industries we saw a similar pattern to those in creative occupations, although the numbers who left the creative industries were smaller in both percentage terms and as a raw number. Approximately 110,000 people left the creative industries between Q1 (January–March) and Q2 (April–July) in 2020, around 8 per cent of the workforce.[4]

When we looked in more detail at specific sub-sectors in the creative industries, or occupational groups – such as publishing, architecture and crafts – we found that for *most* of the creative industries and most creative occupations, there were not large changes in the number of workers in 2020 (Figure 2.2).

However, the shift in numbers working in music, performing and visual arts occupations is clearly significant. The number of workers in these occupations dropped from around 200,000 in January–March 2020 to around 155,000 in April–June and then again to around 140,000 in July–September and to around 134,000 in October–December, a decline of almost 34 per cent since pre-lockdown. When we analysed it from the industry-wide perspective mentioned earlier, rather than the occupational perspective, we found similar, but smaller-scale, results. This is a particularly important finding as over the last few years the number of people working in music, performing and visual arts has increased, albeit with some variation in number from month to month (see Figure 2.3). The post-lockdown decline clearly breaks this pattern.

The impact on working hours

Even for those sub-sectors where we didn't find evidence of high levels of job losses, we found that since lockdown began in March 2020 creative occupations saw significant reductions in the average

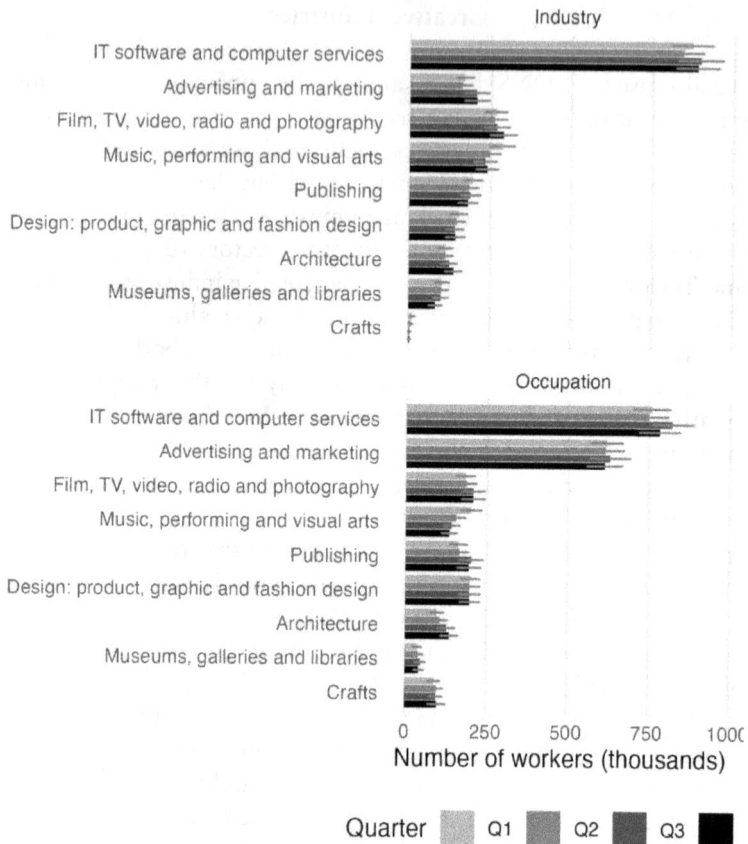

Figure 2.2 Overall size of the workforce in creative industries and occupations in all four quarters of 2020

number of hours worked each week. Figure 2.4 shows the change in the number of hours worked by people in each of the creative occupational groups, comparing the second quarter of 2019 (April–June) with the second quarter of 2020 (April–June). This comparison is to make sure the differences observed are not just due to seasonal variations. This reveals a substantial increase in the number of people that reported working zero hours in the previous week.

The data also show us that the reduction in hours did not fall evenly across the creative industries: those working in crafts, film,

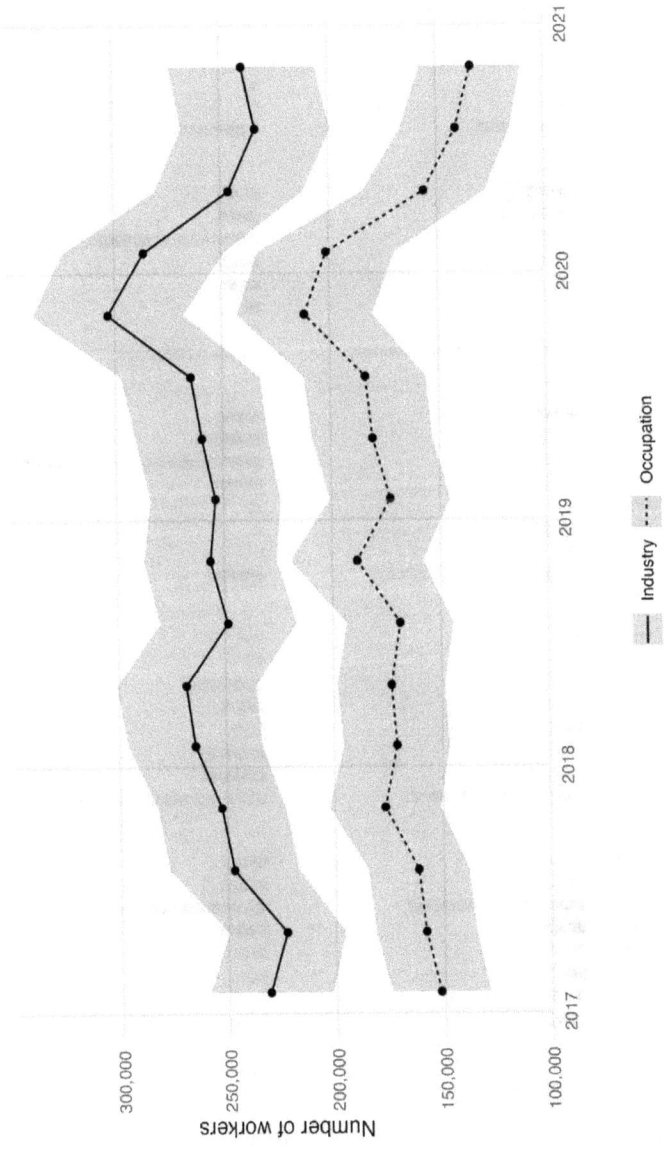

Figure 2.3 Workers in music and performing arts, 2017–2021

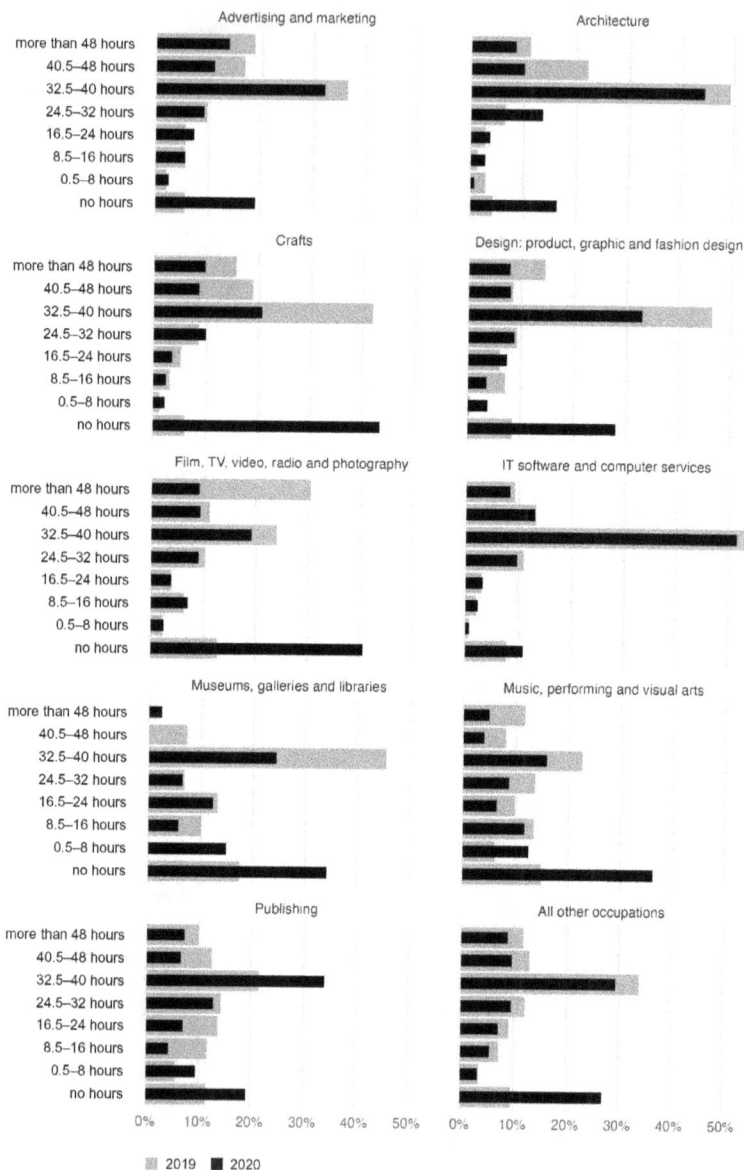

Figure 2.4 Distribution of hours worked, by occupational group

Advertising and marketing

Architecture

Crafts

Design: product, graphic and fashion design

Film, TV, video, radio and photography

IT software and computer services

Museums, galleries and libraries

Music, performing and visual arts

Publishing

All other occupations

more than 48 hours
40.5–48 hours
32.5–40 hours
24.5–32 hours
16.5–24 hours
8.5–16 hours
0.5–8 hours
no hours

0% 10% 20% 30% 40% 50%

2019 2020

TV, video, radio and photography, music, performing and visual arts and design were the most severely affected. Moreover, July–September 2020 data indicates that while there was a slight reduction in the percentage of workers working zero hours in this latter part of the year, the average number of hours worked were still far below pre-lockdown levels. Thus, we can see that workers in the creative industries were hit particularly hard by the COVID-19 pandemic and lockdown. Within this segment, industries and occupations such as music and performing arts suffered most, with a collapse in the number of hours worked and large numbers of job losses.

What were the national and regional differences, and the differences between demographic groups?

In this section, again based on analysis of the ONS Labour Force Survey for the first three quarters of 2020, we dive down below the headline figures to look at the impact on different places and different groups of workers within the creative economy. Firstly, we compare the nations and regions of the UK. We then focus on disabled people; those who are younger; and those who haven't engaged in higher education. This analysis complements work that looked at the impact on other demographic groups, such as women of colour (TUC, 2021).

The nations and regions of the UK

In 2020 there were no clear differences in trends between the four nations. Notably, almost every nation showed some level of contraction in 2020 Q2 (April to June 2020) as lockdown hit (Figure 2.5), and then a small expansion as restrictions eased and the economy reopened in Q3 (July to September 2020). This suggests that the size of the creative labour force is responsive to the type and extent of lockdown conditions.

The exception is Q2 in Scotland, although we should bear in mind that the sample size is much smaller than for England, and for the UK as a whole. Indeed, this is one area where we need much more detailed data to give a more comprehensive picture of the

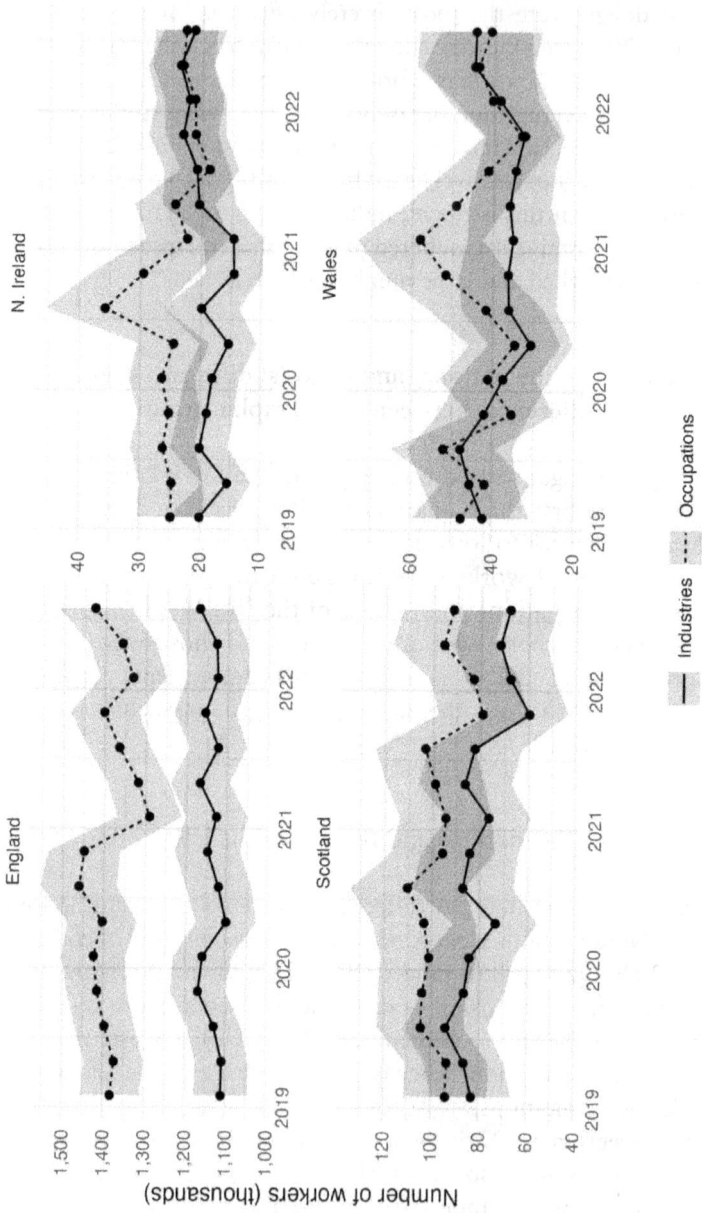

Figure 2.5 Size of the workforce in creative industries and occupations 2019–2022, by nations

Scottish, Welsh and Northern Irish creative economies. The ONS Labour Force Survey collects data on the entire UK economy, with creative industries and occupations representing a significant, but small, proportion of the economy as a whole. Within that, England is by far the largest single national economy. The data for the creative economies outside of England therefore have to be treated with more caution as a result of the smaller sample sizes.

These smaller sample sizes mean that there is limited scope for further regional breakdowns within Scotland, Wales and Northern Ireland. However, we can offer a more detailed analysis of England. London and the South East dominate the geography of the creative industries in England. This holds true even if we account for these regions having larger populations. For most regions there is little evidence of large changes in numbers from the beginning of lockdown onwards. There is some evidence of a particular decline in the South East, although we should bear in mind that the uncertainty around this is large, again due to small sample sizes.

Nevertheless, the nation-level data does suggest that the creative workforce contracted and expanded in line with lockdown restrictions. In other sectors of the economy (Taylor and Florisson, 2020) it appeared that those in contractually insecure jobs, often with lower levels of education, and in lower-paid jobs, were the most vulnerable to job loss during this period.

The impact on different demographic groups

Before the pandemic, a range of academic literature was concerned that there were clear inequalities in creative jobs based on people's demographic characteristics (see Brook, O'Brien and Taylor, 2020 for a summary). The most recent analysis, published by the AHRC Creative Industries Policy and Evidence Centre (Carey, O'Brien and Gable, 2021a, 2021b), shows the long-standing under-representation of women, disabled people, those from working-class backgrounds and people of colour in the creative sector. In terms of changes in the representation of women, disabled people and people of colour, it is too early to say if the pandemic has had any long-term consequences, although we know from TUC (2021) analysis that there has been an immediate, negative impact on employment figures.

There is fairly strong evidence that the proportion of people without degrees working in creative occupations is declining. The pandemic saw a decline in the percentage of workers in creative occupations without degrees from 37 per cent in the year before lockdown to 34 per cent in the six months post-lockdown, a difference which is statistically significant. For context, the percentage in the overall workforce without a degree is more than 60 per cent.

Figure 2.6 uses the longitudinal version of the Labour Force Survey to examine whether people who left creative employment were disproportionately drawn from certain demographic groups.[5] The graph illustrates that while there are some differences, the relatively small sample sizes in the Labour Force Survey for each sub-group means that in most cases we cannot be confident whether these observed changes are real or due to sampling variation.

An important exception, and the one where we see the biggest difference, is among workers aged under twenty-five. More than a quarter (27 per cent) of creative workers under the age of twenty-five left the creative occupations after lockdown, compared with just 14 per cent of workers aged twenty-five and over.[6] Before the pandemic it was also typical to see a higher turnover of workers aged under twenty-five in and out of the creative industries compared with workers of other ages. However, among under-twenty-fives, the rate of leaving since lockdown (around 15 per cent) was higher than what would typically be expected.

We can see the biggest differences in the number of hours worked. In all demographic groups the average number of hours worked decreased, and the percentage of people working no hours increased following the 2020 lockdown. However, there were also clear demographic differences in the magnitude of the changes.

There was a greater increase in the proportion of people working zero hours for people under the age of twenty-five, and for people without a degree, as compared with those over the age of twenty-five, and with a degree, respectively. For those under the age of twenty-five, over 30 per cent of workers reported working zero hours. There are also higher proportions of women working zero hours, as well as disabled workers. Of course, many of these groups were already more likely to be working zero hours pre-lockdown.

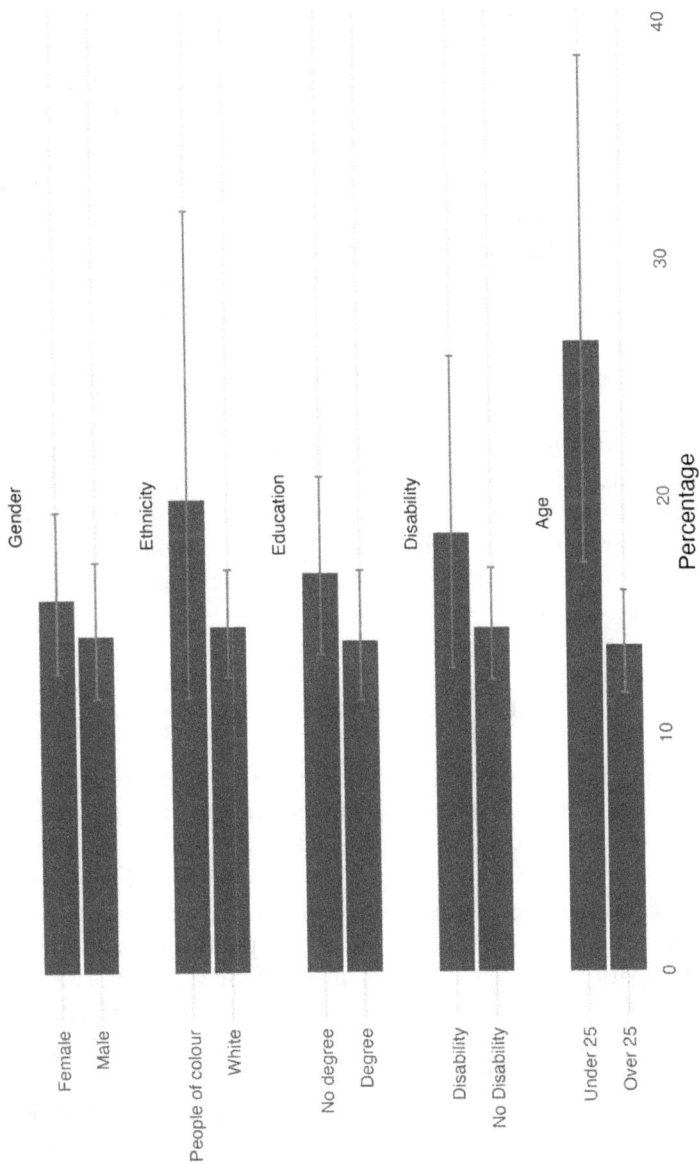

Figure 2.6 Percentage of workers leaving creative occupations per quarter since lockdown

We also looked at changes in hours worked for workers in creative industries and found similar trends. In this case, we found a larger increase in the proportion of disabled workers working zero hours compared with non-disabled workers. These differences in changes in hours worked broadly reflect what we observed in the overall labour force. The exceptions are that under-twenty-fives in creative occupations and disabled people in the creative industries do appear to have greater reductions in working hours than we see in the labour force as a whole.

Although changes in formal or self-identified employment were not large, changes in the numbers of people actually working substantial hours were. To some extent this might indicate that the government support schemes were effective, in that they retained workers within the creative sector. However, it does also suggest that certain demographic groups were more vulnerable to losing their jobs in the first months of the pandemic. It is easy to see how this could lead to even greater inequalities in the sector. Additionally, it seems clear that younger workers were particularly affected. This is of particular concern regarding future inequality in the cultural and creative sector, potentially heralding a missing generation of creative and cultural workers.

The impact on freelancers

Freelancers are especially important to the creative economy, as they represent a high proportion of the workforce compared to other parts of the economy. At the end of 2019, ONS data indicated that around 15 per cent of the workforce were self-employed, but the equivalent figure was 30 per cent of all creative occupations and an astonishing 88 per cent of music, performing and visual arts occupations. Freelancers, as a subset of the self-employed, are highly over-represented in music, performing and visual arts (27 per cent of the workforce) as compared with creative occupations (9 per cent) and the workforce as a whole (3 per cent).[7]

In this section, we explore what the ONS data can tell us about the plight of freelancers. We also drill down to look at trends in three clusters of creative occupations: film, TV, radio and photography; publishing; and music, performing and visual arts. We find that the number of freelancers working in creative jobs decreased significantly during 2020. Moreover, the hours worked by those freelancers who continued to work have also seen a severe decline. Different demographic groups have suffered unevenly, with younger workers and women suffering job losses and reduction of hours at greater rates than their older and male colleagues.

As with creative occupations as a whole, freelancers in different occupations had different experiences of the impacts of the pandemic. For those in media occupations, the flow of job losses seems to have been stemmed with some evidence of recovery. For those in music, performing and visual arts, the crisis continued well into 2022.

Freelancers in all creative occupations

Figure 2.7 shows the number of freelancers working in creative occupations from the start of 2018 to the end of 2020. The grey sections surrounding the central black line in the visualisation shows the confidence intervals that are associated with sample sizes in the Labour Force Survey. We can see that at the end of 2020 the number of freelancers working in creative occupations was lower (around 156,000) than the beginning of 2018 (around 176,000). This suggests that the trend for growth in freelance employment, as part of a growing creative economy sector, stalled as a result of the pandemic. In particular, the number of freelancers in all creative occupations declined by around 38,000 from the start to the end of 2020.

We see similar trends in the numbers of hours worked. By the middle of 2020 there was a steep rise in the numbers reporting working zero hours per week in their freelance creative occupation (and an associated decline of those reporting working over 32 hours). There was some evidence of recovery in the numbers reporting working over 32 hours a week by the end of 2020.

The data from the ONS Labour Force Survey suggests that the crisis for freelancers hit different demographic groups in uneven ways. Age clearly mattered most, with the decline in numbers of freelance workers impacting less severely on the oldest, and perhaps most established, freelancers. Figure 2.8 summarises trends for different age groups, highlighting steep declines in numbers for

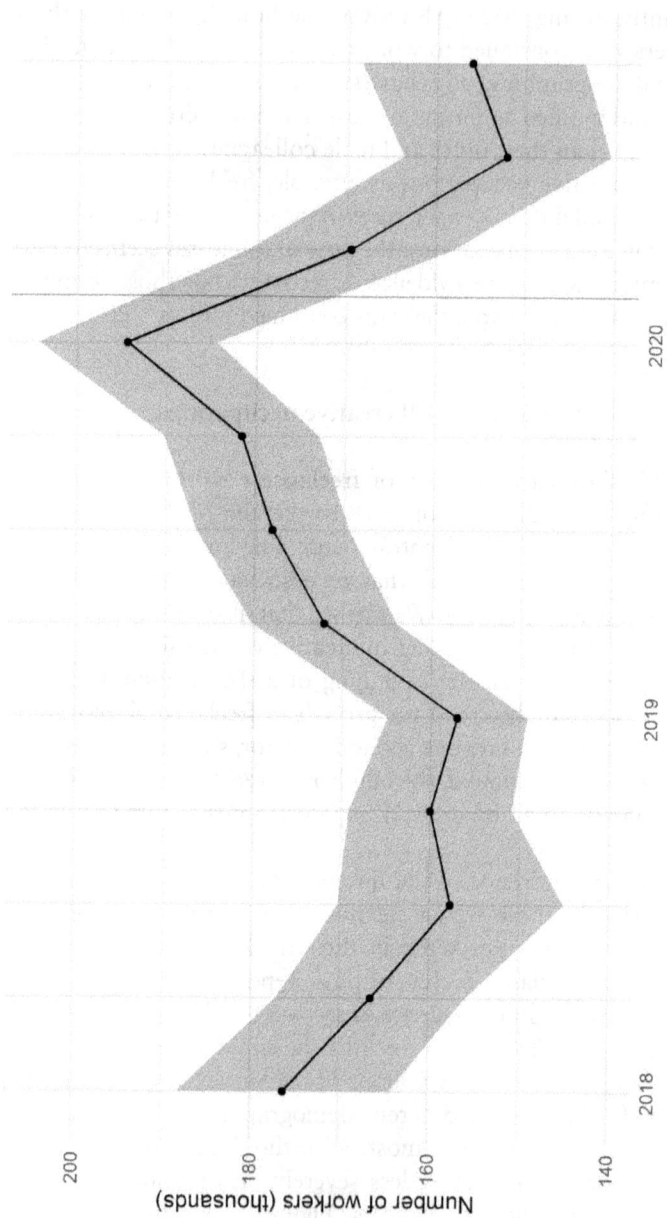

Figure 2.7 Number of freelancers in creative occupations, 2018–2020

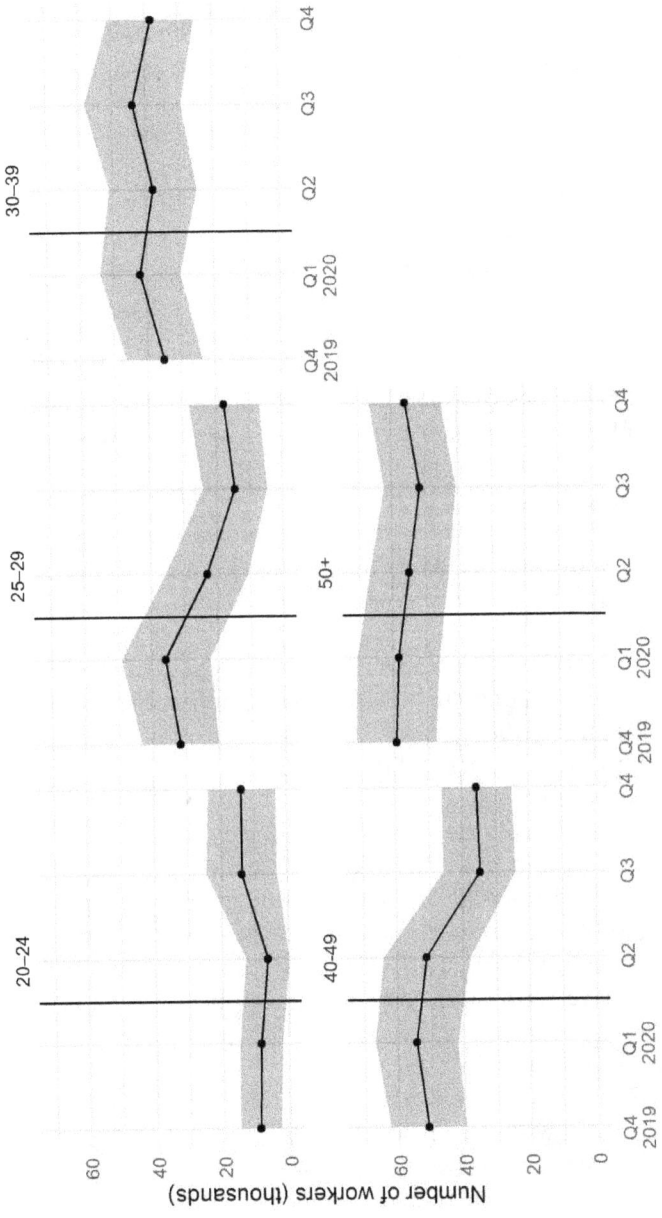

Figure 2.8 Numbers of freelancers in creative occupations by age, 2019 Q4–2020

two age groups. Freelance workers aged twenty-five to twenty-nine in creative occupations declined from around 30,000 to around 20,000 during 2020. Those aged forty to forty-nine also saw a steep decline, from around 50,000 workers to around 38,000.

For the over-fifties, the impact of lockdown, reopening and then the second lockdown was less marked. There is evidence of losses during the year that were similar in number to their younger counterparts, but this is set against evidence of a recovery by the end of the year. While the absolute numbers were similar at certain points in 2020 for the over-fifties, the overall change is less pronounced, given their greater number in the creative sector.

As with all of our analyses, there are many reasons to be cautious, not least of which are issues associated with seasonal churn in numbers and the lack of robust data on freelancers leaving, coming back in and leaving again. The small size of the twenty to twenty-four-year-old cohort also makes us cautious about drawing firm conclusions, given the size of the sample. This data does provide some indications that younger freelance creatives were poorly protected by government and sector interventions.

We now turn to differences between white freelancers and freelancers of colour. The Labour Force Survey data suggest that the number of the latter group remained stable over the course of 2020. This may be a result of there being very low numbers of freelancers of colour in creative occupations more generally, along with other factors such as age, gender and levels of qualifications. We can see this comparison in Figure 2.9.

As a result of small sample sizes, relating in turn to the small number of freelancers of colour in creative occupations, we cannot speculate as to whether this is driven by demographic factors, such as the age profile of those particular freelancers, or occupational factors such as their specific job. Both, however, are plausible drivers. As we have seen above, different age groups were impacted differently. As we will see below, different occupational groups also saw different patterns of job losses.

Figure 2.10 illustrates that there were differences according to gender regarding when the pandemic affected workforce presence. Female freelancers in the creative occupations were hit early on in 2020, in keeping with the seasonal decline in creative occupations and then the impact of the first lockdown. While the decline of male

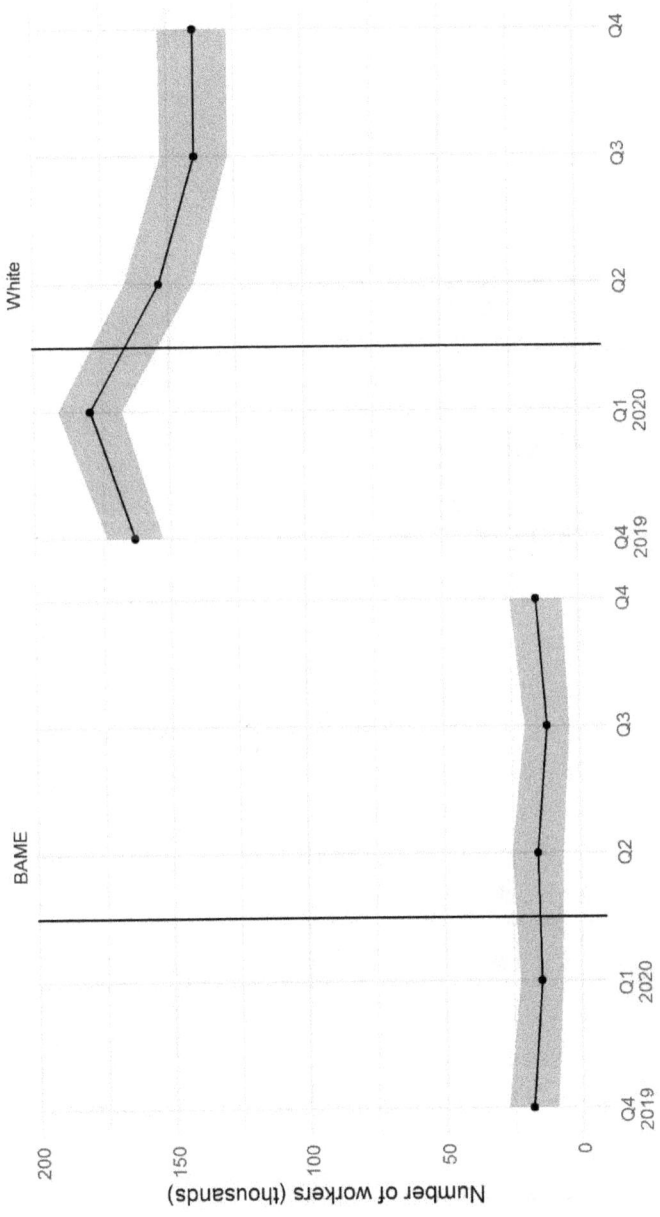

Figure 2.9 Number of freelancers in creative occupations by ethnic group, 2019 Q4–2020

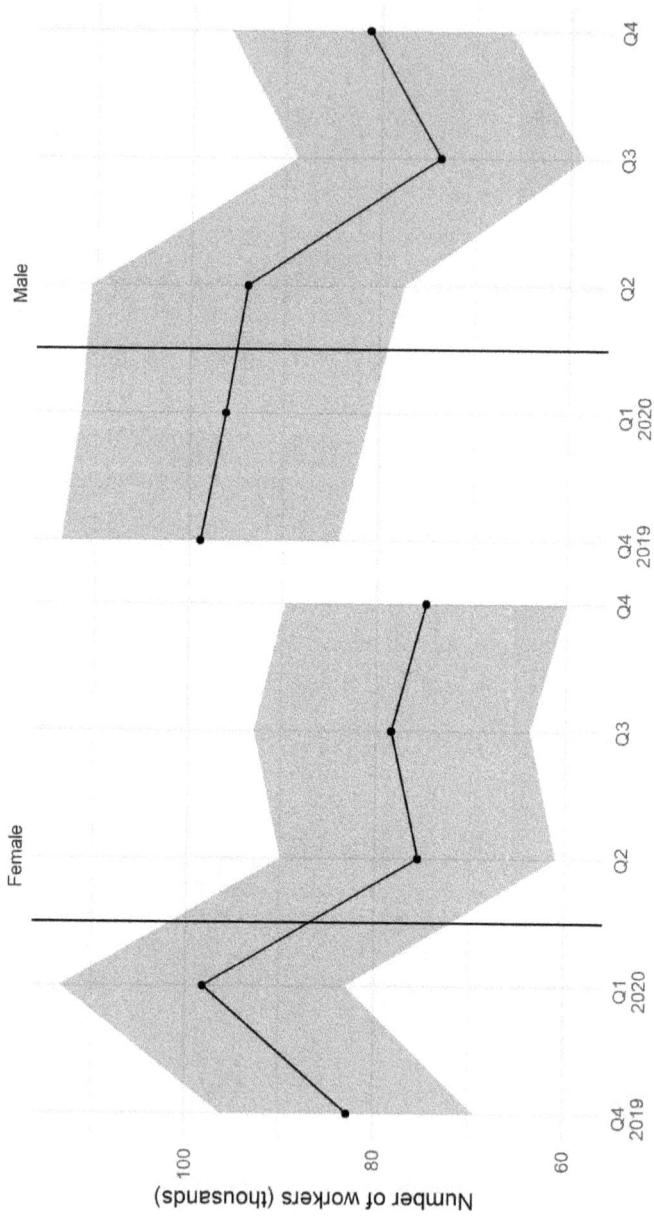

Figure 2.10 Number of freelancers in creative occupations by gender, 2019 Q4–2020

freelancers in creative occupations came later in 2020, the end of the year shows the possible emergence of a gender gap in the recovery for freelancers, mirroring creative economy trends seen after the 2008 recession (Skillset, 2010). Again, however, we should bear in mind the large confidence intervals associated with these numbers.

Different occupations, different impacts?

In terms of specific groups of occupations, there were clear differences within the creative economy. Film and associated occupations saw lockdown declines, but by October 2020 seemed to be on a trajectory of recovery; a similar, if less pronounced, set of impacts happened within publishing occupations. By comparison, music, performing and the visual arts were at the epicentre of the crisis for freelancers, with a trend of decline continuing throughout 2020 that was not at all ameliorated by the brief reopening seen in summer 2020.

There are also important demographic differences within those sets of occupations. Where we have sample sizes robust enough for analysis, we can see pronounced gender differences – for example in publishing, which witnessed a decline in female freelancers of around 14 per cent and a rise for men of 15 per cent across the year. By comparison, there did not seem to be gender differences in music, performing and visual arts, with around 38 per cent declines for men and women alike. While low numbers mean we can't report the changes in the size of the film and related *occupations* workforce by gender, the data in the ONS Labour Force Survey on the film *industry* is very worrying. This suggests a staggering 51 per cent fall in the number of female freelancers by the end of 2020 as compared to the start of the year, compared with a minimal 5 per cent decline for men.

The impact of the furlough scheme

As we have shown above, the COVID-19 pandemic had a profoundly negative impact on employment in key parts of the cultural sector. In this section, we consider redundancies and the government's support for the Coronavirus Job Retention Scheme in the cultural sector. The popularly called 'furlough' scheme was indeed vital to protect jobs in the cultural and creative industries.[8] However, as we saw in the previous section, high numbers of freelancers were not protected.

For this analysis we've used data from the Business Impact of COVID-19 Survey (BICS), a data set that, in March 2021, was renamed the Business Insights and Conditions Survey. This survey collected data every two weeks, using an online questionnaire from a sample of just under 40,000 businesses. It began in April 2020, asking questions about a range of business issues, including finances, workforce and trading confidence.[9] The ONS classifies this data set as 'experimental' and there are many reasons to be cautious about it. For example, it is voluntary, depending on the goodwill of businesses to complete the survey questions. It does, however, offer a unique insight into businesses' experiences over the pandemic period.

The ONS reports BICS findings by industrial sector. This was incredibly useful in getting a picture of the UK economy over the course of the pandemic. However, there have been limitations in terms of understanding the experience of cultural and creative industries. These limitations exist for three reasons. Firstly, cultural and creative businesses and organisations are included in two separate industrial sectors in the ONS reporting: information and communication; and arts, entertainment and recreation. This means that we don't have a single indicator for the sector. Secondly, businesses and organisations that are *not* cultural and creative are also included in these two industrial sectors. An obvious example is that betting shops, golf courses and gyms are included in the 'arts, entertainment and recreation' category.

Figure 2.11 shows the percentage of workers furloughed across all creative industries, and in the economy overall (in a thick grey line). They are placed together on the same chart for ease of comparison. Figure 2.12 presents charts for each individual creative industry, against a backdrop showing the level of lockdown restrictions, from highest to lowest. This allows us to show the levels of the furlough relative to the levels of Covid-related restrictions.

Three sectors – performing and visual arts, museums and galleries, and film and television – are immediately striking. They are at the top of Figure 2.12, reflecting the fact they had very high proportions

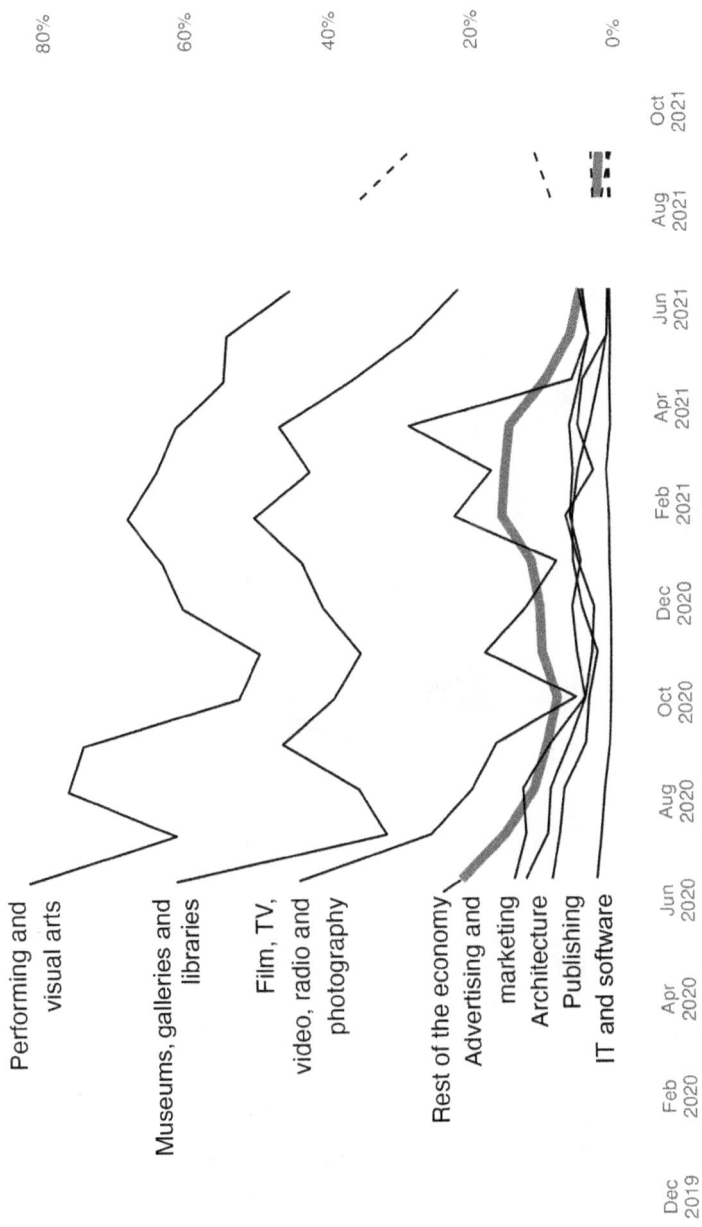

Figure 2.11 Percentage of staff furloughed by creative sector

Performing and
visual arts

Museums, galleries and
libraries

Film, TV,
video, radio and
photography

Rest of the economy
Advertising and
marketing
Architecture
Publishing
IT and software

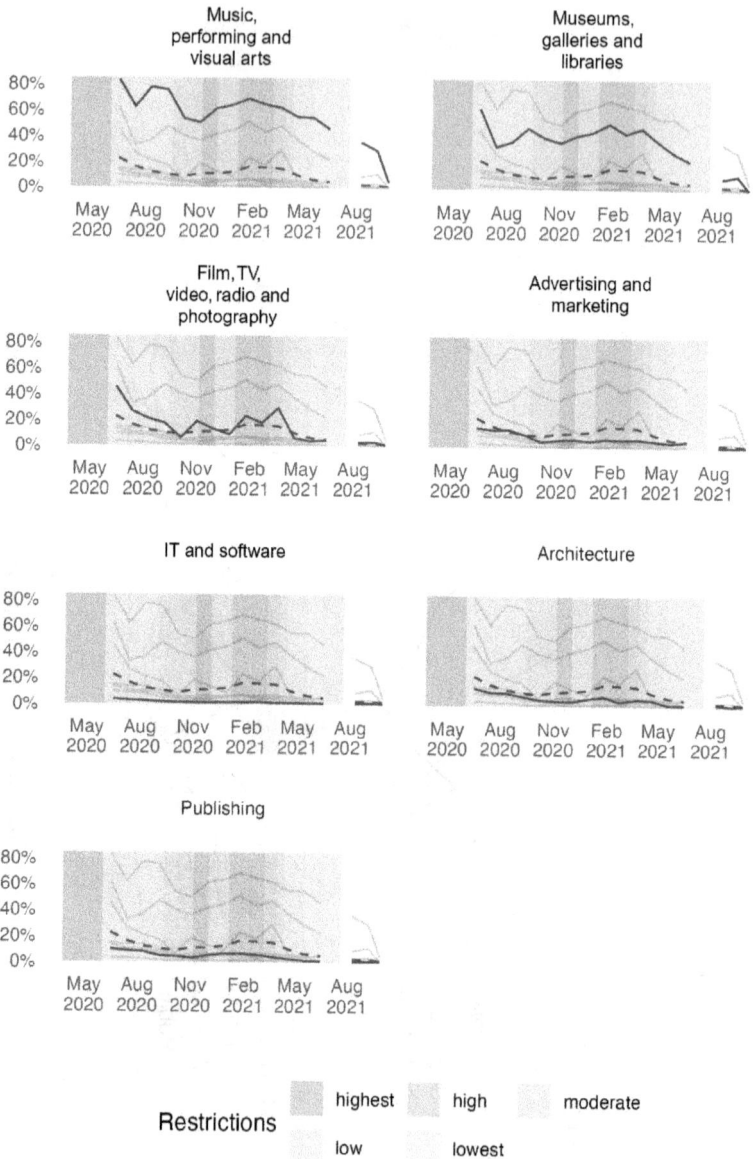

Figure 2.12 Percentage of staff furloughed by creative sector and Covid restrictions

of furloughed staff (over 80 per cent in performing and visual arts and over 60 per cent in museums and galleries) at the beginning of the pandemic. This is a significantly higher proportion than the average across the rest of the economy, which was just over 20 per cent, despite including sectors such as hospitality, which we know were severely affected by pandemic measures.

What is also noticeable about performing and visual arts and museums and galleries is their slow return to 'normal'. In the last waves of the BICS, when furlough was coming to an end, we can see how the performing arts had almost 30 per cent and museums and galleries had over 10 per cent of the workforce on furlough, even as pandemic restrictions were eased and ended, whereas other sectors had only 2 per cent of the workforce furloughed.

The impact of the pandemic on film and television and publishing was less dramatic than for the performing and visual arts and museums, although still on average higher than the rest of the economy, and there was a spike in furlough for film and television at the start of 2021. For publishing, as other analysis has indicated, companies did not see the same levels of impact as those industries that engage physical audiences or work on film and television sets.

Upskilling and retraining in the workforce

One way in which creative workers responded to the pandemic was to enhance their skill levels by developing their qualifications and education. During economic crises the demand for education increases (Barr and Turner, 2015). Workers spend their time strengthening their skills to get an advantage in their profession – *upskilling* – or, alternatively, investing in acquiring new skills that will allow them to change their occupation – *reskilling*. Creative workers have been *upskilling*, taking arts-related education courses to bolster their skills ready for a return to work.

We're again using the ONS Labour Force Survey for this analysis. Figure 2.13 shows that in 2020, the proportion of workers enrolled on either full-time or part-time education courses (excluding for leisure purposes) was higher than in recent years.

The increase in 2020 bucks a relatively steady negative trend in *non-creative* workers' enrolment in education and is more marked for creative workers in 'core' creative occupations. We define 'core' creative occupations as: film, TV, video, radio and photography; museums, galleries and libraries; music, performing and visual arts; and publishing.

It is important to note that this is still a small proportion of the total number of core creative workers. However, the uptick in the numbers suggests a clear response to the sector's economic crisis.

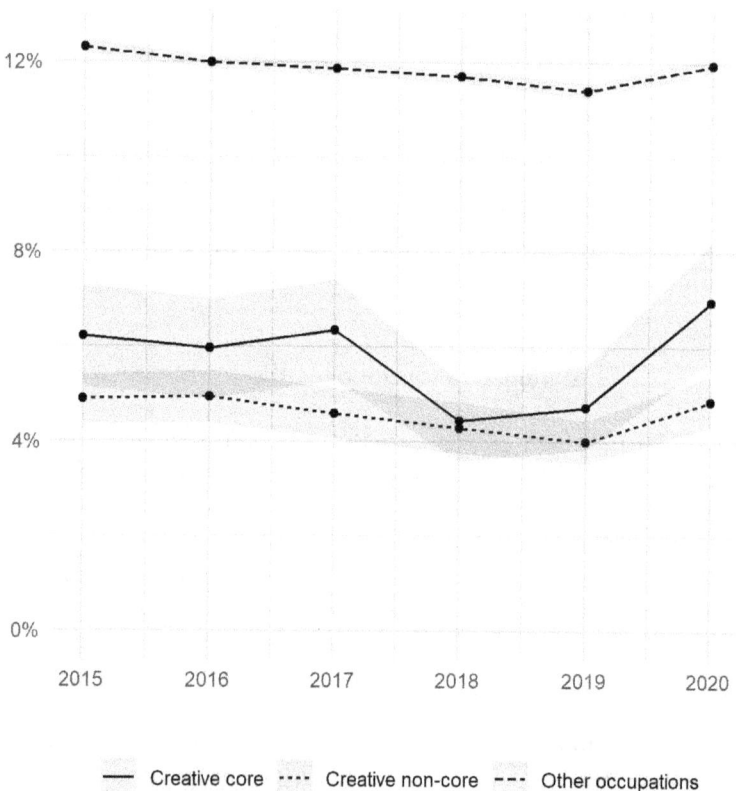

Figure 2.13 Workers enrolled in education courses

Choice of subject

We turn now to look more closely at enrolment in arts-related education, a category that includes various creative fields: fine arts, music and performing arts, audio, visual and media production, design, crafts and general art programmes. Figure 2.14 shows that the proportion of core creative workers enrolled in arts education in 2020 (out of the workers enrolled in any education) was similar to that of 2019, if not even slightly larger. The estimates demonstrate an increase of around 5 per cent in the enrolment in arts education among core creative workers. However, the sample size is small and we should again be cautious when drawing definitive conclusions.

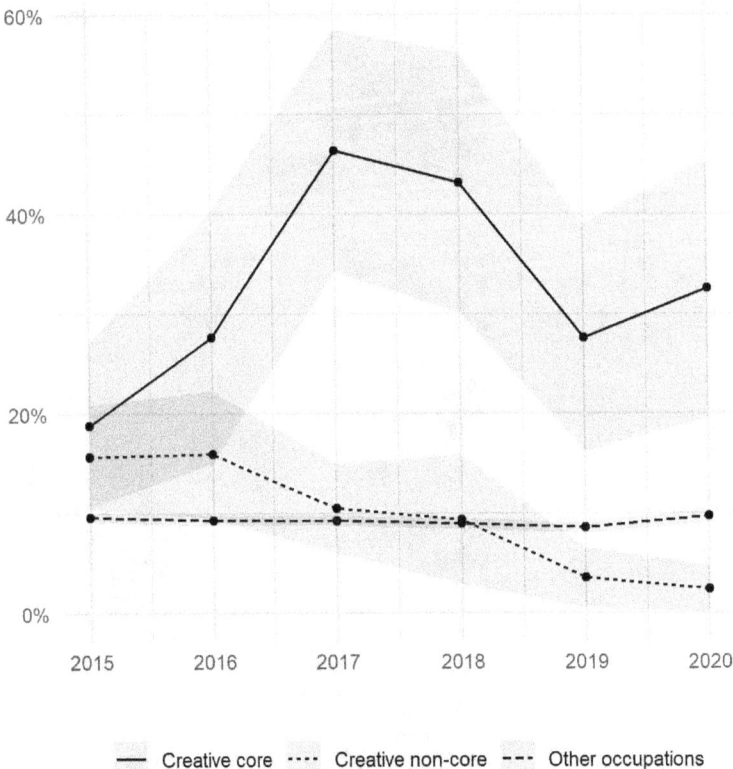

Figure 2.14 Proportion of art education enrolments

We also estimated the number of workers enrolled in arts-related education. This is to verify that the observed increase in the fraction of workers enrolled in arts education is not simply a result of the shrinking of the cultural workforce due to job losses and workers leaving during the pandemic. Our estimates, illustrated in Figure 2.15, show that this is not the case. Even with the contraction of the workforce, the observed increase in arts education is also apparent in absolute enrolment numbers.

In Figure 2.16, we zoom in on the four most popular study fields as they appear in the ONS coding. The bar graphs depict the distribution of studied subjects. We should keep in mind that the total number of workers enrolled in 2020 is higher than in the previous years, so small increases in proportion represent an even more pronounced increase in absolute numbers.

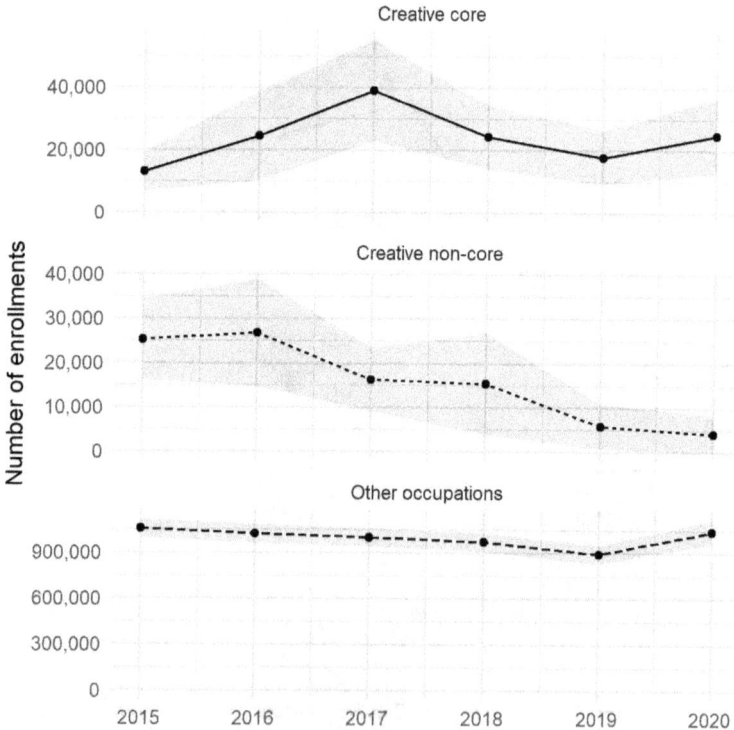

Figure 2.15 Overall numbers of art education enrolments

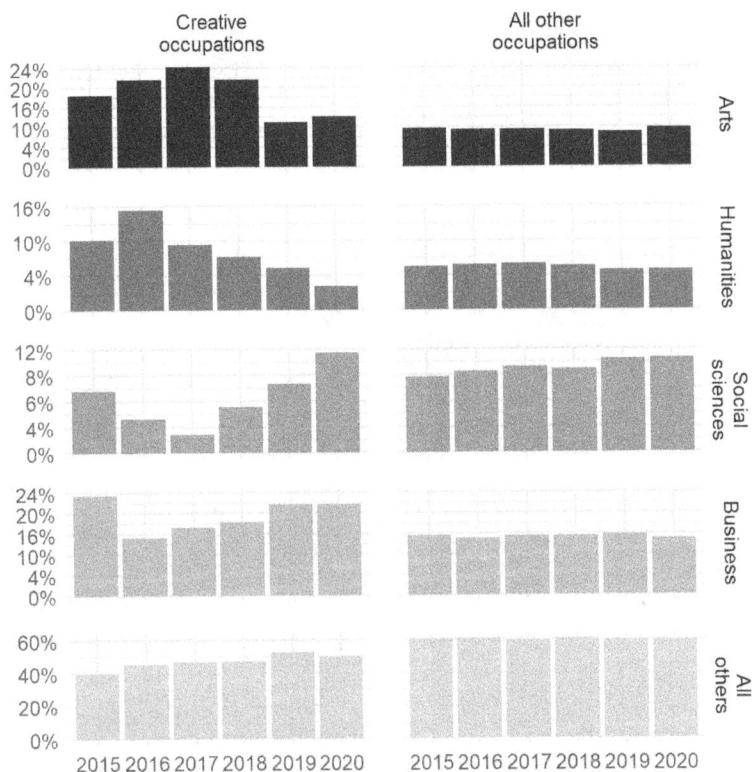

Figure 2.16 Subject choices of all creative workers enrolled in education courses

We merge all the creative workers into one group in this graph since some of the categories contain a small number of respondents. We find no *dramatic* changes in the proportion of creative workers enrolled in different educational programmes. The most pronounced changes over the period are not among cultural workers enrolled in arts courses. Instead, since 2017, we can see increases in enrolments in social sciences programmes and decreases in enrolments in humanities programmes. This result indicates once again that creative workers were not turning in big numbers to other fields of study to train themselves in alternative occupations.

Postgraduate and specialist skills

Creative workers tend to have higher levels of educational qualifications than the average worker and are more likely to attain postgraduate degrees (Oakley *et al.*, 2017). Figure 2.17 shows the level

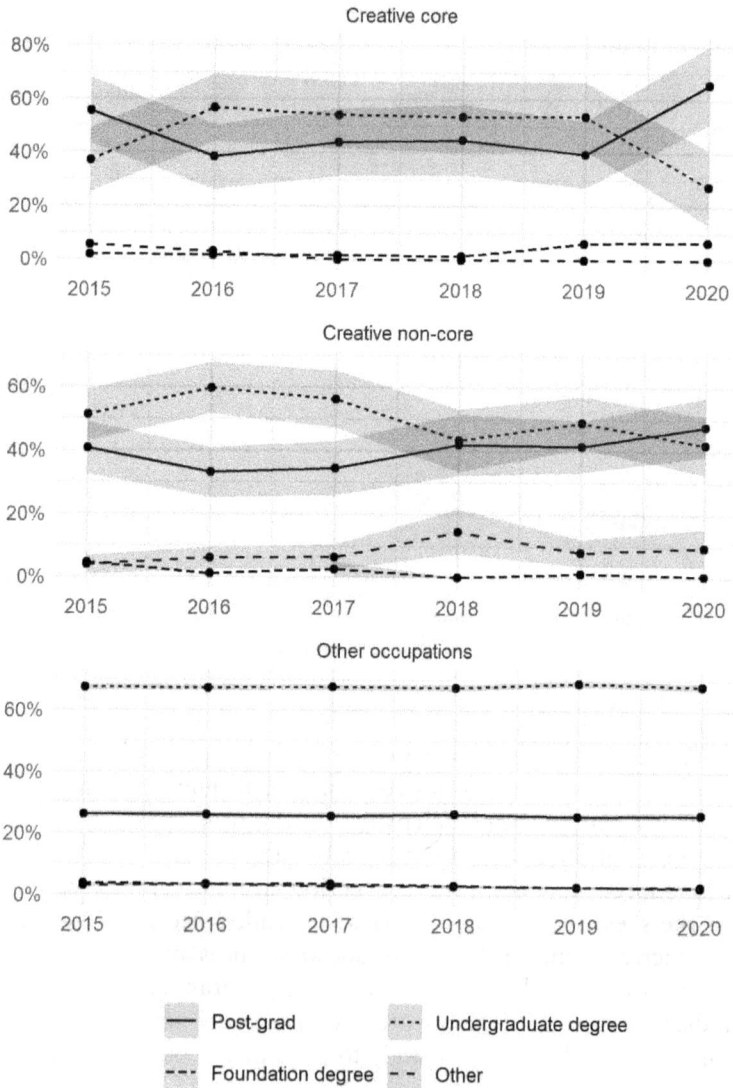

Figure 2.17 Level of qualification being studied

of degree programmes that workers who study art-related subjects are enrolled in. It suggests that the impact of the pandemic has been to motivate core creative workers to extend their art-related education. Figure 2.17 shows that, consistently over time, the proportion of creative workers studying for arts-related postgraduate degrees is about double that of other workers. In 2020, for the first time since 2015, the number of core creative workers studying for an arts-related higher degree (66 per cent) surpassed that of undergraduate degrees (27 per cent).

In October 2020 a government advert with a picture of a young ballet dancer and the headline 'Fatima's next job could be in cyber (she just doesn't know it yet)' went viral in the media, receiving a large amount of backlash. The ad was read by many as a recommendation from the government that artists change their profession, against a backdrop of concern over the future of the creative industries. The pandemic does seem to have pushed many creative workers to think about their professional future and enrol in educational programmes. However, it seems that the goal of the educational activity of those core creative workers most impacted by the pandemic was not *reskilling* for alternative professions but rather *upskilling* to reap the possible benefits of more education within creative occupations. The *upskilling* trends seen in 2020 continued at least to the first months of 2021.

2021: doing more with less

By the end of 2021 many parts of the economy and society had fully reopened. However, our analysis of ONS data demonstrates that the performing arts workforce still had not fully recovered. As illustrated in Figure 2.18, in terms of the size of its workforce, even at the end of 2021 the performing arts were recovering much more slowly than other sectors of the creative industries, lagging behind publishing, the screen and media sector, museums, galleries and libraries.

Although music and the performing and visual arts was the second largest of these sectors before the pandemic, we can see that it lost over 40,000 workers since its peak at the end of 2019. In terms of the total number of hours worked per week, it was also still behind pre-pandemic levels, showing a sharp decline in the final

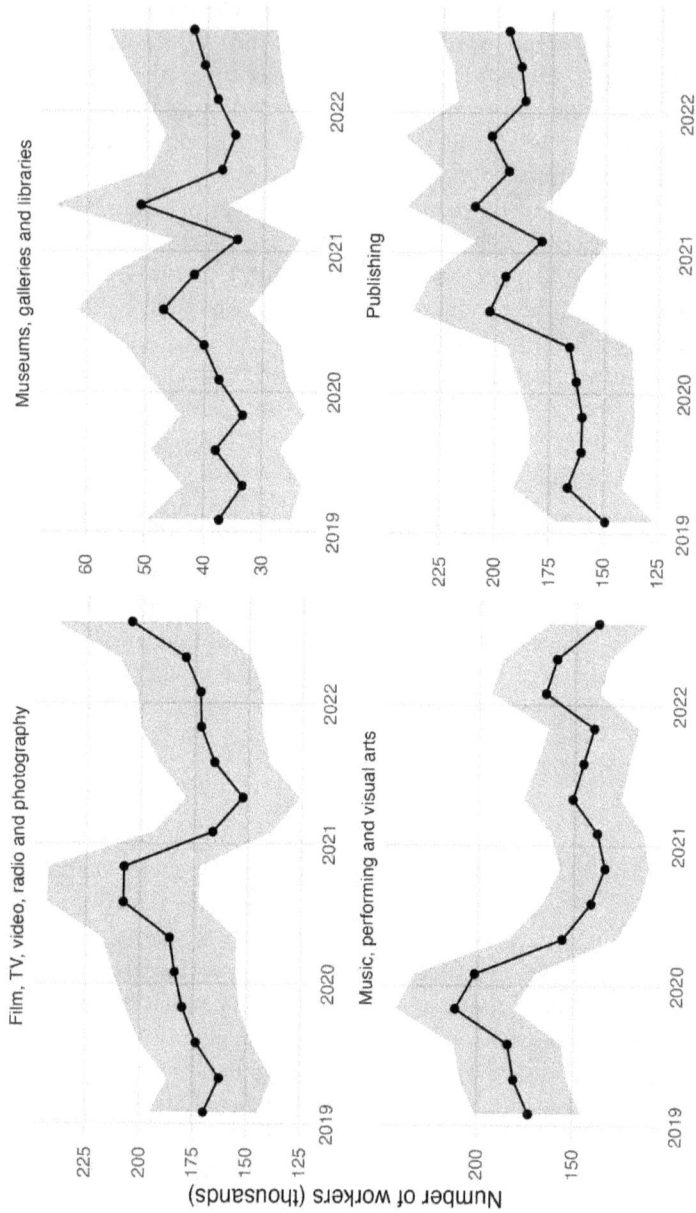

Figure 2.18 Number of workers in different creative sectors, 2019–2022

half of 2021 – but notably not as sharp a decline as museums, galleries and libraries.

Fewer workers working harder

However, as we can see in Figure 2.19, levels of activity as measured by average hours worked per week recovered substantially in 2021, just tailing off again in the last three months of 2021. This essentially means that those people working in music, performing and visual arts who weren't made redundant or didn't leave their occupations were working harder than ever. This has significant implications for the future infrastructure of the sector and specifically for:

- Diversity – there are fewer jobs around.
- Recruitment – how can the sector attract new people to an overworked sector?
- Retention – how many more workers will choose to leave the sector?
- Burnout – how will those left behind be able to sustain these levels of work?

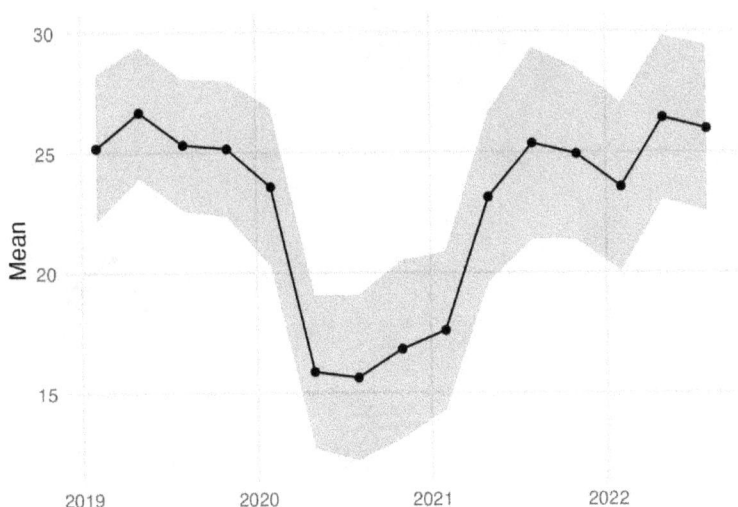

Figure 2.19 Mean hours worked per week in music, performing and visual arts, 2019–2022

In order to take a more micro view, we use actors as a particular case study, analysing the occupational category 'actors, entertainers and presenters'. Although the numbers are too small here and the confidence intervals too wide to draw any definitive conclusions, we can see in Figure 2.20 that this particular creative workforce decreased steadily throughout 2021, despite a positive end to 2020 as some venues reopened and the British winter 'panto season' took off in force.

Conclusion: 2022 and beyond

Finally, we can reflect on the most recent data available as this book went to press. Against the backdrop of concerns of a looming global economic recession, by 2022 the cultural workforce was showing signs of an almost full recovery to pre-pandemic levels of activity. However, the appearance of 'things going back to normal' masks the harmful longer-term effects of the pandemic in exacerbating the cultural sector's structural and ingrained inequalities (Brook, O'Brien and Taylor, 2020).

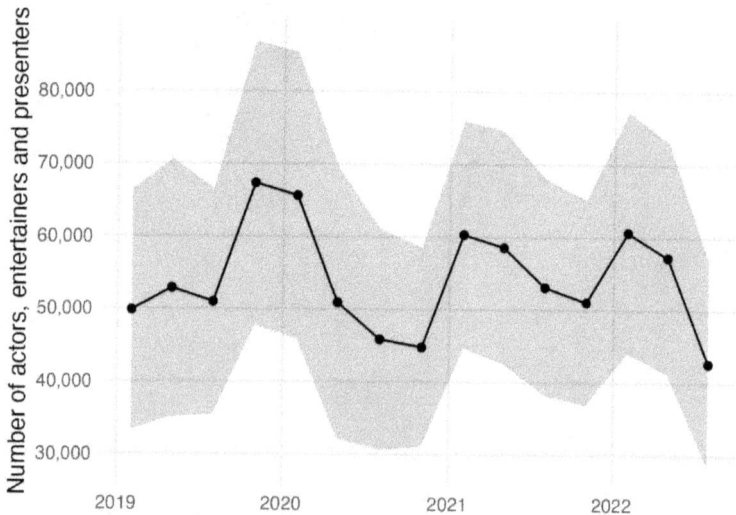

Figure 2.20 Number of actors, entertainers and presenters, 2019–2022

2022 opened with a positive trend of an increase in the number of workers in creative occupations (see Figure 2.21). We see this positive trend also in the music, performing and visual arts sector, which suffered the most from the pandemic's impact. At

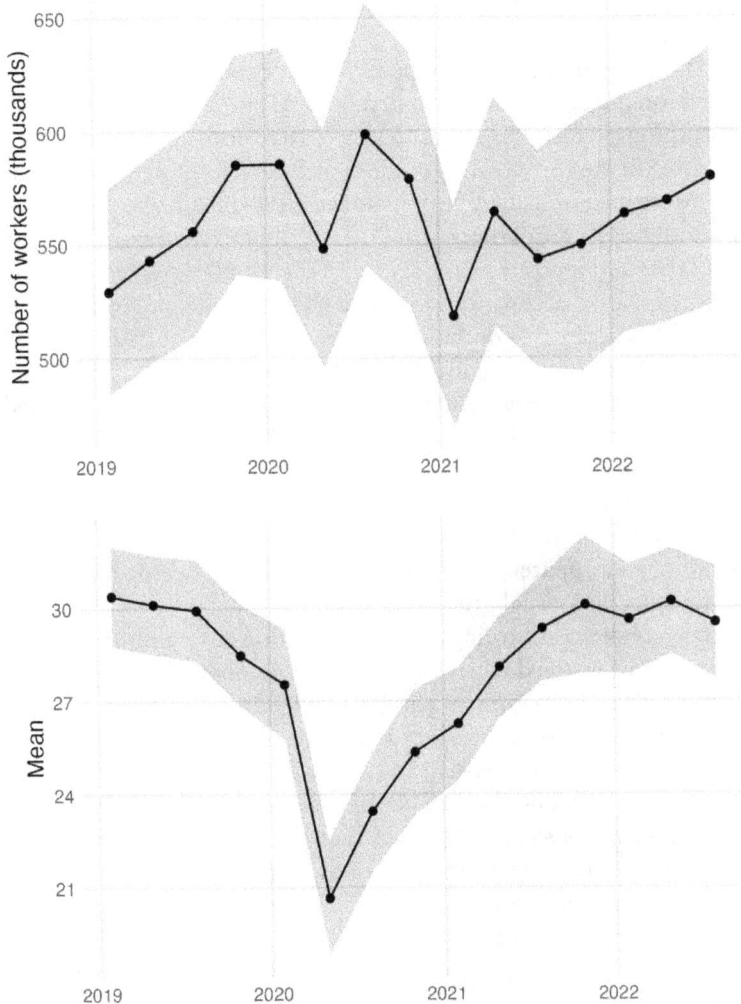

Figure 2.21 Number of workers in the core creative occupations and mean hours worked per week in the core creative occupations

the same time, the intensity of cultural work, measured by mean hours worked per week, which had been increasing since hitting an all-time low in 2020, is showing signs of coming to a plateau (see Figure 2.21). Our estimates, based on ONS data, show that the volume of activity in the core creative occupations in the second quarter of 2022 (April–June) reached a record level of 16.5 million weekly hours, which is higher than its highest level in 2019 of 16 million weekly hours.[10]

This may sound like good news for the cultural sector. However, when looking at specific socio-demographic groups, we see a rather disturbing picture. Figure 2.22 shows that both men and women working in the core creative occupations were negatively affected by the pandemic, in its first year, in a relatively similar way. However, since the second quarter of 2021 the number of men and women has taken an opposite trend. By 2022 the number of men working in core creative occupations matched its pre-pandemic level. Yet the number of women is declining and in the middle of 2022 reached a number even lower than its level during the pandemic. We must remember that the core creative occupations are an aggregated group of different occupational groups. The existing gender inequalities in specific occupations (Brook, O'Brien and Taylor, 2020) has continued, with gender inequalities in employment numbers most notable in the film, TV, video, radio and photography occupations, and apparent in the other occupations except for music, performing and visual arts.

The concerns regarding a 'lost generation' of cultural workers appear to be justified when looking at the number of workers in the core creative occupation by age groups. Figure 2.23 shows that the number of workers in the thirty-five to fifty-three category, and to a lesser degree also the fifty-five and above category, is growing steadily since 2021, while the number of young workers (aged eighteen to thirty-four) is steady. The fact that the number of older (aged fifty-five and above) workers has even surpassed its pre-pandemic levels suggests that more established and experienced workers are replacing younger, early-career workers. Younger, early-career workers were disproportionately hit by redundancies during the pandemic, and now are not returning at the same rate as their older counterparts. As a result, we can see the first indications of a long-run 'lost generation' effect.

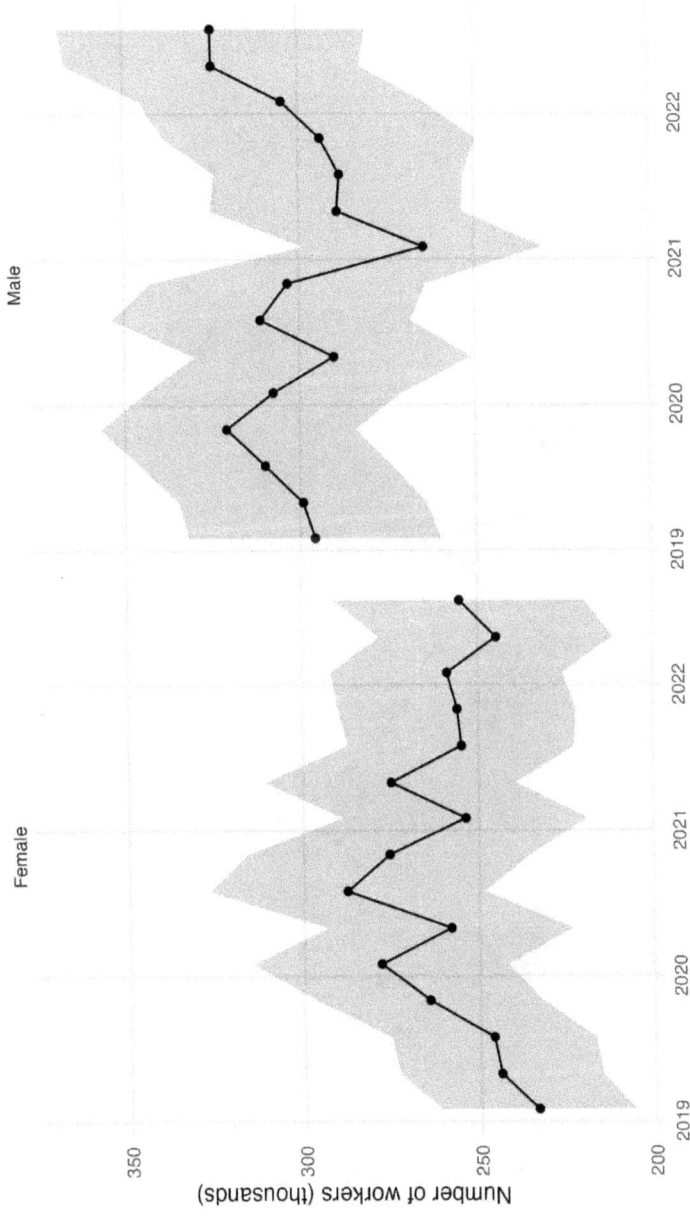

Figure 2.22 Number of workers in core creative occupations by gender

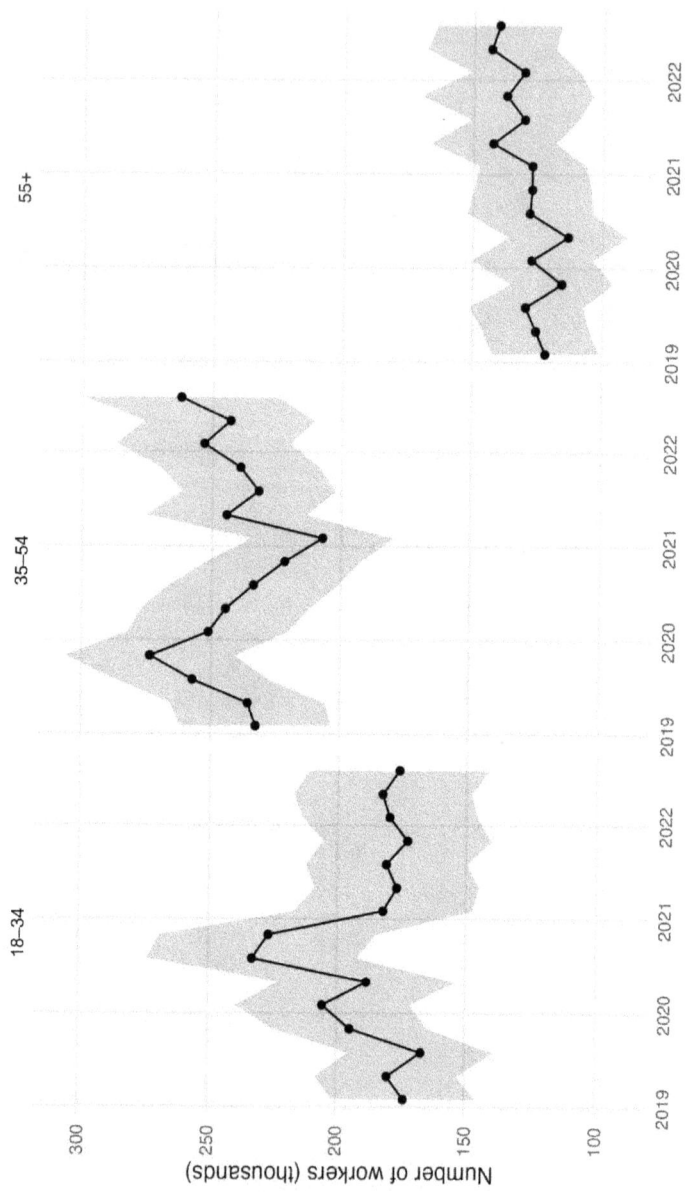

Figure 2.23 Number of workers in core creative occupations by age group

We find similar results in the case of ethnicity and education. It seems that the recent increase in the number of workers reflects existing patterns of inequality; employment growth is driven by white workers and by workers with higher education levels. We also find that most of the growth in the number of workers is attributed to self-employed workers, who face more precarious working conditions compared to employed workers. The ability to participate in creative labour markets is being further concentrated in those groups who have the resources to withstand potential precarity.

Overall, this analysis, and the most recent data, reinforces the narrative of the uneven nature of the pandemic's long-term impact. Ultimately, 2020 compounded the already existing problems of Britain's cultural labour market. These problems are true globally, as we see in the concluding chapter, as well as within the specific case we have analysed here.

We can end this pessimistic review of the situation in the core cultural occupations on a positive note with one silver lining brought by the pandemic: we found that the number of disabled workers in the core creative occupations has grown in the aftermath of the pandemic, as shown in Figure 2.24. We believe that the expansion

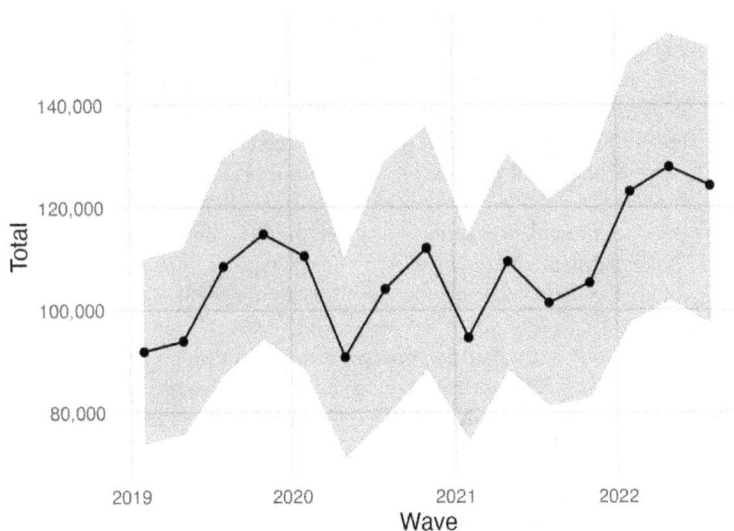

Figure 2.24 Number of disabled workers in the core creative occupations

of opportunities for remote work, encouraged by the pandemic, has opened new and more accessible pathways for disabled people to participate in the cultural workforce. It is essential that these new opportunities, rather than the return to the unequal pre-pandemic normal, are central to both cultural policy and the cultural sector.

Notes

1 This is approximately 260,000 people (95 per cent confidence interval – 210,000 to 310,000), which is (statistically) significantly higher than the estimated 170,000 (130,000 to 210,000) people who were newly working in creative occupations in Quarter 2, indicating that the total number of people working in creative occupations has declined.

2 Although these numbers come with some uncertainty, as our data come from a sample of the population, the confidence intervals on the graph do not overlap. This means that we can be confident that more people have left the creative industries than would normally be expected at this time of year.

3 Defined as people without a job who have been actively seeking work in the past four weeks and are available to start work in the next two weeks.

4 This number is only those who left the creative industries and not the net change in size of the workforce.

5 For the purpose of this chapter we have used fairly broad socio-demographic groupings: the numbers of cultural and creative workers in the survey as a whole are small, which makes it difficult to draw conclusions about the population. It is important to bear in mind that there is likely to be considerable diversity within our groupings, even if we are not able to explore this given the data that we have available.

6 We experimented with a variety of age groupings. However, we report differences between under-twenty-fives compared with the rest of the population as this was where we saw the most substantial differences.

7 The Labour Force Survey captures a range of different forms of self-employment. Respondents saying they are self-employed can choose up to four options from the following to capture their self-employment status:

1. Paid salary or wage by employment agency
2. Sole director of own ltd business
3. Running a business or prof practice

4. Partner in business or prof practice
5. Working for self
6. Sub contractor
7. Freelance work
8. None of the above.

In our analysis we're looking at people who have indicated they are 7) freelance workers. Therefore, they are only a small subsample of the overall number of self-employed workers.

8 The Coronavirus Job Retention Scheme was designed to cover wage and associated employment costs where businesses were unable to operate as a result of public health measures. Employees were given temporary leave, or 'furlough', and businesses and organisations were able to claim grants from the government for the costs of continuing to employ them.

9 More information about the BICS is available at: www.ons.gov.uk/surveys/informationforbusinesses/businesssurveys/businessimpactofcoronaviruscovid19survey

10 However, we have to be cautious as this difference is not statistically significant.

References

Barr, A. and Turner, S. 2015. Out of work and into school: labor market policies and college enrollment during the Great Recession. *Journal of Public Economics*. 124(C), pp.63–73.

Brook, O., O'Brien, D. and Taylor, M. 2020. *Culture is bad for you*. Manchester: Manchester University Press.

Carey, H., O'Brien, D. and Gable, O. 2021a. *Social mobility in the creative economy: rebuilding and levelling up?* [Online]. London: Creative Industries Policy and Evidence Centre. [Accessed 8 January 2024]. Available from: https://pec.ac.uk/research-reports/social-mobility-in-the-creative-economy-rebuilding-and-levelling-up

Carey, H., O'Brien, D. and Gable, O. 2021b. *Screened out: tackling class inequalities in the Screen Industries*. [Online]. London: Creative Industries Policy and Evidence Centre. [Accessed 8 January 2024]. Available from: https://pec.ac.uk/research-reports/screened-out-tackling-class-inequality-in-the-uks-screen-industries

Oakley, K., Laurison, D., O'Brien, D. and Friedman, S. 2017. Cultural capital: arts graduates, spatial inequality, and London's impact on cultural labour markets. *American Behavioral Scientist*. 61(12), pp.1510–1531.

Skillset. 2010. *Women in the creative media industries*. [Online]. [Accessed 24 August 2022]. Available from: www.screenskills.com/media/1507/women_in_the_creative_media_industries_report_-_sept_2010.pdf

Taylor, H. and Florisson, R. 2020. *UK labour market sees record redundancies*. [Online]. 15 December. Lancaster University. [Accessed 6 February 2023]. Available from: www.lancaster.ac.uk/work-foundation/our-work/insecure-work/uk-labour-market-sees-record-redundancies

TUC. 2021. *Jobs and recovery monitor. Issue #3: BME workers*. [Online]. London: TUC. [Accessed 8 January 2024]. Available from: www.tuc.org.uk/sites/default/files/2021-01/Recession%20report%20-%20BME%20workers%20(1).pdf

3

The same people seeing more: audiences' engagement with culture during the COVID-19 pandemic

Oliver Mantell, Anne Torreggiani, Ben Walmsley, Jenny Kidd and Eva Nieto McAvoy

Introduction

The COVID-19 pandemic has disrupted cultural production and engagement in ways we do not yet fully understand. It manifested as an interlude, an acceleration and an inflection all at the same time. Little remained the same: some things reduced then returned, while others reduced for good; some things kept changing in the direction they were already heading, and some sped up; others changed in new ways that have persisted beyond the immediate crisis. This observation holds as much for audience trends and dynamics as it does for institutions and practitioners. It is difficult to divine whether we will witness a gradual return to old patterns of engagement or a radical switch, pushed to further extremes by the cost-of-living crisis. The prolific shift to digital distribution made a wealth of new arts content available to audiences stuck at home, but did it have the democratising, game-changing effect on audiences that many thought they were witnessing?

This chapter investigates how audiences and the wider UK population engaged with cultural content during the pandemic, in both live and digital spaces, and explores how their behaviours and attitudes are evolving as we emerge from the COVID-19 crisis into the cost-of-living crisis. It presents, contextualises and discusses the findings of the Cultural Participation Monitor, a bespoke longitudinal tracking survey of the UK population that analysed changing digital engagement habits and attitudes towards re-engagement. Led by The Audience Agency, the Cultural Participation Monitor has been asking a representative sample of the UK population across multiple waves about their cultural experiences and expectations before, during and beyond the pandemic. Our exploration of audiences' digital behaviour change includes a deep-dive analysis of social media by Jenny Kidd and Eva Nieto McAvoy at the moment the UK went into national lockdowns in March 2020. The chapter interrogates how society's relationship to arts and culture may have shifted over this time of significant change and tells a story about the kinds of cultural content and interactions that people found valuable in a period of unprecedented uncertainty and anxiety.

The chapter concludes by assessing the signs of longer-term trends in audience behaviour and engagement and by exploring the implications of these trends for artists, cultural organisations, funders and policy-makers.

Methodological reflections on our population survey

To understand and analyse any possible relationship between digitisation and democratisation of cultural engagement and to move beyond a perspective mediated entirely by cultural practitioners and commentators, we felt that it was vital to engage directly with the general public. As new rules and regulations for social distancing came into law, there was an outbreak of audience surveying as organisations and umbrella bodies rushed to understand the potential impact of each new wave of restrictions. Many surveys were hastily concocted, posing narrow or parochial questions, one-off and close-up exercises, based on dubious samples, sometimes intent on 'proving' what the sector thought it was witnessing. Others were well-crafted and considered but inevitably biased towards committed cultural audiences. In this deluge of more or less reliable intelligence, it seemed important to develop a statistically significant, universal understanding of the impact of the pandemic on people's cultural engagement across the UK's four home nations. Our aim was to provide an ongoing, real-time barometer of the public's response, fleeter of foot and more responsive to change than existing studies such as Taking Part, the national statistical survey on participation (DCMS, n.d.), but more independent and impartial than the sector's urgent DIY research.

Accordingly, we chose a population-wide survey. The survey was carried out online for practical reasons, despite some risks of sampling bias. We attempted to mitigate these by making it nationally representative by region, age, gender, ethnicity and Audience Spectrum, The Audience Agency's ten-category segmentation model, often and accurately used to track significant differences across a spectrum of cultural attitudes and behaviours. Audience Spectrum enabled us to differentiate between privileged segments 'highly engaged' with culture of the formal, publicly funded variety, less frequent or medium-engaged groups, and those 'less engaged' with formal arts and cultural offers. The research design also reflected our interest in the widest range of cultural and creative activity across society rather than a limited range of institutional offerings.

Our primary interest was in the scope and degree of change in cultural habits over both the short and long term. We could not assume that those regularly attending before COVID-19 would do so after it – and understanding potential new audiences would be as important as understanding newly lapsed ones. Similarly, we were looking for shifts in 'everyday creativity' (see Wright, 2022), evolving interaction with digital cultural content and evidence of other cultural or creative pursuits not mediated by public institutions. We therefore included questions about how much spare time people had and what they did with it before and during the pandemic, and what they anticipated doing after it. These core questions were repeated across roughly quarterly waves for eighteen months and offered a sense of how public attitudes were changing. To these we added spot-questions to understand sudden changes – in policy, attitude, the news, etc. – as they emerged. Having this fresh information at our fingertips became increasingly valuable as the sector became more adept at adapting; and since the rate of change has scarcely slowed, we continued the Monitor beyond the period of the original research, into 2022–2023. This unforeseen extension to the survey contributes something of a sequel to the original research story and facilitates a longer-term observation of audience trends.

The evolution of cultural engagement through the pandemic

In terms of a direct response to the impact of the pandemic on external activities, a clear picture emerged from the first wave of the Monitor in November 2020. Nine months into the crisis, with one lockdown behind us and another one on the cards, it was clear that just over a third of the population had no intention of going out to do cultural – or indeed any other kind of – activity. Another third were only likely to do so under strictly controlled conditions, while a final group – just under one-third – were keen to go back to doing in-person activities. Perhaps predictably, these divisions of opinion corresponded to age and life-stage, with older audiences significantly more cautious than younger ones, especially those with young families. We mapped a similar divide between rural and urban communities: our survey highlighted how people in large metropolitan centres – especially London – were far more gung-ho. Intriguingly, it seemed that the different COVID-19 policies across the nations may also have driven public confidence and perceptions of risk, with the proportion of people willing to return in Scotland, Wales and Northern Ireland being far lower than in England throughout the pandemic and despite factoring for age and other demographic influences.

Remarkably, however, the vast majority – over 95 per cent in repeated waves of the Monitor, including those keen to get back to normal attendance – continued to think that social distancing was important and to be respected. Very few people suggested that distancing measures spoiled their experience – at least not enough to put them off returning to cultural venues – and 90+ per cent of respondents repeatedly rated arts and cultural organisations as doing a good job with the measures they put in place. Of all the measures, those allowing flexibility, such as offering ticket refunds and the chance to move time slots, were the most highly rated. This reflected our finding that what people liked best about digital opportunities was their 'always-on' quality – the chance to engage as and when people wanted and on their own terms. A side story about the appeal of more flexible, customer-considerate ways of working emerged in our analysis.

Contrary to popular belief, the COVID-19 pandemic was not unremittingly devastating for the arts and cultural sector – at least from an audience and funding perspective. In fact, the population's interest in and support for arts and culture seemed considerably consolidated by the pandemic, with 57 per cent of people reporting that it was important to their wellbeing, 63 per cent saying they were more willing to support public funding for cultural institutions and 56 per cent confirming that they were more likely to donate personally to organisations to help them operate with COVID-19 restrictions in place. The plight of public organisations through the crisis clearly touched a nerve and we might speculate that the creative, social engagements that some organisations turned to with their communities, as highlighted in various chapters in this book, made a significant public and civic impact.

Meanwhile, as reported widely in the media, people got used to staying in, discovering the joys of hunkering down and getting creative or consuming lots of new cultural content – and sometimes both at once. However, it emerged that very few people actually took up *new* creative hobbies or developed a *new* digital cultural habit during the pandemic. Our research demonstrated that people who were *already* keen everyday creatives and/or digital culture enthusiasts engaged more than ever before. This generally applied to more privileged, more arts-engaged people who fell into the group with more time on their hands. However, these trends started to drop off relatively steeply after lockdown as a significant proportion of the population returned to the office (and the gym, commuting etc.). This suggests that removing physical barriers to engagement such as lack of time, lack of money and the need to travel is not in itself an effective way to open up cultural and creative opportunities to a more diverse audience base. This confirms existing research by Stevenson (2019), which identifies the presence of the 'disinterested' cultural participant but challenges the finding by Brook (2016a) that spatial equity can have a significant impact on cultural participation.

The segmentation of audiences by levels of confidence – a third staying in, a third remaining cautious and a third getting out – was remarkably persistent throughout the pandemic and it was only by the very end of 2021 that we observed a small but significant shift. By November 2021, a residual 37 per cent were still staying in and, as of September 2022, 26 per cent of people said they still did not want to return. This highlights a significant lag between the actual level of risk and people's perception of it, which is continuing to hamper ticket buying and thus to hinder the recovery of the cultural sector itself. The enthusiastic 'keen to get out' group, however, did indeed flock back to venues as they reopened, with many of them reporting higher levels of engagement than pre-pandemic.

The cost-of-living shockwave

Despite the lag effect on perceptions of risk, by autumn 2022, the majority of people were willing to go out, although a net 20 per cent of people were still anticipating that they would do less overall in future than before the pandemic. Considerable differences between forms of cultural engagement began to emerge: at one end of the spectrum, 20 per cent of people reported that they were expecting to attend more outdoor experiences than before the pandemic, while at the other end 34 per cent were expecting to go to the cinema less often than they used to. Divining lasting impacts has become complicated by the new shift in behaviour precipitated by the cost-of-living crisis. By the end of 2022 some organisations, particularly metropolitan venues, were reporting attendance back at pre-Covid levels. However, most respondents to the seventh wave of the Monitor in September 2022 indicated that they were worried about the effects of the cost-of-living crisis on them and their household (86 per cent said they 'agree' or 'strongly agree', with almost half strongly agreeing). People also told us that this will directly impact their cultural activities, with as many as 92 per cent intending to scale back on entertainment spend outside of the home as a result, especially among mid-engaged, middle-aged and less urban groups. When we asked about the range of areas people were expecting to cut back spending on, entertainment and leisure outside the home was in a small group of areas second only to 'non-essential retail' (or what we might call 'shopping for fun'). Although the picture remains complex, the outlook for healthy audience figures across the cultural sector looks bleak.

Inequality and exclusion

We have long known that cultural engagement is socially stratified: people's socio-economic class, wealth and education levels are the most significant predictors of their propensity to attend publicly funded arts and cultural events (O'Brien, Brook and Taylor, 2019). The Monitor confirmed this established pattern (by Indices of Multiple Deprivation, by occupation type and by socio-demographic profiles). Notably, when focusing in on precisely those groups who were structurally disadvantaged, the survey highlighted some of the ways in which COVID-19 actually exacerbated this effect. For example, those with professional backgrounds were more likely to be better off as a result of COVID-19, cutting costs, such as holidays and commuting, without losing income. Older groups were also least likely to see a change in income, as those who were already retired could not be furloughed or lose their jobs. But those who were younger, disabled and/or in semi-routine or routine occupations were likely to end up worse off financially and encounter more disruption to their routines. On this latter point: this was because these groups were both more likely to have less time (working longer, reduced public transport, looking after children, etc.) and also more likely to have more of it (due to furlough or unemployment, for example).

We saw these inequalities reflected in cultural engagement, as the divide between cultural haves and have-nots widened considerably. Pressure on the income and time of less-well-off, frontline workers was of course greatly exacerbated by the sudden scarcity of arts and cultural opportunities, and the complicated new ways in which they could be accessed. Other chapters in this book document the inspired acts of many organisations that managed to support and cheer their communities in creative ways but there were not enough of these valuable interventions to show up in a population study like the Monitor.

It looked as though this effect was starting to level off by early 2022. However, as we have noted, as the cost-of-living crisis deepened it impacted less affluent people in a disproportionately negative way, meaning that people in lower socio-economic groups were even less likely to spend money outside the home. One particular concern is that the groups most affected by the cost-of-living crisis (younger, urban, family and lower-income groups) were in many cases those whose levels of cultural activity had bounced back furthest since COVID-19. The new crisis has seemed particularly targeted at those whose attendance has proved most resilient following the previous one, thereby maximising the total impact of the two challenges combined.

The impact of age, life-stage and lifestyle

Across the phases of the research, several key factors recurred as the drivers of different levels of engagement (and also factors we

know to be linked to different behaviours, attitudes and motiva-
tions). We saw consistently higher engagement – and more elas-
tic 'snap back' – from those who were younger, urban, highly
engaged and with dependent children. These audiences attended
more online, returned soonest when small windows of opportunity
emerged mid-pandemic, and returned first and in greater numbers
once venues started to open more fully, especially from autumn
2021, for live events. Their willingness to engage persisted throughout 2022, generating implications for what the 'new normal' might
look like.

In many ways, this echoes previous research by The Audience
Agency (2016) which identified notable differences between the
'Baby Boomer' age cohort (with a large population 'bulge' entering retirement and taking on an increasing proportion of cultural
engagement, especially at ticketed events) and those who were
younger. Back then, we anticipated increasing reliance on this group,
until a point – perhaps fifteen years in the future – when there would
need to be a shift towards a younger audience, one which the sector
had not, up to that point, been incentivised to prioritise. This, we
warned, could result in difficulties adapting and a loss of purpose if
organisations did not start to adapt well in advance.

COVID-19 may have sped up this process. The loss of Baby
Boomer audiences due to COVID-19 (risk, change of habits, accelerated 'ageing' of lifestyle) has brought forward the point when a
reduction was expected due to age and ill-health. Since older (core)
audiences have different needs, interests and behaviours, this affects
both the immediate impact of the pandemic and future developments for the sector. For example, many organisations' revenue
and planning anticipates behaviours that Audience Finder tells us
are strongly associated with older audiences such as early booking,
donating, subscriptions, in-venue dining and attending matinées.
This will disproportionately affect art forms with older audiences,
notably classical music, theatre and opera. It also presents a conundrum for many organisations who will need to work harder to retain
older core audiences while learning new habits and developing radically different offers for younger audiences with divergent tastes. To
some extent, a renewed focus on younger audiences post-pandemic
could potentially alienate and therefore exacerbate the demise of core
older audiences on whom the cultural sector has relied for decades.

Family audiences

After age, the most striking difference in our survey analyses was between those with or without dependent children in the household (hereafter: 'families'). The family experience of the pandemic was different in several notable ways, including home schooling, looking after children's wellbeing and development in difficult and novel circumstances, and greater exposure to infection via children and their social contacts. These factors combined to give a strong incentive to engage with culture outside the home once this became an option. Even before COVID-19, there was latent demand for more family arts content and once again the pandemic turned up the dial on this trend.

There are several benefits to family engagement. Attending with (and for) children gives a motivation (or excuse) for adult audiences to visit unfamiliar venues and spaces. It also makes entering those spaces easier: people know that they can at least play the role of 'parent', whatever other unfamiliar roles might be projected onto them in a novel environment. As a result, we see a far more diverse range of audiences (e.g. by social group and ethnicity) for family arts events compared to many other art forms. This is significant in the context of urgent policy drivers to diversify cultural organisations. As attending cultural activities at an early age is also associated with later engagement (even if there might be a period of non-engagement in between), building family audiences also helps to build audiences in the longer term, so emerges as a strategic priority for cultural organisations.

Digital and hybrid future

Small comfort though it was, the cultural sector quickly realised that lockdown presented an extraordinary laboratory situation in which to carry out a giant and arguably long-overdue experiment in designing digital and hybrid experiences. The opportunity to test the potential of digital content and digitally enabled visitor journeys was unprecedented, albeit not entirely planned for nor properly resourced. In effect, COVID-19 created a classic 'burning platform', pushing the sector beyond its usual caution and justifiable reservations about digital. With time on our hands and a nation in need, what was to lose? Many organisations also said that they had increased their digital offer during lockdown to help maintain or strengthen their audience relationships and the Monitor suggests this was generally successful, with just over 50 per cent of our sample saying they had used digital content created by an organisation they had visited.

These forays into the unknown were not of course carried out under strict laboratory conditions, especially in terms of gathering good data, and it seems that the sector was also prey to optimism bias. Many organisations who put a lot of time and effort into their new digital offers were convinced that this work was opening up access for new, hitherto excluded audiences. Other stakeholders were also optimistic: the rationale was that when apparent barriers to live engagement such as transport time, high ticket costs and 'threshold anxiety' were removed, new audiences would emerge onto new and existing digital platforms to enjoy cultural content from their own homes, with little else to occupy their time. However, the Monitor showed clearly and consistently that this wished-for democratisation failed to materialise at the macro level. In fact, it showed that the net increase in people engaging with cultural content was less than 3 per cent. This became the headline about the pivot to digital content, a story of failure in many eyes and one that is still circulating.

The full story is, however, far more complex. Because consumption of cultural content did inevitably increase massively, some core attenders showed a big appetite, some new audiences were indeed found and, importantly, digital content and platforms did provide much appreciated new access. As illustrated in Figure 3.1, 58 per cent of our sample had engaged with a digital experience created by a cultural organisation. People who already had an interest in digital culture offerings did a lot more during the pandemic and were ready and willing consumers of the online, hybrid and social media content and experiences produced by cultural organisations. 87 per cent rated their digital experiences positively, with 79 per cent reporting that they exceeded their expectations.

While it should not really come as a surprise that the most likely to engage with digital were urban, super-arts engagers and supporters, and tech-arts early adopters, it is still significant that

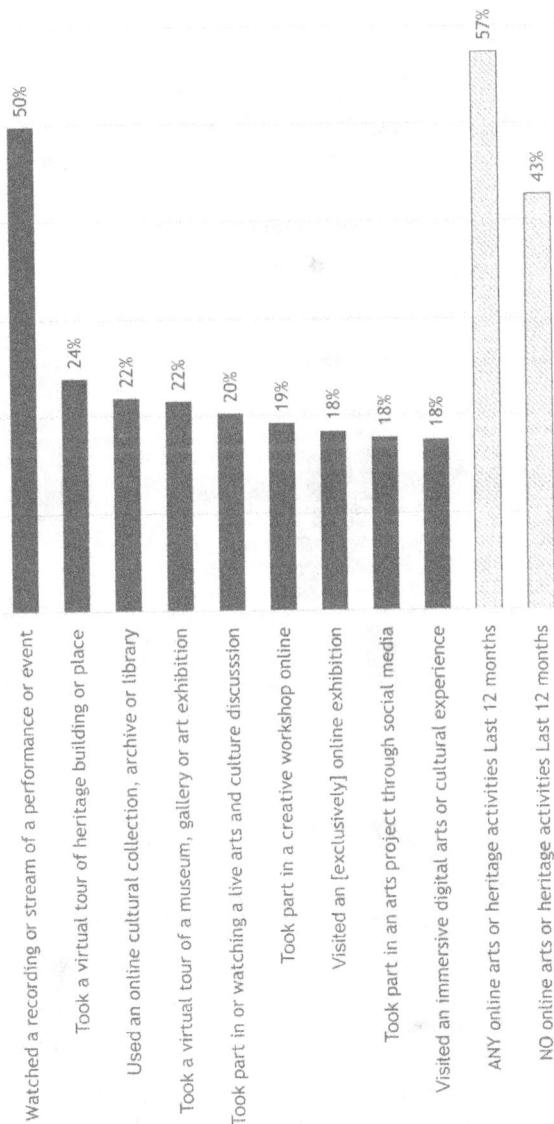

Figure 3.1 Digital engagement with culture, November 2021

Watched a recording or stream of a performance or event — 50%

Took a virtual tour of heritage building or place — 24%

Used an online cultural collection, archive or library — 22%

Took a virtual tour of a museum, gallery or art exhibition — 22%

Took part in or watching a live arts and culture discussion — 20%

Took part in a creative workshop online — 19%

Visited an [exclusively] online exhibition — 18%

Took part in an arts project through social media — 18%

Visited an immersive digital arts or cultural experience — 18%

ANY online arts or heritage activities Last 12 months — 57%

NO online arts or heritage activities Last 12 months — 43%

the profile of these enthusiasts is significantly younger, with much higher representation among people of colour than the audience for in-person arts and museums. As depicted in Figure 3.2, younger people were also far more likely to take part in participatory and immersive kinds of experiences. Although there has been a gradual tail-off in the amount of time younger audiences are now spending online, at the end of the lockdown significant numbers said they thought they would engage more with digital culture in future. By September 2022, a net 12 per cent of the whole sample said they would do more if more online culture were available and the percentage was far higher among under-thirty-fives and people with families – for example, 22 per cent of the younger, educated Gen

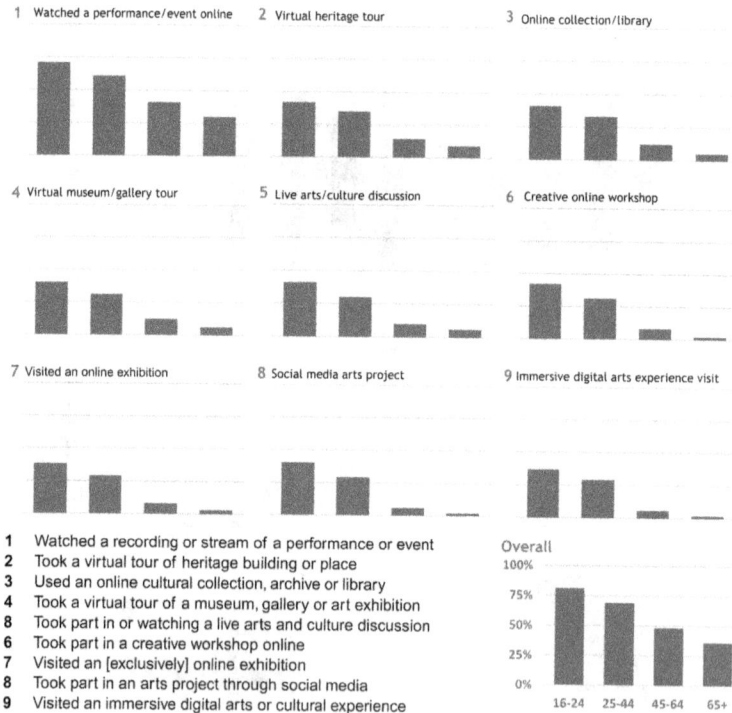

1	Watched a recording or stream of a performance or event
2	Took a virtual tour of heritage building or place
3	Used an online cultural collection, archive or library
4	Took a virtual tour of a museum, gallery or art exhibition
8	Took part in or watching a live arts and culture discussion
6	Took part in a creative workshop online
7	Visited an [exclusively] online exhibition
8	Took part in an arts project through social media
9	Visited an immersive digital arts or cultural experience

Figure 3.2 Digital cultural activities people engaged with in the last 12 months, by age group, November 2021

Y/Z segment 'Experience Seekers'. 20 per cent of our participants said they would do more if they could find what they were interested in. Again, this figure was much higher for under-thirty-fives and even higher for people with young families.

One of the most important discoveries was that digital really did open up access for disabled audiences, many of whom had been campaigning for more equitable access to cultural content for some time. A significantly higher proportion of disabled people engaged online than they had in person. They engaged far more online than the non-disabled people: 74 per cent of disabled under-twenty-fives, compared with 48 per cent of non-disabled under-twenty-fives. This unprecedented access has increased their appetite for future activity, with 25 per cent of disabled twenty-fives to sixty-fours versus 9 per cent of non-disabled respondents strongly agreeing that they wanted more digital culture. Indeed 62 per cent of arts-going disabled twenty-fives to sixty-fours thought they were likely to replace most or some of their in-person engagement with digital in future. Combined with our findings about younger audiences, this reinforces the strategic need to develop more online cultural content for younger and disabled people and families to build future audiences.

This enforced innovation in digital practice reached beyond the UK population participating in the Monitor. As showcased in Chapter 5, many organisations were delighted to find new niche audiences in far-flung places across the globe, and they were often surprised to connect with them by increasing their social media and gone-digital events. Meanwhile, at the other end of the global–local scale, there were inspiring stories of community-embedded organisations who chose to focus on the hyperlocal and target those furthest from opportunity. Often out of concern for the vulnerable people they work with, practitioners were prompted to try new digital routes to engage with surprising consequences. These creative forays into online engagement demonstrated how for some it can be less intimidating to meet on Zoom than in a public space, that WhatsApp can be an inclusive conduit for a migrant community's creativity, that digital archiving is a great way to start and connect a new community, and that museums make far more compelling school resources than most. There were many other stories of unexpected and transformative emergent practice, all of which demand further investigation.

In short, we must conclude that, seen in a more nuanced way, there is a considerable and untapped market for digital content and digitally enabled experiences in a hybrid mix that is set to grow significantly in the future. While the pandemic may not have solved the digital business model conundrum, the sector was at least able to test demand and build a better understanding of what kinds of experiences work for whom. We saw how digital could enable more accessible, flexible visitor journeys, be a channel for dialogue and community building both locally and globally, draw large numbers, and cement and extend relationships. Although it did not diversify audiences on the macro level, it did attract more younger and disabled audiences and deepen engagement and loyalty among existing audiences. This supports existing research highlighting how digital platforms show more potential in enhancing engagement among existing audiences than in attracting new audiences (Walmsley, 2019). However, we should note that digital experimentation is still in its infancy in the arts and cultural sector and therefore warrants much more strategic investment, research and evaluation.

Social media engagement

As part of our audience research we conducted a systematic analysis of a six-week snapshot of Twitter activity from 19 March to 5 May 2020, the early weeks of lockdown in the UK. The findings presented here are grounded in a mixed-methods analysis of 9,000 tweets shared across the hashtags #MuseumAtHome and #CultureInQuarantine.[1] This approach enabled an assessment of social media interactions that extends far beyond the elementary metrics which cultural institutions typically report on, such as likes, comments and shares – the so-called 'vanity metrics' that, it is argued, often amount to little more than 'success theatre and projection' (Rogers, 2018, p.454). While we used these metrics as a starting point, our aim was to better understand the quality and depth of interactions on Twitter – rather than just their reach – through an analysis of themes, tone and values in the tweets.[2]

Most tweets were from accounts representing cultural institutions or those working in the creative/cultural sectors. Members of the public accounted for only 7 per cent of the tweets in our sample, and only a minority of these (as far as we could tell) were new audiences. Tweets featuring video were more likely to register as high on traction, that is, in the top ten tweets for numbers of likes, retweets or quote tweets (thus most visible).[3] This is perhaps unsurprising given the amount of video content we encounter now in social media environments, but it is really pronounced in our sample, echoing research reporting on cultural institutions' successes in using video content to spark interaction (Najda-Janoszka and Sawczuk, 2021). The sample was international, but mostly representative of the English Twittersphere, and for tweets located in the UK, London and the Southeast were the most active regions.

Some institutions, notably museums and galleries, proved more agile in pivoting to the social media environment during lockdown, quickly moving to produce new content and activities which privileged empathy and intimacy over traditional production values (see also Kidd, Nieto McAvoy and Ostrowska, 2021). A significant proportion of tweets from institutions tried to spark and celebrate the value of curiosity by asking questions and encouraging people to explore and experiment digitally. Other types of cultural institutions (e.g. theatres, opera houses, etc.) were more likely to be conducting traditional promotional activities around events. Regardless, we found that most members of the public were positive about the offer on social media, mentioning pleasurable and enjoyable interactions with content or events.

We found an overall increase in the number of tweets that tried to inspire interaction as compared to previous research (e.g. Kidd, 2011), either asking for engagement or issuing a call to action for people to respond to (in 26 per cent and 17 per cent of tweets, respectively). Strategies included asking people direct questions or inviting them to take part in quizzes or crowdsourcing projects. We also found examples of calls for users to be creative at home, either by providing links to downloadable activities or asking people to engage with everyday objects and to tweet or post the results back to institutions (for example, the Getty Museum Challenge). These examples point to the importance of 'hybridity' – that is, efforts to bridge the traditional physical–digital divide. As institutions closed their doors, we found a heightening of ongoing efforts to connect users with the materiality of cultural institutions in ways that go beyond mere representation (cf. Galani and Kidd 2020; Noehrer et al., 2021; Walmsley et al., 2022). Other examples of hybrid or blended approaches included work with online exhibitions, virtual and 3D guided tours, workshops and lessons for adults and children, and live-streaming of concerts, theatre and other performances. We also found 'behind-the-scenes' moments and snapshots of surrounding outdoor venues (like museums' gardens) that attempted to connect audiences with (closed) cultural spaces as well as nature.

Wellbeing and everyday creativity

Shaped by its real-world contexts during this period, popular content connected powerfully, playfully and/or emotionally with the themes of the pandemic. 'Arts as a way of coping' was present in 59 per cent of qualitatively coded tweets.[4] This included tweets that were Covid inspired or related, as well as tweets which specifically referenced the arts in relation to wellbeing and care. Pre-empting the subsequent findings of the Monitor, many of those tweeting spoke about the potential of culture and the arts to make lockdowns and the related isolation they were experiencing more tolerable. Also of related interest was a grouping of tweets that referenced support, advocacy and funding for the arts in particular. Although not quite so prevalent, references to nature were also present, often cited in relation to art and wellbeing and linked to the value of reflection.

A significant proportion of tweets championed the value of creativity and celebrated practical engagement with the arts. We found plenty of examples of institutions encouraging users to be inspired by objects in their collections to create artistic responses at home to share online. One of these initiatives was National Galleries of Scotland's call for users to respond to a challenge and create #arttogether on 25 March 2020:

> It's time to get creative and make some ART TOGETHER! [emoji smile] [emoji palette] Inspired by Paolozzi's gigantic 'Vulcan', here's your chance to make and share your own fantastic Vulcan sculptures using whatever you can find around the house. Here to inspire you is one we made earlier! #arttogether.[5]

Users responded well (twenty-seven replies, eleven of which were creative contributions, some by children). This tweet offers a perfect example of the hybrid approach mentioned earlier. We also found a number of responses to the responses, demonstrating the value of playful interaction in the social media environment.

Other values that were celebrated in the sample of tweets included social value (discussed below), playfulness (often demonstrated through the use of emoji and GIFs) and considered reflection (including nostalgia, admiration and resilience). We saw only very few tweets which debated or made the case for the arts' economic value.

Place and community

Arts and culture were connected dynamically with place in our sample (mostly locally or regionally rather than nationally, especially through the use of hashtags). Tweets reaffirmed the heightened importance of community and local green spaces during the early weeks of lockdown.

Perhaps unsurprisingly, museums and galleries were most likely to share information about collections, but they were also the most likely group to be sharing 'behind-the-scenes' insights. These attempts to open up institutions via behind-the-scenes snapshots proved popular in our sample, perhaps demonstrating a longing within audiences for the reassurance and familiarity the physical space and place of a museum building seems to suggest, to some people at least, even remotely. This is interesting, as it highlights the importance of place and locality in the sample and underscores active attempts by organisations grounded in communities to be visible, and to engage, collaborate and support. In this respect, we may have seen a more nuanced consideration of what specifically social media 'community' means for these organisations, an examination of which, according to Wong (2015), is long overdue.

During this initial period of lockdown many tweets promoted and celebrated social values. Some promoted initiatives for local place-based communities, while others referred to wider civic and societal issues. Many sought to solicit a sense of belonging or togetherness among followers, offering comfort, enrichment and connection digitally while their doors were closed. There was a sense of benevolence from institutions sedimented into our sample, a wish to be public-spirited, helpful and 'of' the communities they represent. As such, tweets that might provoke or anger users were avoided. It has been noted elsewhere that the pandemic has seeded or nurtured civic-mindedness within institutions – a 'pivot to purpose' (Walmsley *et al.*, 2022) – and our analysis suggests that digital teams have played an important role within that endeavour (see also Kidd, Nieto McAvoy and Ostrowska, 2021).

Changing ideas of the local

Attitudes to local engagement reflect other trends. As well as respondents indicating that they expected to engage more locally after the pandemic than before it, they also indicated that they had become aware of more cultural things to do as well. This effect was most pronounced for younger, highly engaged groups in urban areas, highlighting that there is less likely to be 'spill over' from cities to surrounding areas. This trend is likely to intensify the existing geographical inequalities between areas.

Working from home (WFH) is another trend already changing attendance habits and it looks set to have a lasting impact. We know from previous research, including Brook's (2016b) analysis of Audience Finder data, that working people are most likely to attend either where they live or work. When these become the same place, there is likely to be a greater concentration of local audiences. Moreover, not only do many of those who have been working from home expect to continue to do so, they also prefer it (and hence are incentivised to maintain it where possible). In practice, as debates have continued about the future of home working, changes to office accommodation (with many organisations downsizing), working practices (familiarity with online working) and location (e.g. remote hiring) mean that many changes are already 'baked in'. The Monitor showed us a strong correlation between those that anticipated WFH most or some of the time and high levels of cultural engagement. We can be sure, then, that this is likely to shift the profile of audiences significantly for some venues and organisations and could well have a positive impact for smaller organisations that are located further away from iconic city-centre buildings and shiny creative districts (Florida, 2002). This shift implies that cultural organisations should maintain a more local presence and reimagine and re-engage their local audiences.

Conclusions and implications

The most significant finding from our investigations into audience behaviour and perceptions over the course of the COVID-19 pandemic is that the removal of what have traditionally been perceived to be spatial and financial barriers to engagement failed to diversify who engages with publicly funded arts and culture in the UK. This confirms existing research into cultural engagement but challenges studies that advocate for more local arts venues as an audience development strategy.

Our analysis of social media tells an important story about the kinds of content and interaction that users found valuable during this time of crisis. It therefore helps us to understand and articulate the value of cultural content on social networks more broadly as we emerge from the pandemic. It presents a rich and nuanced snapshot of social media activity and highlights emergent debates that demand further consideration in those contexts relating to hybridity, the value of user creativity and connection, digital inequalities and the limitations of traditional engagement metrics. Our analysis raises a number of questions as we consider implications for future digital engagement and for research in that field: How has the pandemic impacted institutional assessments of the value and importance of social media activity? How do those assessments inform digital strategy, resourcing and training within institutions, and across the sector? Can cultural institutions continue to centre place-based and community initiatives online, as well as work towards inclusion and social justice, in the midst of a post-pandemic recovery that sees cultural infrastructure being squeezed? As social networks continue to evolve, and as their own priorities shift post-pandemic, how will cultural institutions respond?

Overall, our research demonstrates that the sector's efforts to stand by their communities paid off. Support for the cultural sector and public understanding of its value have increased significantly since 2019. Perhaps it took the pandemic to show many of us how important culture and creativity really is, especially when enjoyed in the company of others. In many senses, then, the case for culture has never been stronger. This makes the plight of organisations caught between the after-effects of the COVID-19 tsunami and the current storm of the cost-of-living crisis seem particularly unjust. It is probably still too soon to call what the lasting changes on audience and engagement trends are likely to be, especially given the new volatility generated by the cost-of-living crisis. As we conclude our analysis, there are four clear issues emerging from our research that we ignore at our own peril.

The first is that the widening gap between the nation's haves and have-nots is particularly problematic in the context of cultural engagement: the Monitor shines a spotlight on the structural inequalities that continue to determine who does and who doesn't engage with publicly funded arts and culture in the UK. Despite the sector's growing confidence and skills in building meaningful relationships with people traditionally less engaged with formal arts and culture, the setbacks wrought by the pandemic and now the cost-of-living crisis are severe. We know that in times of crises like these, people need both bread and circuses and yet many organisations are ill-equipped to provide accessible and attractive cultural content, creaking as they are under the pressure to maintain their social commitment while increasing revenue.

This reality appears particularly challenging in the face of the second trend: the general changes in habit which are likely to diminish the core audiences the sector has relied on for far too long. We have seen a measurable change among less committed, less confident audiences, which will only be consolidated by the cost-of-living crisis. The Monitor shows us that a significant group – largely older, away from the big cities – were already predicting they would be engaging less in person in future. This trend has been masked in some places by large numbers of younger people doing more in a post-Covid rush, but the cost-of-living crisis is disrupting this shift: the autumn 2022 wave of the Monitor showed that the large majority of the population (particularly younger people and those with young families) think they will be spending less on culture as a result. This is especially worrying given that these groups were emerging from the pandemic as segments with the highest potential to engage with culture, as revealed in our earlier analysis. Ultimately, the pandemic has helped to put a spotlight on the generation gap and the critical importance of not assuming that each generation wants the same thing. Future-thinking organisations will need to pay close attention and apply their ingenuity to address the increasingly divergent habits and preferences of the next generations of audiences.

In this environment, it is also essential that organisations are mindful of the third issue: the changing dynamics in how we relate to the places where we live and work. The Monitor gave us many clues that this change is on the cards, although it may be subtle, long term and hard to perceive. Again, future-proofing will require organisations to become fully enmeshed in the DNA of their place, to be vital partners in cultural co-production and engagement, and places of community, joy, solace and sanctuary.

The fourth major trend – the shift towards public expectations of high-quality digital and hybrid content and experiences – is arguably the most critical. Poised, as many predict we are, on the brink of the Fourth Industrial Revolution, the technically enabled 'imagination age' (Moin, 2022) seems to be the factor we can least afford to ignore. Frustratingly, then, while many organisations learned from and gained new confidence from their pandemic digital experiments, many have 'snapped back' to business as usual: some because they framed their digital offers as a temporary way of getting through the crisis rather than as a way of anticipating seismic change; others because, despite a sense they were on to something good, they lack capacity to keep pushing forward on all fronts.

Our research clearly signals that change, showing us that early adopters at the front of the curve are highly responsive to emerging digital offers; that digital can provide new solutions to old problems; that the next generation want not just digital content but digitally transformed cultural experiences that are immersive and participatory; that we can and must offer the smarter, more flexible, more personalised visitor journeys that automation, AI and immersive and responsive technologies can enable.

It is hard to see how this potential can be properly met by organisations who still struggle for survival and lack the deep pockets required to convert their pandemic learning, let alone accelerate the rate of experimentation or collaborate with others, to seriously scale the sector's reimagination. There is an obvious role and responsibility for cultural funders and policy-makers here, and elsewhere we have set out our recommendations for these key stakeholders (see Culture Commons and Centre for Cultural Value, 2022). In summary, the cultural sector urgently needs targeted support to capitalise on the digital learning from the pandemic and attract the next generation of cultural audiences. We know that this will be a more hybrid generation and hope that it will be a more diverse and representative one.

Notes

1 A thematic analysis was conducted on a sub-sample of 450 tweets.
2 A full overview of the study's methodology can be found in Kidd, Nieto McAvoy and Ostrowska (2021).
3 51 per cent of tweets in the full data set (n. = 9000) included photographic/image resources, and 8 per cent included videos.
4 Tweets coded as educational in theme (42 per cent of coded tweets) also tended to garner particularly high levels of interest and traction.
5 https://twitter.com/NatGalleriesSco/status/1242788701391945730

References

Brook, O. 2016a. Spatial equity and cultural participation: how access influences attendance at museums and galleries in London. *Cultural Trends*. 25(1), pp.21–34.

Brook, O. 2016b. Location, location, location. *Arts Professional*. [Online]. 15 February. [Accessed 16 December 2022]. Available from: www.arts professional.co.uk/magazine/article/location-location-location

Culture Commons and Centre for Cultural Value. 2022. *Impacts of Covid-19 on the UK's culture sector: implications and recommendations for policy-makers*. Leeds: Centre for Cultural Value.

Department for Culture, Media and Sport (DCMS). n.d. *Taking Part Survey*. [Online]. [Accessed 8 July 2023]. Available from: www.gov.uk/guidance/taking-part-survey

Florida, R.L. 2002. *The rise of the creative class and how it's transforming work, leisure, community and everyday life*. New York: Basic Books.

Galani, A. and Kidd, J. 2020. Hybrid material encounters: expanding the continuum of museum materialities in the wake of a pandemic. *Museum and Society*. 18(3), pp.298–301.

Kidd, J. 2011. Enacting engagement online: framing social media use for the museum. *Information Technology & People*. 24(1), pp.64–77.

Kidd, J., Nieto McAvoy, E. and Ostrowska, A. 2021. *Implications of the COVID-19 digital 'pivot' in museums and galleries: lessons from practitioners*. [Online]. Creative Industries Policy and Evidence Centre. [Accessed 11 January 2023]. Available from: www.pec.ac.uk/discussion-papers/pivot-to-digital-how-museums-and-galleries-responded-to-covid-19

Moin, S.M.A. 2022. *Creativity in the imagination age: theories, practice and application.* Cham: Palgrave Macmillan.

Najda-Janoszka, M. and Sawczuk, M. 2021. Interactive communication using social media: the case of museums in Southern Poland. *Museum Management and Curatorship.* 36(6), pp.590–609.

Noehrer, L., Gilmore, A., Jay, C. and Yehudi, Y. 2021. The impact of COVID-19 on digital data practices in museums and art galleries in the UK and the US. *Humanities & Social Science Communications.* 8(1). https://doi.org/10.1057/s41599-021-00921-8

O'Brien, D., Brook, O. and Taylor, M. 2019. The creative economy, the creative class, and cultural intermediation. In: Jones, P., Perry, B. and Long, P. eds. *Cultural intermediaries connecting communities: revisiting approaches to cultural engagement.* Bristol: Policy Press, pp.27–43.

Rogers, R. 2018. Otherwise engaged: social media from vanity metrics to critical analytics. *International Journal of Communication.* 12, pp.450–472.

Stevenson, D. 2019. The cultural non-participant: critical logics and discursive subject identities. *Arts and the Market.* 9(1), pp.50–64.

The Audience Agency. 2016. *The generation gap.* [Online]. [Accessed 11 January 2023]. Available from: https://theaudienceagency.org/resources/feature-bridging-the-generation-gap

Walmsley, B. 2019. *Audience engagement in the performing arts: a critical analysis.* London: Palgrave Macmillan.

Walmsley, B., Gilmore, A., O'Brien, D. and Torreggiani, A. eds. 2022. *Culture in crisis: impacts of Covid-19 on the UK cultural sector and where we go from here.* Leeds: Centre for Cultural Value.

Wong, A. 2015. The complexity of 'community': considering the effects of discourse on museums' social media practices. *Museum and Society.* 13(3), pp.302–321.

Wright, J. 2022. *Research digest: everyday creativity. Version 1, May 2022.* Leeds: Centre for Cultural Value.

4

Pandemic drama: how England's theatre organisations responded to the COVID-19 pandemic

Karen Gray and Ben Walmsley

Introduction and context

Before the COVID-19 pandemic, the UK's theatre sector was generally thriving. Audiences were buoyant and it was widely regarded as world-leading for the quality of its production, its resilient infrastructure and its notable economic impact. However, as highlighted in Chapter 2, workers across the performing arts were among those most negatively affected during COVID-19 and over 80 per cent of the performing arts workforce before the pandemic were self-employed. Some of these negative impacts relate to historical structural issues including inequalities within the workforce, funding gaps and disparities, and unsustainable business models. During the crisis, the theatre sector was forced into making and accelerating changes to the strategies and modes it used to make work and to engage with its audiences, which inevitably led to a strong focus on digital adaptation and distribution. Alongside the enforced and repeated closure of buildings, this shift challenged organisations of all scales to make radical decisions about their business models and tackle issues of productivity, quality, capacity and skills that are likely to have significant implications for policy, management and training for many years to come.

Lockdown experiences of making and watching theatre have raised important questions about the future roles of physical spaces, shared or synchronous experiences and definitions of authenticity, and regarding audience perceptions of the relative value of digital and live performance. They have drawn closer attention to inequalities of access of all kinds. Some organisations have 'leaned into' their learning and engagement functions to maintain and sometimes deepen audience relationships that otherwise may have been fractured during the crisis. Innovative and adapted models for engagement using remote, hybrid and blended formats have been trialled. Combined, this activity reflects the intensified attention being paid towards the social and civic role of theatre in the mid-twenty-first century.

In this chapter, we examine these phenomena and discuss their implications across the timeline of the pandemic. We highlight some of the convergences and divergences within the sector and between it and other cultural sectors. We build on research engaging with theories and concepts drawn from arts management, cultural leadership, cultural value, cultural policy studies and audience studies, specifically the public role of arts and culture, which identifies a 'relational turn' (Walmsley, 2019). We highlight repercussions for communication, building solidarity and tackling inequalities within the sector's workforce. At the chapter's heart are the insights gained from over fifty semi-structured depth interviews undertaken throughout 2020–2021 with theatre professionals across England, a sample drawn from different organisation types, geography, business models and roles, and including freelance theatre professionals. The lived experiences of these primary stakeholders are explored in depth via three short illustrative case studies comprising a large national organisation, a mid-scale regional theatre and a smaller company with an innovative place-based model. We also draw on complementary strands of the wider project, including audience research and analysis of the UK's Office for National Statistics' Labour Force Survey.

Impacts on the workforce

Chaos and uncertainty

The advisory and then enforced building closures and introduction of social distancing that followed the announcement of the first lockdown on 16–17 March 2020 left UK theatre and its workforce in a state several interviewees called 'absolute chaos'. Immediate practical tasks were pressing: buildings needed to be secured and mothballed, touring productions dismantled and sets moved and

stored, while cast and crew were dispatched without any indication of when or if they might be called again. Programming had to
be rescheduled and ticketholders informed, compensated and their
expectations managed, all despite the absence of any clear picture
of when theatres might reopen. But once theatres had fully shut
down, their leaders were left to deal with the human implications
of the crisis. In almost all cases, theatres had not undertaken any
significant risk assessment or scenario planning for a pandemic and
managers were poorly served by human resources (HR) staff. It
was estimated that more than 15,000 theatrical performances were
cancelled in the following twelve weeks, leading to over £300m
in lost box office revenue (UK Theatre and Society of London
Theatre, 2020). In many cases, managers turned to their boards
to bring in urgent legal and HR support to guide them through
rapidly devised government policies on furlough and existing legislation on redundancy. As one leader commented: 'The board
really stepped up amazingly, were really keen and willing to meet
as much as needed and that ended up being at the hardest points
fortnightly.' Reassurance was provided, 'even if it was just hearing
them say "no one has ever done anything like this, so there is no
playbook"'.

A punishing and extended period of uncertainty began for everyone, while there was little indication of what additional support, if
any, would be made available to fulfil the needs of the people working in a sector, which – unlike hospitality or retail – was never going
to be able to easily remobilise from a standing start. Subsequently,
throughout the crisis, senior leaders found themselves on a constant
treadmill of financial planning and replanning to support multiple
funding applications, working to very short deadlines and constantly
shifting reopening dates. At the same time, organisations needed to
focus on their vanished audiences and their displaced artists and
volunteers. They also had to lobby for funds and negotiate with
sector partners – urgently assessing freelance contracts, complex
co-production agreements and even capital development projects,
while simultaneously appealing to audiences to remain loyal and
donate lost ticket sales. This all placed a heavy burden on organisation life, and on leaders in particular, causing heartache and stress
and leading to feelings of guilt. If before the pandemic cultural leaders
required a range of skills and attributes 'little short of the miraculous'

(Leicester, 2007, pp.6–7), now they were operating in a whole new sphere and by the end of 2020 many were very close to burnout.

There were new and evolving rules and ways of working to negotiate and a lack of clear precedent or regulation in place to guide employers. Interviewees talked of 'stumbling through' and 'constant firefighting'. As for financial or strategic forward planning, one compared the process to 'crystal ball gazing'. Where tired, static business models left some largely unable to pivot, as one director of a small studio theatre put it: 'it just became an office job – the most boring desk job in the world … all about keeping a business alive that isn't really even doing anything'. In short, the theatre sector was overwhelmed and faced a perfect storm from all directions: the traditional business model, inculcated over centuries, disappeared overnight. However, and perhaps most urgently of all, theatre managers and leaders had to deal with their own staff.

Many employees were initially apprehensive and frightened, and this uncertainty exacerbated the inherent management challenges. But in many cases this situation resolved quite quickly following the announcement of the Job Retention Scheme, which most leaders regarded as a lifeline. Regardless, organisations experienced significant challenges around the pivot to home working, which required them to overcome years of presenteeism and woefully low investment in IT. A positive repercussion, however, was the establishment of more regular internal communications as rapid improvements in IT infrastructures generally enabled better visual and verbal staff engagement. Organisations also had to make difficult decisions about who to keep on, who to furlough and who, if anyone, they might need to make redundant. Confirming the quantitative data presented in Chapter 2, redundancy hit younger workers the hardest, particularly those with under two years' employment who therefore enjoyed fewer rights; however, older workers were also disproportionately vulnerable and/or chose to accept voluntary redundancy packages, which left some larger organisations bereft of a generation of traditional stagecraft skills.

The plight of freelancers

Most painfully perhaps, and as earlier chapters in this volume demonstrate, the crisis exposed long under-acknowledged issues caused by precarity and exacerbated by the inequitable ways in which theatre's workforce is structured and remunerated (Comunian and England, 2020; DCMS, 2020). It has since been claimed that 'no other industry outsources its creative leadership or its innovation to such a degree' (Freelancers Make Theatre Work, 2021, p.8). When the pandemic hit, the twin central pillars of the UK Government's pandemic policy response – lockdown and then the implementation of the Job Retention Scheme – created an inequitable situation for those across the performing arts who were self-employed, and for the many portfolio workers or those employed on casual or zero-hours contracts (DCMS, 2020). In many building-based organisations, those in the latter group included staff employed in important components of mixed business models, such as hospitality or retail. Our interviews documented how, while many leaders sympathised with their freelance and temporary workers, most moved instinctively into 'survival mode' and turned their focus inwards: as one director told us bluntly, '[freelancers] can't have the same expectation of continuing employment with an organisation as a permanent staff member'. Similarly, while casual staff may have initially been supported in some organisations, this eventually proved unsustainable, with most quietly 'falling off the books' as venue closures extended into 2021, thereby often leaving the remaining workforce even less diverse than it had been before the pandemic.

Other research suggests that many freelance theatre workers responded with typical resilience, developing innovative practice, skilling themselves up or moving sideways into digital work, starting courses of further education, and seeking or expanding previously held portfolio roles outside theatre (Maples *et al.*, 2022; Shaughnessy *et al.*, 2022). However, despite the introduction of the Coronavirus Self-Employed Income Support Scheme (SEISS) in March 2020, the complex nature of employment in the sector meant that a significant number of freelance theatre workers still fell through the gaps, leaving them unable to claim support and seeking alternative work or turning to Universal Credit (Maples *et al.*, 2022). Anxiety and frustration were expressed on social media and elsewhere at the inequalities implicit within policy responses, with the experience of freelancers and smaller organisations often pitched against that of bricks-and-mortar organisations and what Culture

Secretary Oliver Dowden MP had damagingly termed the nation's institutional 'crown jewels' when introducing the sector's £1.57bn rescue package in July 2020. Our interviews also pointed out a difference in experience between those working in the subsidised and those in the commercial sectors. Indeed, one director of a large commercial theatre told us that it felt the national narrative was consistently driven by the subsidised sector.

A lack of understanding of the respective positions and circumstances occupied by those working within different parts of theatre's ecosystem was highlighted regularly by interviewees. Harnessing such concerns, the Freelancers Make Theatre Work movement was formed to provide a collective voice for freelancers, campaigning to industry and government and demanding a seat at the table in discussions about support, recovery and reset. Faced by the real hardship being experienced by many individuals, we did hear stories of larger organisations proactively working across their theatre ecologies to support smaller companies and freelance artists both financially and in terms of professional support – for example, to apply for alternative sources of funding. Various organisation-backed initiatives with similar aims also sprang up. For example, in May 2020, 150 performance companies and venues signed an open letter addressed to freelance workers, followed by a pledge to sponsor an individual member in working as part of a Freelance Taskforce intended to strengthen the voice of the freelance community (Fuel Theatre, 2020) in all key conversations. Organisations often noted their involvement in collegiate initiatives such as Greater Manchester's Artist Hub (see Chapter 9). Many also expressed a personal sense of responsibility and reported engaging in pro bono as well as funded mentoring, advice and development support for freelance colleagues during the crisis.

Overall, our research identified a sharp rise in collegiality across the cultural sector and this was certainly true in the theatre sector where existing networks strengthened almost overnight and new networks quickly emerged to offer moral and operational support. Theatre workers were keen to share their stories and help each other and perceived networks as 'silently looking out for each other'. One interviewee described the tangible impact of these networks as profound: 'It did feel like those networks did have some actual influence …the amount of pressure that was put on the government from the whole theatre sector ...I genuinely don't think that money would have been anywhere near what it was if the sector wasn't ... collectively lobbying the government.'

However, for many theatre freelancers, time and labour already sunk into development of future work (generally unpaid) meant that many were already significantly out of pocket when the pandemic struck. While some commitments for cancelled work were honoured immediately following the initial lockdown, this was not uniformly the case, with distressing results. One creative producer, for example, voiced frustration and anger at a major building-based organisation that, she said, had simply backed out of a project that had been four years in the planning: 'The two lead artists said to me they felt disposed of.' Any new work on offer necessarily leant towards learning and participation or digital programming. So, for those already well networked or with these in-demand skill sets, the pandemic generally bit less hard. Indeed, some theatres found themselves directly employing more freelancers than previously: delivering learning and participation work online took greater resource than its in-person equivalent and they reported an increase in collaboration with local authorities and statutory support and third sector organisations, providing targeted support for groups such as economically disadvantaged children, young people and families.

As the crisis extended, some freelancers felt that 'transparency and communication' from organisations finally reached a level that many had been demanding for years. However, opportunities handed out to freelancers still sometimes felt, as one venue's senior leader termed it, more like 'crumbs' from the table; others argued that, as usual, cultural recovery funding simply failed to 'trickle down' from larger to grassroots organisations or to individuals in the way that some had clearly anticipated.

Experiences of employed and furloughed staff

For those who remained employed, the stresses were different, although many also found themselves reflecting on the fragility of the industry, its unsatisfactory career structure and the inflexibility of its normal working conditions. Additionally, interviewees pointed to disparities between the experiences of those furloughed and those who remained working. Those working often found themselves ill-equipped and in unfamiliar territory; they were required to take on multiple and different roles, to use different skills and to bear heavier workloads: 'All the usual structures and boundaries and parameters that we usually adhere to went out the window and we all had to get stuck in', one senior manager told us. As a venue director confided: '[M]y role ... doesn't resemble any job description I have ever seen ... it's all about interpreting and enacting government guidance.'

Some staff, in particular members of facilities and technical teams, were furloughed well into 2021. Furlough was capped for most, affecting those on higher salaries. While many organisations made efforts to include furloughed colleagues in regular communications, there was widespread understanding that many may have felt frustrated and isolated. However, there was also some resentment among those who remained working. This was part fuelled by the knowledge that furloughed colleagues were not exposed to the same pressures and had perhaps even picked up additional work in other sectors while some of those remaining working had taken pay cuts to keep their organisations afloat.

Those with existing skills at the intersection between live and digital or with assets ready to be made into digital native performance were well placed to benefit. In contrast, interviewees expressed particular concern around prospects for independent technical, facilities or backstage specialists, many of whom could be offered no possibility of work for extended periods. A hint at the difficulties that might accompany a full reopening came when several commercial production companies were part of Operation Sleeping Beauty, an ill-fated (most closed before opening night) attempt to rehearse and stage panto in 2020, supported by the government and underwritten by the National Lottery. A director involved in one of these productions that we interviewed struggled to bring back technical and front-of-house teams since many had found alternative work. Those who remained employed often found themselves questioning their career choice, as did freelancers and those who were furloughed and could not find rewarding work in other more agile sectors. As one freelancer mused: 'Why am I working in theatre? It doesn't offer any security ...pay rises in theatre just don't exist.

The Equity rate goes up so, so slowly …. It's a mad industry to work in anyway, and then to have something happen like this…'

Throughout 2020 and 2021, feelings of exhaustion, dislocation and anxiety about what might happen as a consequence of failure were common for those who continued working. Interviewees with caring responsibilities described 'flexible' hours extending into late nights and early mornings while working from home: 'I think it's important to acknowledge that the personal really does impact on the professional at the moment', one manager told us. Interviewees frequently expressed a sense of duty and generosity towards colleagues and their local and wider communities: 'It's been relentless. I think everyone has found that. … And the energy of constantly reimagining and feeling like you want to do so much more is really hard in itself.' Such feelings perhaps reflected Alacovska's (2020) argument that cultural work should be viewed 'as a labour of compassion as opposed to a labour of passion' (p.728); and compassionate and emotional labour takes a heavy toll: there were reports of increased sickness rates and new or exacerbated mental health conditions, with some organisations seeing high levels of uptake in their creaking wellbeing and counselling services (when they were fortunate enough to have these). Others talked of training employees in 'mental health first aid'. Each new lockdown created fresh scars, as hopes for returns to normality were raised and then dashed. Everyone felt most keenly the absence of the thrill of live theatre and the physical presence of audiences and of colleagues. With ghost lights flickering in many empty theatres, it was hard to keep delivering work that, for many, smacked of compromise.

Case study: Theatre Absolute

'To be honest, we have not stopped working', Theatre Absolute co-founder and director Julia Negus nevertheless confessed in January 2021. Embedded in its local community, Theatre Absolute opened a small shop-front theatre space in central Coventry in 2009 as a short-term project; the company never anticipated that it might still be there thirteen years later. Project funded, with a small core team supported by a network of associates, the theatre creates cross-disciplinary performance, offering audiences and performers opportunities to explore radical or disruptive narratives.

In March 2020, just three days before the opening night of a long-planned project, the first lockdown forced the shop-front theatre space to close. The resulting loss was creatively and emotionally challenging for everyone, and while backing from funders Esmée Fairbairn was never in danger, significant income from the bar and hires was lost, ticketholders had to be contacted and reimbursed, and the two leaders were very conscious that staff, freelance artists, all those involved in future planned commissions, and the theatre's audiences might all need support.

The organisation adapted immediately: 'We're storytellers at the end of the day, so we created a raft of work both so that we could keep commissioning freelancers …but also be with our communities.' Importantly though, alongside multiple funding applications, the core team took time out to nurture their own artistic practice and reflect strategically, working with a consultant on the company's mission, vision and values. A series of online workshops for Coventry-based writers culminated in a series of micro-commissions and an online sharing event. Emergency Response Funding from Arts Council England meant that they could also offer mentoring and a one-to-one online script dramaturg service: 'We could have run that four times over!' Mindful of the strong correlation between everyday creativity and emotional wellbeing (Wright, 2022), Theatre Absolute also made and posted out 300 Writing Boxes filled with stimuli and prompts to support creativity at home.

Across multiple lockdowns, the shop-front space remained an asset, despite being closed to the public. Its large street-facing windows formed a changing exhibition space, engaging passers-by with film, photography, poetry and textiles. Local artists were offered short solo residencies along with a small bursary – no strings attached – allowing them to make work or just to be in the space. The company had never viewed its work within and with its local communities and the shop-front space as separate because the space wouldn't exist without those who make and come in to see its work; its creation was 'a deliberate act of civic theatre'. The pandemic saw Theatre Absolute renegotiate its relationships with its audiences while developing a heightened sensitivity towards inclusion and the barriers to it. The company felt that some relationships deepened through the use of digital technology: 'There are lots of people who won't engage in the physical space, for lots of reasons.'

As part of plans for the regeneration of Coventry city centre, the building in which the shop-front theatre is sited is scheduled for demolition in 2023 and the theatre will close. It is clear though that the pandemic will be writ large in the company's future plans because of its role in highlighting the inaccessibility and lack of inclusivity affecting many cultural spaces and places. At the time of writing, these plans included short residencies in community and public spaces around Coventry alongside digital and online delivery. The company is also determined to make work that can form an exemplar for care and compassion, for themselves as theatre producers, for those with whom they work and for those living their lives around them.

Organisations: mission, vision and citizenship

As the effects of lockdown prompted many organisations to focus more regionally, local cultural ecologies consolidated and this led to new collaborations on funding bids and pioneering community projects. In the very early days of the pandemic, there were instances of fractiousness as the stress of unpicking artistic contracts and co-production deals began to take its toll. There was inevitably some 'unpleasant financial wrangling' with collaborators, which damaged some existing business relationships in the short term. As noted above, relationships with freelancers were sensitive and in some cases not helped by certain unions who, wittingly or not, quickly sowed seeds of division.

Emergency relief income (Economic Resilience Fund[1] and Culture Recovery Fund) saved many theatres and producing companies from bankruptcy, but some smaller organisations found the application process 'insanely complex' and felt that it wasn't designed for them. As the lockdowns eased, organisations started to reassess their financial positions and get on with the business of programming and reprogramming, with some interviewees admitting to making safer choices. Many organisations used the break in producing and presenting work to focus on schools and/or community engagement: 'We've really leant into our L&P [learning and participation] work. It was always a really vital part of our creative programme, but at the moment it *is* our creative programme.'

Policy-makers initially responded slowly, with some demonstrating limited understanding of the complex logistics, operations and infrastructure of the sector. This resulted in a set of poorly researched COVID-19 restrictions, all of which presented a raft of new challenges for live theatre. Not least of these were the 1–2m social distancing measures which essentially made live performance financially untenable. These presented a particular challenge for commercial venues, which were not eligible for relief funding. The government's tiered approach to Covid restrictions played out differently across the country; theatres in some regions (including London) could open for most of autumn/winter 2020 and much of 2021, whereas others (especially in north-west England) remained closed for months on end. Some theatres struggled to deploy box office, front-of-house and hospitality staff as even many of those who had been furloughed had either found other (often better-paid) jobs and/or enrolled in higher education courses to skill up. This recruitment crisis endured into 2023.

Confirming our findings from the Cultural Participation Monitor (see Chapter 3), existing audiences proved slow to return to live events. Many theatres felt as though they were almost developing audiences from scratch: one director commented 'I think we have to think about our theatres as if, it's almost as if we are opening them for the first time. It's not a kind of everybody's ready to come back through the doors, it's like going into a place of low engagement and deciding you're going to build a theatre and opening campaign.' As another interviewee put it: 'turning up and just expecting people to come to the theatre is old-fashioned now'. Although we know that audiences didn't broaden or diversify on a macro level, many theatre companies did see new audiences emerge to them, as existing cultural audiences became increasingly omnivorous and hungry for cultural content and engagement. Moving towards full reopening in 2021, therefore, many organisations also took time to review how they were engaging with their publics. The results included plans to ditch printed brochures, initiatives to deepen relationships with existing patrons and strategies to re-examine ticket pricing models that might encourage new or cautiously returning audiences.

Case study: The National Theatre

As elsewhere, shutting down was a traumatic experience for the National Theatre (NT). This was the first time in its then forty-four-year history that the NT had closed its building and its shutdown was not just unprecedented; it was also unplanned and occurred in a vacuum of public information. As one interviewee put it, 'there was skeletal information and a heightened sense of fear .... The HR team were out of their depth. We all made mistakes and communicated badly.' The stress was 'phenomenal' – decisions had to be made within hours, including closing the theatre and sending staff, actors and audiences home before that evening's performance. Staff had to track down 150 colleagues working across the large site and communicate complex information rapidly and sensitively. Staff and audiences had fundamentally different levels of understanding about the pandemic at the time and there were vulnerable people to consider among both groups.

The pandemic brought immediate change and speeded up planned strategic developments. Before COVID-19, NT was reliant on 85 per cent capacity to balance its finances and it quickly had to reconsider this unsustainable income model. In the words of one director, 'The P&L [profit and loss financial statement] was not robust: we were reliant on a bit of luck and a prevailing wind.' As another director confided: 'It dismantled the business ... it's been about survival, not strategy and it's knocked any sense of certainty out of the business.' The immediate financial impact was 'grim beyond belief' and the organisation only survived thanks to its £15m reserves, emergency government funding and a loan of £20m. In this sense it was a victim of its own success and had to radically rethink its business model alongside its concept of its own resilience. NT realised how key its strong national networks were; this meant they could quickly be harnessed and mobilised to address the immediate challenges and collectively lobby for support.

On the positive side, the pandemic forced a wider range of staff to engage with the business model, encouraging greater understanding of the need to manage budgets very tightly and take 'a more business-like approach to cost management'. It also encouraged a more entrepreneurial use of the venue's spaces, with the Lyttleton being temporarily transformed into a lucrative film studio, producing in-house content for global film media networks. The organisation responded much more rapidly and radically than it ever would have in normal times, where pressures on box office income historically delimited opportunities for business model development. Innovation notably included the launch of National Theatre at Home, representing a shift not only in the business model but in the ethos of the entire organisation to embrace domestic engagement with theatre. Over 10,000 people subscribed to the streaming platform in the course of several weeks, forcing the theatre to redesign its intellectual property policies, its evaluation metrics and analytics and its entire audience engagement model.

The organisation quickly came under pressure to support its significant number of freelance staff and accessed its Benevolent Fund to support freelancers who were at risk of losing their homes. As one senior manager pointed out, the pandemic immediately 'shone a light on who has career security'. The discrepancies between different cohorts of staff – those who were furloughed versus those who weren't; those who were made redundant versus those who kept their jobs; employed versus freelance – inevitably created tensions and feelings of guilt: 'It feels like an incredibly bruised organisation: there's a sense of survivor's guilt.' This sense of injury was confirmed by another interviewee who confided: 'Wounds have been left; people feel like they have been through a traumatic time and we're trying to heal the wounds as quickly as possible.' The 'survivors' were soon pivoting to home working and working harder than ever, covering for vanished colleagues and cancelling annual leave. Redundancies were significant and took an artistic as well as psychological and operational toll: 25 per cent of permanent roles had to go to achieve cost savings of 30 per cent, culminating in an overall loss of 50 per cent of staff who were on the payroll in February 2020; the diversity of staff decreased from 19 per cent to 15 per cent against a target of 30 per cent; and a whole generation of stagecraft was lost almost overnight, compromising skills and institutional memory.

Exhaustion soon set in, but this was tempered by a shared sense of a more nimble organisation facing unique opportunities: 'I've achieved things that it would have taken me years to achieve ... and it forced us to rethink inclusion.' Former Executive Director Lisa Burger summed up the strategic challenges as follows: 'We'll have to rethink everything and we're tapping into the energy of change …. The ambitions are undimmed, but the resources are much less.' Despite these ambitions, the interviewees all communicated the need to do less but struggled to identify what might have to go. Although the official line in 2020–2021 was 'people not stuff', by the end of 2022 there were no clear plans of how to scale back activity – apart from touring perhaps.

When asked to envisage the future of the sector for prospective cultural workers, one staff member commented: 'It's too hard to exist in this business; it's just not worth it. Unless you're middle-class and you have some sort of financial backing, it's impossible, especially in London.' If theatre is to survive, he added, it will need to be 'less nostalgic and complacent. It will need to wake up, modernise and take its place in society if it's to become a twenty-first century business'. His colleague was more upbeat: 'It'll be a tougher ride than ever before but if you're willing to ride the storm, then do it!'

A pivot to civic?

Reflections on the social value and civic role of theatre took place in a heady atmosphere that included heightened awareness of structural inequalities and of economic precarity resulting from the combination of national and global pandemic impacts and the resurgence of the Black Lives Matter (BLM) movements following the murder of George Floyd. Although diversity (or rather the lack of it in the arts) was already high on the agenda prior to the pandemic, theatre organisations told us they felt positively challenged by BLM. They described anti-racism and diversity action work accelerating during the pandemic pause. One common manifestation of this were attempts to diversify boards of trustees. The newly ubiquitous use of video-call meetings reportedly helped this drive, with organisations finding that the technology encouraged and enabled attendance from a wider group of people: 'I don't feel we are limited any more by our location', the director of a small theatre on the east coast of England told us. This director had also taken the disruptive opportunity offered by the pandemic to commission new and more diverse work than its usual programming strategy would have allowed. Another interviewee described how, as a trustee, she had invited a young person to shadow her during the pandemic, with the aim of demystifying the board process and demonstrating a place within governance for alternative voices. Whether or not any changes to the make-up of those boards during this time have lasting impact on the overall governance of culture in the UK (cf. O'Brien, Rees and Taylor, 2022) remains to be seen.

As our earlier case studies suggest, freed from their business-as-usual delivery mode, theatre-makers and organisations whose doors were closed for almost eighteen months found themselves ruminating on alternative business models, organisational structures and processes, fundamental questions of value, and on what closure and the likely legacy of the pandemic would mean for their long-term visions and missions. In alignment with the dynamics of current cultural policy and the funding associated with it prior to the pandemic, some theatres had already embraced roles as place-making institutions or community hubs. However, some larger organisations in particular expressed a newly awakened 'sense of civic duty ...and a bit of local pride' in bringing theatre back to their communities and felt motivated by the chance to be 'a better citizen', as one director put it. Others, particularly some of those more commercial organisations unused to civic or community engagement work, told us they were overwhelmed by the loyalty displayed by their audiences and buoyed by messages of support from members of their local publics; it was comforting 'knowing how loved you are by the city'. However, our research discovered that for others, an apparent shift towards the civic arose to fulfil more utilitarian and short-term purposes, often to the consternation of smaller companies, some of whom had been operating in this space for decades.

Regardless of motivation, many organisations started to examine opportunities for an involvement in pandemic response and recovery in their local areas. This pivot reflected Mintzberg's (2009) observation that community-minded leaders 'see themselves as being in the centre, reaching out rather than down' (p.142). It was notable that even regional commercial theatres experienced the crisis as a motivating force to join these conversations, something one interviewee from the commercial sector described as a 'silver lining'. Engaging more deeply with local communities meant that organisations could deliver on existing commitments while offering employees and free-lancers tangible and meaningful work. They could obtain or some-times flex or justify existing funding by channelling it into education and community outreach projects. They could also increase or main-tain their awareness with important stakeholders within the local economy, thereby staking a place at the table for discussions around 'reopening'.

However, while delivering services of civic or public value was helping to build or cement relationships with local authorities, with voluntary and third sector partners, and with leaders representing other sectors within their local civic infrastructure, our research sug-gests that, in contrast to the museum and gallery sector, in delivering this work fewer organisations appeared to see this replacing their traditional core role. When asked what they considered this role to be, interviewees frequently reflected on a vision of themselves as, above all else, providers of live entertainment.

Maintaining and repurposing buildings

The stability of this vision meant that for many, the closure of physi-cal buildings was particularly painful. Seeing their buildings dark was challenging, particularly for members of staff whose working lives were so closely tied to them. As one senior leader mused: 'The building is the engine room and I can't do anything until it's pro-ducing great shows again.' For commercial venues, the decision to mothball during the pandemic was simple: 'Obviously those massive productions don't come out of the goodness of their heart, so for us to work, we need to be profitable to producers.' Unused spaces, which still needed to be secured and maintained so that they could reopen as quickly as possible, presented a consuming concern for all theatres. Many older theatres were in dire need of capital refurbish-ment before the pandemic, and there were worries that this capital stock had further depreciated during closures. Certain buildings – like Wakefield Theatre Royal's historic Charles Matcham audito-rium – simply could not function either front- or backstage given the requirements of social distancing. Faced with this, some theatres, including The Lowry in Salford, moved their work outdoors and into communities, or carved out alternative uses for their theatre spaces.

Case study: The Lowry

Losing 95 per cent of its income, moving staff to working from home and closing its doors to audiences overnight was a scenario that no one at this large Salford-based theatre and gallery complex could have planned for. In the decade prior to the pandemic, the managing charity had made successful strides towards complete financial sustainability. In March 2020, like many other building-based organisations, The Lowry faced the perverse situation that the less it did, the more sustainable it would remain.

Emergency Response Funding from Arts Council England and the furlough scheme proved vital support. Then, in autumn 2020, Culture Recovery Funding allowed The Lowry to sustain its artistic programme into 2021. Furlough continued for many, but staff were asked to take pay cuts, hours were reduced and some opted for voluntary redundancy. Even these actions could not compensate fully for the £200,000 per month cost of running a mothballed building.

The organisation began exploring options early for alternative uses of the space, settling finally on a relationship with the Ministry of Justice that saw its smaller Quays Theatre used for criminal hearings as it functioned as a 'Nightingale Court' between September 2020 and August 2021. Relieved to find a solution that would help it survive, The Lowry was undoubtedly naive in not foreseeing the backlash – 'when people threaten to burn your building down' – that it, and fellow Nightingale Court venue, Birmingham Rep, faced, with local communities and some creative partners accusing them of breaking trust with groups and individuals likely to experience the court system as unjust. In early autumn 2020, the move also felt somewhat 'against the Zeitgeist' as elsewhere the sector was cautiously reopening. With hindsight and following renewed lockdowns at the end of 2020 and throughout early 2021, its caution felt justified.

Supporting vulnerable young people is core to The Lowry's mission and its learning and participation work continued throughout the pandemic. However, in delivering it, staff had to develop new digital skills at speed while also finding ways to address issues of digital exclusion. As it became evident how badly the pandemic was affecting young people's mental health, activity moved from online to face to face (where possible), but in community venues: 'We're on people's doorsteps more than we ever have been.'

The team also extended its work and deepened its relationship with local statutory and voluntary bodies, including the local authority. It joined with other Greater Manchester providers in developing creative packs as part of Free School Meal provision. Strong relationships with schools also continued, including through digital artists-in-residence placements. A programme of in-person creative work delivered outdoors was well received. As a result, the organisation has found itself able to fast-track plans to continue similar programming that will extend its presence beyond its walls and the immediate 'Media City' locale. Effects of this could be longer lasting than any moves to digital during the pandemic, most of which it found difficult to exploit financially.

When we spoke in 2021, The Lowry was emerging from the pandemic bruised. The crisis had been incredibly challenging for all its staff, whether furloughed or dealing with heavier workloads, fewer resources and the pressures of working from home. Some key team members were lost and in 2021 skills gaps arose in functions such as development, fundraising and marketing. The organisation and its employees are now facing the need to exercise pay restraint for several years as part of a commitment to servicing the £7.3m Culture Recovery Fund Repayable Finance loan it secured in 2021. Financially, there is little doubt there will be an extended and potentially painful journey to full recovery. Audiences were slow to return in 2021 and producer confidence remained unpredictable. Since any smaller and more challenging work will necessarily need to be heavily subsidised by commercial shows, it was clear there would be knock-on implications for future programming.

Despite these challenges, The Lowry feels more able now to articulate its ethical and artistic voice. It, and its senior leaders, have recognised anew the value that its many ancillary staff generate. Its experiments with building use mean that it understands how space can be 'an adaptable tool in our armoury' and it is now moving further out into the communities that surround it. In addition, there is a strong sense that civic and community engagement during the pandemic has created a distinctive platform for future work, reinforcing The Lowry's value to partners such as the local authority, to the local cultural ecology (including freelance creatives), to philanthropic donors and funders, and to Salford residents and audiences.

Touring

The future of touring provided another common topic for discussion. Here, interviewees reflected not only on the effects of the pandemic but also on those linked to rising supplier costs, concerns around sustainability and climate change, and on barriers to free movement within Europe post-Brexit. The Cornwall-based touring company Kneehigh Theatre was perhaps one sideways casualty of the enforced time for reflection while their subsidy encouraged them to continue producing work during the pandemic. In June 2021, Kneehigh announced that changes in artistic leadership had led trustees to reflect 'on a possible new future but [conclude] that it was better and more responsible to close Kneehigh and ensure an orderly wind down' (Kneehigh Theatre, 2021). Elsewhere, rumblings of concern about touring among those we interviewed were widespread: even successful mid-scale touring companies confirmed that the level of guarantees and fees offered to them and smaller companies was likely to hamper any recovery, as the reserves required to underwrite touring would need significant rebuilding for even the very biggest of national operators: 'it's a broken system', one interviewee claimed. Several suggested the period post-pandemic might provide the perfect opportunity to develop 'slow touring' or located-residency models, enabling touring companies to embed their work and ethos within specific communities and to connect work more closely with audiences and their associated everyday, sensory, political or economic contexts. However, potential practical repercussions of shifts like this, others worried, were that rural or already culturally disadvantaged regions might further miss out on theatre within their local areas.

The rapid shift to digital

Many organisations focused on training, revisioning and restrategising – for example by 'thinking about audiences in a more holistic way' – while others experimented, to varying degrees of success, with digital production, distribution and engagement. Interview data revealed a theatre sector excited about the potential of digital but struggling to monetise it, especially in the face of competition from national companies. The story feels familiar (at least on the surface) to that experienced across other parts of the cultural and creative sector (see Chapter 8), with organisations and individuals finding themselves greatly accelerating their digital activity in the first months of the pandemic. As in other sectors, where resources were available to put online or stream, these were not always of high quality; crucially for theatre, there were few platforms available through which organisations or individuals could effectively market or make money from them and this remained an abiding concern throughout the pandemic. While streaming free content online might have been good for staff morale – and it did, interviewees told us, sometimes result in good engagement from audiences – it solved few financial problems and, worse, may even have contributed to 'digital burnout'. Many companies lacked a sufficiently high-quality digital archive to stream for free. Additionally, they described struggling not only with the skills required for and technicalities of filming digital content, but also with ethical and legal questions around how to recompense those who had been involved in original productions and with navigating copyright requirements for music and other assets. The NT At Home ('it did stop local theatres really being able to enter that landscape') and Netflix effects ('we can't recreate *Bridgerton*; we don't have the budget') left theatres wary about the nature and purpose of their digital output. In the end, a singular disinclination to engage with it was expressed in different ways by many interviewees; as one producer clarified: 'We make theatre. It's what we do.'

Despite this general sense of resistance to digital formats for performance, success stories did emerge. Indeed, some digital native productions succeeded in addressing a need and desire in audiences for a shared experience. For example, in collaboration with a studio theatre, one small Bristol-based theatre company co-produced an interactive murder-mystery on Zoom: 'It's the kind of thing that wouldn't really work in the theatre, it's not like the artists are having to compromise to go online.' By July 2021, two iterations of the show had resulted in sell-out performances that reportedly reached more than 20,000 people. While audiences dropped away when hospitality businesses reopened, in 2022 the company experimented with innovative technology allowing remote audience members and actors to appear co-located on the screen (Telepresence Stage, 2022).

Elsewhere, the NT claimed schools' engagement through free digital as one of its pandemic success stories, and other organisations noted high levels of engagement for Christmas performances livestreamed free into care homes or schools. Additionally, productions that may have attracted only a small or niche audience in live performance reportedly received wider worldwide interest when streamed online; examples include a 2021 production of *Overflow*, a monologue from the perspective of a trans woman set in a toilet, staged at the Bush Theatre in London, and a video-conferenced production of *The Tempest* on Zoom from Creation Theatre that even generated a small profit for the company (Aebischer and Nicholas, 2020). For learning and participation programmes, existing activities aimed at young people or other targeted groups were moved online, with varying degrees of success. Technology certainly kept the activities afloat, which meant that theatres continued to serve their communities; but for most of those involved in delivering these programmes, it was often viewed as second best to in-person participation: 'We've done some stuff, it's not brilliant. It doesn't replace meeting in a room and having a cup of tea.'

However, there are signs that the experience was formative in demonstrating which groups might genuinely benefit from a blend of technology and in-person activity. There were increased opportunities for accessibility and inclusion offered to groups and individuals who might otherwise be unwilling or unable to cross the threshold of physical spaces and their sometimes surprising (to providers) take-up of the offer. Successful examples included online writing workshops involving disabled people or for women experiencing domestic violence, and sessions that brought together community groups sharing similar backgrounds and experiences but who remained separated by geography. Crucially, alternative formats did not just mean sessions solely delivered online: interviewees described running activities with older people over the telephone or in mixed groups with some people using Zoom; they talked about maintaining pastoral provision for young people using WhatsApp and of conducting slow performances involving the exchange of postcards or letters. A good number claimed such experience had increased their understanding around the potential of hybrid or blended provision for inclusion and suggested this might be a long-term legacy of the pandemic. However, as other researchers have suggested, such a legacy will need careful maintenance if its gains are to be sustained (Feder *et al.*, 2022; Misek, Leguina and Manninen, 2022).

Thus, despite some positive experiences, theatres experimenting with providing a space for digital work more frequently expressed a sense of the experience being difficult and even dispiriting. The problem was exacerbated by skills gaps in marketing the work and an insufficient understanding of audience behaviour in digital spaces. An overwhelming desire to return to live theatre and the sense that there is as yet no satisfactory model for reliable revenue generation from digital provide powerful counteracting forces that appear likely to dissuade theatre-makers from further experimentation and investment. This, as well as a lack of evidence for a significant increase in online public cultural participation during the pandemic, suggests that the sector has a lot to learn if it is to understand how and why audiences might take up future digital offers. It also needs to differentiate between the fundamentally different activities of digital production, digital marketing and digital engagement and appreciate the different skills involved in each (Cirstea and Mutebi, 2022).

Conclusions and implications

Our research with theatre professionals across the UK illustrates how the painful experiences of the pandemic often led to pioneering ideas and initiatives brimming with potential. While all theatre organisations had to be incredibly agile to survive during the pandemic, the smaller ones certainly benefitted from not having to 'turn a big tank of an organisation'. Among the larger organisations, The Lowry's increased sense of being able to express its value within its local community and beyond its walls points to ways in which changes (and mistakes) made during the pandemic might leave the sector leaner but perhaps more articulate. Meanwhile the National Theatre showcased how digital theatre can function effectively in people's homes and has proven the concept of digital theatre subscription.

While Theatre Absolute's team and their associates struggled with personal and professional loss and exhaustion, the company also benefitted from the enforced pause. In this, they were not alone: through our research, we saw other organisations undertaking transformative work on their visions, structures and processes, including diversifying board representation and actively seeking to change recruitment practices. Perhaps, as several interviewees suggested, shifts in leadership or representation for diverse voices will only truly take root when space is carved out within funding cycles to allow for a more measured, moral and relational approach to developing and supporting those working within the sector. Helpful here too, we observed, were business models whose success was not predicated upon large or unequal labour structures and organisational models that included community or cooperative ownership and compassionate leadership, meaning that skills, responsibilities, accountability and losses could be more equitably balanced and shared.

Theatre in the UK and indeed globally has been at crisis point and it remains in a place of transition and flux. Although many theatre companies have reignited their relationships with local schools, communities and providers of public and voluntary services, their core audiences are proving cautious to return and the current cost-of-living crisis will only exacerbate this caution. Some theatres have seen hard-won reserves wiped out or are now servicing significant loans in an era of rising interest rates; the pandemic has taught them that relying on box office and retail income no longer guarantees resilience. If the sector is to maintain its position as a mainstay of people's leisure time and a significant contributor to both the population's wellbeing and the national economy, it will need to continue to collaborate, innovate its business and production models, and revolutionise the way it engages audiences old and new. As one of our interviewees reflected, it will also need to convince the public and policy-makers of its ongoing relevance and be clear about its cultural value and impact:

> We have to come up with a stronger argument and a better language so that people who don't go to the theatre a lot understand why it's worthwhile and the value of it, whether that's linked to mental health or civic duty and pride. Essentially we talk about protecting culture and protecting society like the arts is a culture of a country ...; if you don't protect the creative industry making shows and making art, there isn't really a society.

Note

1 The Economic Resilience Fund (ERF) was offered to businesses in the hospitality, leisure and attraction sectors that were materially impacted by a greater than 50 per cent reduction of turnover between 13 December 2021 and 14 February 2022.

References

Aebischer, P. and Nicholas, R. 2020. *Digital theatre transformation: a case study and digital toolkit.* [Online]. Oxford: Creation Theatre. [Accessed 12 July 2022]. Available from: https://ore.exeter.ac.uk/repository/handle/10871/122587

Alacovska, A. 2020. From passion to compassion: a caring inquiry into creative work as socially engaged art. *Sociology.* 54(4), pp.727–744.

Cirstea, A.M. and Mutebi, N. 2022. *The impact of digital technology on arts and culture in the UK.* [Online]. POSTnote Research Briefing. London: UK Parliament. [Accessed 8 August 2022]. Available from: https://post.parliament.uk/research-briefings/post-pn-0669/

Comunian, R. and England, L. (2020). Creative and cultural work without filters: Covid-19 and exposed precarity in the creative economy. *Cultural Trends.* 29(2), pp.112–128.

Department for Digital, Culture, Media and Sport (DCMS). 2020. *Impact of COVID-19 on DCMS sectors: first report.* London: The National Archives.

Feder, T., McAndrew, S., O'Brien, D. and Taylor, M. 2022. Cultural consumption and Covid-19: evidence from the *Taking Part* and *COVID-19 Cultural Participation Monitor* surveys. *Leisure Studies.* 42(1), pp.38–55.

Freelancers Make Theatre Work. 2021. *The Big Freelancer report.* [Online]. [Accessed 12 July 2022]. Available from: https://freelancersmaketheatrework.com/wp-content/uploads/2021/03/The-Big-Freelancer-Report.pdf

Fuel Theatre. 2020. *An open letter to theatre and performance makers.* [Online]. London: Fuel Theatre. [Accessed 12 July 2022]. Available from: https://fueltheatre.com/an-open-letter-to-theatre-and-performance-makers/

Kneehigh Theatre. 2021. *Web archive.* [Online]. [Accessed 14 July 2022]. Available from: https://web.archive.org/web/20210603163127/www.kneehigh.co.uk/

Leicester, G. 2007. *Rising to the occasion: cultural leadership in powerful times.* St Andrews: International Futures Forum.

Maples, H., Edelman, J., FitzGibbon, A., Harris, L., Klich, R., Rowson, J., Taroff, K. and Young, A. 2022. *Freelancers in the dark: the economic, cultural and social impact of Covid-19 on UK theatre workers. Final report.* [Online]. University of Essex. [Accessed 12 July 2022]. Available from: https://freelancersinthedark.com/publications/freelancers-in-the-dark-end-of-project-report/

Mintzberg, H. 2009. *Managing.* San Francisco: Berrett-Kohler Publishers.

Misek, R., Leguina, A. and Manninen, K. 2022. *Digital access to arts and culture.* Loughborough: Loughborough University. [Online]. [Accessed 12 January 2024]. Available from: https://hdl.handle.net/2134/20025731.v1

O'Brien, D., Rees, G. and Taylor, M. 2022. Who runs the arts in England? A social network analysis of arts boards. *Poetics.* 92(A).

Shaughnessy, C., Perkins, R., Spiro, N., Waddell, G., Campbell, A. and Williamon, A. 2022. The future of the cultural workforce: perspectives from early career arts professionals on the challenges and future of the cultural industries in the context of COVID-19. *Social Sciences and Humanities Open.* 6(1), pp.1–12.

Telepresence Stage. 2022. *Telepresence Stage case study March – April 2022: Sharp Teeth Theatre.* [Online]. Bristol: Telepresence Stage. [Accessed 14 July 2022]. Available from: www.telepresencestage.org/residencies/sharp-teeth-theatre

UK Theatre and Society of London Theatre (SOLT). 2020. *Written evidence submitted by UK Theatre and Society of London Theatre/ Federation of Scottish Theatres/ Creu Cymru/ Theatre and Dance Northern Ireland to the DCMS Select Committee Inquiry: impact of COVID-19 on DCMS Sectors.* [Online]. [Accessed 14 July 2022]. Available from: https://committees.parliament.uk/writtenevidence/3564/html/

Walmsley, B. 2019. *Audience engagement in the performing arts: a critical analysis.* London: Palgrave Macmillan.

Wright, J. 2022. *Research digest: everyday creativity. Version 1, May 2022.* Leeds: Centre for Cultural Value.

5

Beyond the digital: notions of belonging and the impacts of COVID-19 on festivals in Scotland

John Wright

Introduction

Festivals in Scotland have a long history and play a significant role in the socio-cultural discourse of the nation. From the ancient origins of the Highland Games and the nineteenth-century inception of Burns Night to the contemporary development of globally significant festivals such as the Edinburgh Fringe, festivals seem intractable from the Scottish collective consciousness. Indeed, a cursory glance at Visit Scotland's landing page revealed the value of the 'live' festival experience as a central pillar of the tourist board's promotion (Visit Scotland, 2022). A fundamental aspect of any festival is in the act of 'gathering' with others – an embodied experience described by Monica Sassatelli as a 'multifaceted sociable experience' (2011, p.25). Many of the interviewees referred to fundamental notions of 'gatherings' within which the traditions of their festivals were rooted. Returning to places on an annual basis, the language that they used was rooted in ideas of belonging.

However, faced with government restrictions on gatherings in the course of the pandemic, festivals had to quickly adapt and change both their structures of management and operations. Work from home policies also implied viewing from home, which forced most festivals to rapidly develop digital content for their audiences. However, as restrictions evolved, and parts of society opened up, festivals started to experiment with hybrid forms of management and production. In many cases this led to collaborations with local authorities, communities and other festivals. Festivals started to share resources and knowledge with each other and informal networks developed in order to cope with the crisis.

Drawing on empirical data from interviews with Scottish festivals, this chapter explores the effect that digital and hybridised programming, performing and gathering have had on different aspects of belonging and evaluates the extent to which this changed or shifted how festivals might approach future planning. The chapter draws on a thematic analysis of the festivals included in the study and includes a case study in order to explore the complex relationship between ideas of belonging and shifts to digital and live or hybrid festivals. The first section comprises a thematic analysis of the role of place and complex notions of belonging across the festival cohort. The second section constitutes a case study utilising a comparative analysis of Orkney Music Festival and Burns Big Supper, which focuses on the complex relationship between place, people and culture to draw out themes of identity, collaborative and participatory practices, shared resources and tradition.

Notions of belonging

Literature on belonging is extensive and has been effectively applied to many different fields of research. Belonging is frequently associated with emotional attachment and is described by Nina Yuval-Davis (2006) as 'an act of self-identification or identification by others' and of feeling at 'home' within a specific context be that physical, virtual or spiritual place (p.199). Yuval-Davis identifies an important distinction between belonging and the politics of belonging, suggesting that 'the politics of belonging comprises specific political projects aimed at constructing belonging in particular ways to particular collectivities that are, at the same time, themselves being constructed by these projects in very particular ways' (p.199). In other words, belonging only becomes political when it is seen in relation to others within society. Belonging within this broader context is interrelated with notions of identity and the concept of nations (Anderson, 1983); people, geography and places (Woodman and Zaunseder, 2022); and friendship and support structures (Condorelli, 2014). This was evident throughout the interviews we conducted but overtly characterised by one interviewee within a borderland festival who said that 'our sense of place has been strong; throughout [the pandemic] we were compelled to do stuff by our membership and our community … in our digital work we wanted to show people who we are and where we live and getting people curious about that'. There was a real sense of belonging to communities beyond the immediate close relationships which constitute the festival. This was about the festival both reflecting the identities of a locality and being part of the continual change of those identities.

As noted by Yuval-Davis, the concept of 'home' within the broader discourse of belonging presents a complex knot of tensions and interconnections. Mary Douglas (1991) conceptualises a home through grounded empirical research. Douglas states that 'for a home neither the space nor its appurtenances have to be fixed, but there has to be something regular about the appearance and reappearance of its furnishings' (p.289). It is this sense of regularity and organisation of space which plays out in the festival context and helps frame this chapter.

Both these notions of belonging are important to our analysis of Scottish festivals because the pandemic disrupted norms of engagement and a sense of regularity and yet opened up the potential for connections beyond local and regional geographic proximities. The neutrality of belonging shifted and was thus charged with an urgency to identify with others through the concept of the festival. A sense of 'longing' to be with others was expressed by many of the interviewees alongside a need to create this sense of belonging through different modes of action, which in themselves led to many of the decisions that are discussed within this chapter.

Methodology

The following analysis draws upon empirical data gathered from semi-structured and partially transcribed sector interviews carried out between October 2020 and September 2021. The interviewees have been anonymised for ethical reasons, but their roles in the festivals remain visible as this is pertinent to the analysis. Our research also employs relevant secondary sources pertinent to the festivals. This chapter utilises case study and comparative analysis to draw out key themes. The case studies have been selected for their comparable size and geographic locations in order to effectively draw comparisons.

Drawing on the work of Yuval-Davis and others, this chapter utilises a conceptual framing of belonging through three distinct analytical forms as outlined by Yuval-Davis. These consist of 'social location', which takes into account the relational and power dynamics between social, economic and geographic groups. Another is the 'identification of emotional attachments' through stories that we tell. Although this chapter focuses on this in a collective sense, this can go further and be about individuals in relation to collective identity. These 'identity narratives can be individual or they can be collective, the latter often a resource for the former' (Yuval-Davis, 2006, p.202). Then there are the 'ethical and political values' of belonging that emerge in relation to others in society and how they are judged. Each of these are applied within the chapter to explore the different intersections between belonging and festivals but are not exhaustive and present areas for further research.

Place, virtual festivities and belonging

The festivalisation of culture is a phrase which refers essentially to the way in which culture is produced and consumed within society but it also reflects the steady spatio-temporal dislocation of the periodic staging of festivals (Taylor and Bennett, 2014). Festivals are no longer entirely constrained to the seasons, to common land or as part of wider religious holidays. Instead, they are contradictory places where the commodification of culture and the temporary annexation of public space (in terms of physical festivals) lie in tension with the disruptive and transgressive forces forged in traces by collectivisation (Bakhtin, 1963; Bourdieu, 1984). In other words, festivals are places where people come together to escape everyday life. Yet, festivals are often understood by funders, organisers and other stakeholders in economic terms rather than in social or cultural terms. Festivals become profitable and attractive to investors by temporarily enclosing public space and implementing ticketing systems or by creating exclusive events within commercial properties and spaces and, as a result, have increasingly been separated from the common access to space and time with which they were traditionally associated.

The pandemic dramatically changed this state of play and has in some cases forced a reimagining of what festivals should be and how they operate. Throughout the cohort of festivals in Scotland included in this research, these tensions and pressures emerged within specific activities. It became apparent early on in the interviews that all of the interviewees had experienced a sense of loss as their respective festivals were either postponed or cancelled. This experience was further intensified by a sense of survival panic both as a basic human need in the face of danger and on a broader socio-economic plane as festivals and livelihoods came into jeopardy. As a result, many interviewees described the realisation that their usual modes of practice and production were no longer viable. One interviewee described this moment as profoundly changing their role within their community, 'from organising leagues, printing brochures, etc. to giving advice to our members, writing Covid risk assessments and readjusting insurance arrangements'.

This shift in activity became a shift in purpose for many festivals as they adapted their priorities. Their immediate locality in the communities that form the festivals and that they serve became the primary focus in many cases. Notably, this was felt across the entire cohort, whether they were a highly commercial mega festival, cooperative or a smaller rural festival. This shift in the socio-cultural perspective of festivals manifested in many different ways, but significantly it represented a movement away from the all-encompassing economic drivers. At this point it is important to stress that this was not a complete negation of economic drivers but rather a renegotiation of the festivals' role within society.

This realignment brings with it a sense of the interconnectedness and interdependence of festivals and their communities through notions of belonging. This was profoundly enacted by several festivals in their support and coordination within their localities. In particular, an island festival producer in the west of Scotland stated that they felt compelled to work with the local food bank. The festival established 'food bank Fridays', which were regular live-streamed 'gigs' to raise money, awareness and help for the local food bank that became more vital during the pandemic. They stated that they were 'trying to help everyone else', motivated by an emotion of caring and a sense of social responsibility because their community was under threat. This was about much more than managing food provision; it reflected a sense of belonging to a place formed in the festival's interconnectedness with its community as epitomised in the phrase: 'the island all pulls together', which was repeated multiple times during the interview.

In Yuval-Davis's 'Belonging and the politics of belonging', this sense of the interconnectedness between communities, culture and sharing of resources when under threat is described as a state where 'the emotional components of people's constructions of themselves and their identities become more central the more threatened and less secure they feel' (p.202). This depth of feeling is described within the discourse of belonging as emotional attachment. Another interviewee summed this up in terms of an 'emotional and artistic hit, felt very immediately'; during the early lockdowns they 'felt very cut off, not going to live events, private views and seeing people'. For this interviewee, there was a doubling effect of isolation as they did not live in the geographic location of the festival where they worked. This meant their sense of belonging to the festival was less interconnected with local communities as they identified more strongly with their immediate colleagues and their professional life as an audience manager within the brand of the festival. The sense of belonging between these two interviewees is significantly different: the former is embedded within a local Scottish island context and the latter working remotely for a festival that is located in a large city, yet their respective festivals play a role in their individual constructions of identity through these emotional attachments. Importantly, this identity is never fixed, as articulated by Yuval-Davis: 'Of course, not all belonging/s are as important to people in the same way and to the same extent. Emotions, like perceptions, shift in different times and situations and are more or less reflective' (2006, p.202).

Of course, what festivals do in their various forms is provide a sense of place for all involved. This sense of place and togetherness in which people experience collective joy has been theorised by many sociologists and anthropologists including Émile Durkheim in the form of 'collective effervescence' and by Victor Turner as 'communitas' (Turner, 1977; Durkheim, 1995). This place is at least a partial alternative to 'everyday life' albeit both complicit, imperfect and intertwined. However, this sense of place is rooted in the collective memory, traditions and cultures of regular comers, local communities, organisers, artists and newcomers. In short, although festivals are always changing in their content and construction, they provide a nexus for people to feel a sense of belonging because there is a regularity to their appearance, which was characterised by Douglas as 'memory institutionalised ...capable of anticipating future events', be they seasonally located, same groups of people who attend, art form specialty or geographic location. This was expressed by an interviewee as follows: 'it's that coming together to be able to enjoy yourself ...it is all down to that community spirit, the hardiness of us Scots, that just get it done'.

All the festivals that we studied were rooted in their physical locations and due to social distancing and restrictions on gatherings were either forced into a form of hibernation or developed new ways of working, often using digital and live-streaming technologies. A plethora of different approaches emerged in the interviews, ranging from repurposed archival footage of previous festivals to live-streamed and Zoom events. One festival even created a series of socially distanced 'garden gigs' for the local community, which were then filmed and uploaded as digital content. What was most striking about this activity is that in the early part of the pandemic, it was often free to access. Festivals that adopted this approach emphasised that the feedback that they received from both members of their local community and also from festivalgoers living further away was largely positive, with audiences suggesting that it was the first time they were able to attend the festival because of access issues such as disability or the remote location, including the distance to travel if they were travelling internationally. Indeed, many rural festivals were able to increase their reach in terms of the visitors that could now access their content online.

This openness was created both through the necessity to connect with their communities and also through a willingness to experiment creatively. Much of this initial content and activity, although free to access, relied on other forms of provision, charitable models and reserves, and so was not sustainable in the long term. This raises questions about the socio-economic devaluation of culture and sustainability regarding this free-to-access content, which many of the festival producers keenly expressed in their interviews. This supports the notion that 'paid for' cultural consumption (particularly on a scale of mass consumption) is privileged over free-to-access content (Abbing, 2002). Many of the interviewees based in non-profit or smaller partly commercial festivals expressed fears that offering free-to-access content online would decommercialise their cultural production and practice. However, in the Scottish festivals context there is little evidence to suggest this situation has manifested. Of course, this 'fear' is part of the economic threat brought on by the pandemic and related to the value of festivals as a commodity, rather than their social value as a place of belonging. Regardless, the pandemic provided many festivals with the skills, knowledge and resources to develop future digital content to run alongside their live events in what has become known as hybrid delivery.

Belonging: comparing Big Burns Supper and Orkney Folk Festival

Festivals in Scotland are both abundant and heterogeneous in nature: it seems that every region has some form of gathering or festival associated with its locality. This implies that festivals cannot be described in generic terms and that they need different forms of support structures including how they are managed and how they are funded. This specificity became acutely visible when government restrictions on social distancing and gatherings came into force in March 2020. The following analysis of Big Burns Supper and Orkney Folk Festival provides insight into the challenges festivals faced and continue to navigate.

Big Burns Supper is a multi-artform festival which takes place annually over eleven days at the end of January. Located in Dumfries and Galloway, the festival is one of the largest in the south of Scotland in terms of its community platform (Big Burns Supper, 2022). The festival's location is multi-centred in the sense that it occupies venues in small towns across the region. In contrast to Big Burns Supper, Orkney Folk Festival is a rural festival located in an archipelago off the north-eastern coast of Scotland. Unlike Big Burns Supper, its programming and delivery is much more contained within a specific locality and has a shorter duration. Taking place over three days in May, the festival's history is intertwined with the fishing port of Stromness, where most of the events are held in small venues.

Orkney Folk Festival decided to cancel its live performances after frantic twice-weekly meetings throughout March 2020 as venues and events were closing down. The festival team decided to postpone until May 2021 due to their relatively early position in the festival season and they made the decision to pivot to a digital offering. They stressed that this was not to replace the festival but rather to help mark the occasion. Indeed, both Orkney and Big Burns Supper were forced to take, in their words, a 'fallow year'. However, both produced digital offerings which were experimental in terms of the specialist skills that were required and also the content which was developed.

There were major differences between the approaches in the festivals' usage of digital platforms and technology. Big Burns Supper had already begun to pilot the use of digital platforms in its broader programming throughout the year. This was partly a result of the fact that the festival belongs to a parent charity called Electric Theatre Workshop, which is managed through a cooperative model constituted by volunteers and thus embedded in the social structure of governance from the outset. The cooperative's work extends beyond the festival and was 'already testing digital' on a smaller workshop-based programme. By contrast, Orkney Folk Festival had previously decided to run as an exclusively live event and thus had to drastically shift its policies and approaches to a digital model when the pandemic hit.

It is notable in the different approaches to the use of digital platforms that both festivals stated that they were able to learn from other festivals and support organisations such as audio-visual studios and local arts organisations through knowledge exchange and the development of peer-led collaboration. In the case of Orkney, the festival started working with several audio-visual studios which had been set up during the pandemic to provide specific audio-visual resources for festivals and live events production organisations while touring events were cancelled. These studios provided high-quality digital production resources for festivals and events teams to broadcast live to audiences in a Covid-safe environment. Crucially, these studios also provided knowledge exchange regarding how to use the equipment and so passed on new skills, enabling festivals to become autonomous in their use of these resources. These studios were specifically established to share expertise and equipment for a reasonable fee, subsidising access to high-quality equipment for smaller festivals and events organisations that would not be able to afford high-priced broadcasting equipment.

Further, in the case of Orkney Folk Festival this was a mutually beneficial relationship that flourished in a non-hierarchical environment because the expertise and intellectual understanding available in the festival team was shared with the studio engineers. This form of interrelationship between the festivals offers an example of how social location and belonging to highly interwoven parts of the music ecology in these specific areas of Scotland became vital for all parties to adapt their working practices and produce festivals in a new way.

These notions of belonging through social connection and location emerged more clearly as the interviewees talked about the broader networks which developed rapidly over the pandemic. Collaboration and connections between festivals became an important strategy for both Orkney and Big Burns Supper during the pandemic. This is perhaps the most surprising aspect for the festivals that we investigated because they often saw themselves in competition with each other because of the funding landscape (this aspect was seen across the study and specifically in relation to Chapter 6 in the Northern Irish context). In terms of notions of belonging, these connections and relationships were mostly informal spaces for knowledge exchange but crucially they became support structures. As discussed by Condorelli (2014), these forms of informal close collaborations are abundant in the arts sector. Although primarily focused on the field of contemporary art, Condorelli's ideas are applicable across art forms and at different scales. Condorelli states that '[t]he notion of support is examined as the physical, economic, social, and political structures that are art's conditions of possibility' (Condorelli, 2014, p.2). Condorelli goes on to suggest that in the arts, notions of care are rooted in friendships and close ties which can go beyond the transactional and economic to something close to emotional attachments of belonging. This was particularly highlighted in the second round of interviews with an interviewee at Big Burns Supper who stated that: 'It's got even better, there is a project we are working on with partners throughout the UK …there was this kinda block before – I cannot go to Dundee you know – that's 70 quid and I won't see the team all day! Communication has totally changed.'

Being able to work with others virtually, especially for a rural festival, has meant that these conversations and connections were able to happen more frequently, which has helped to maintain networks. Indeed, there was a deeper sense of belonging in the way that the interviewees talked about pre-pandemic working, which was characterised as often closed off to sharing ideas, or in the way that they felt like they were not 'in the club' compared to some urban or city-based festivals. Now they felt that the pandemic's impact had broken down some of these barriers, and, as noted by Yuval-Davis (2006), a loose form of collective solidarity had led to multi-unexpected collaborations in the face of a real threat to their livelihoods. Interviews with people from both festivals revealed that these bonds were forged in a deeper sense through the pandemic. Interviewees from both festivals stated that they would not have been able to survive without coming together with other cultural workers and festivals to share resources including equipment, information about Covid-safe practice, logistics, applications for emergency funding and personal stories. This finding supports the ecosystem analysis of Greater Manchester presented in Chapter 9.

At this juncture it is important to return to the interrelationships between belonging and change over time. Big Burns Supper started to work closely with other third sector organisations and local authorities to help manage cultural and social resources throughout the lockdown periods. Specific examples of this occurred during the initial six to twelve months of social restrictions when Big Burns Supper rolled out a digital choir and a socially distanced theatre workshop and also extended its digital services to schools. Interviewees suggested that although working with local authorities, schools and other third sector bodies was difficult at times and fraught with tensions, particularly regarding public health needs and venue capacity, the pandemic had in fact forced an openness in these negotiations about sharing risk and resources, particularly for the benefit of the local community.

The instrumental value of cultural provision shifted in the festival's thinking as a result of the pandemic. Although Big Burns Supper was already moving towards these forms of practice prior to the pandemic, the crisis accelerated this action. The festival had time to reconsider its role in the community and investigate how it could best utilise the festival's resources to care for people's needs. This reveals the ethical and political values of belonging at the crux of these decisions. Defined as much by the festival's activity within the wider locality as by internal decision-making, these actions were somewhat reflexive as they were forced upon the festival due to social distancing measures and postponement of their events. Nonetheless, they reveal a shift in the purpose of the festival beyond its traditionally intrinsic concept of cultural value and hint at a reimagining of the festival's relationship with its community. In the interviews the phrase 'we don't serve the community, we *are* the community' suggests that the festival, its parent organisation and the local population are in fact interrelated rather than entirely distinct entities. This is further illustrated in the festival's governance model and statement: '[a]s a unique social co-operative, we have over 170 voluntary members who contribute to our social model through volunteering, sponsorship or advocacy. Anyone can join our membership organisation' (Big Burns Supper, 2022).

By being an open and free-to-join organisation, the festival encourages local people to be part of the delivery of the festival itself, ensuring in theory that the needs of the local community align with the direction of the festival. This social value became central to the direction of the festival during the pandemic and it describes one of its main goals as to 'improve the lives of our community who are experiencing high levels of social and rural isolation' (Big Burns Supper, 2022). Here we have the complexity of the politics of belonging, which was a distinct self-identification by Burns Supper to become community led and root itself in Dumfries and Galloway as a place. Yuval-Davis (2006) describes this complexity as 'any construction of boundaries, of a delineated collectivity, that includes some people—concrete or not—and excludes others, involves an act of active and situated imagination' (p.205). Here a collective imaginary of the festival can find a social location within some form of shared values, even if these values differ on an individual level. This was exemplified in the interview data: 'we really listened to our stakeholders ... our community and it was about bringing people together through art ... to bring a bit of joy in a really bleak time'.

Although Orkney Folk Festival is structured in a similar way through a volunteer model it does not describe itself as a 'social co-operative' in the same way as Big Burns Supper. Instead, the focus is on the festival itself and how the act of staging the festival can bring together different communities of artists, audiences and local people. This is one of the fundamental differences between the two festivals. The festival states that '[o]ne of the most important characteristics of the first festival that stands true today is the balance of visiting and local artistes [sic]' (Orkney Folk Festival, 2022). It is clear that akin to Big Burns Supper there is a level of care in their practice, but the difference lies in the delivery of a programme which is solely focused on the 'gathering' itself, rather than direct work within the local community.

The most vital stakeholders within festivals are of course the festivalgoers themselves. Orkney Folk Festival was able to create a reduced-price ticketing scheme for its online festival in 2021 because its overhead costs were greatly reduced. Reducing the cost removed a possible disincentive to engage with the festival and broadcasting across free-to-access online platforms such as YouTube ensured broader access than its previous physical iterations. This practice extended further, as articulated by Woodman and Zaunseder in their research on alternative festive gatherings. The authors state that 'all-comers can potentially join: no tickets, no entry barriers, no security, nothing for sale' (Woodman and Zaunseder, 2022, pp.108–109). However, in the case of Orkney there were still some potential disincentives, such as a small cost. This aspect of relative freedom in the processes of joining and gathering was further emphasised in the interview with the festival: 'We heard stories of people getting dressed up at home and watching it ... texting their friends and family.' This sense of community and communal viewing is key to belonging and indicative of emotional attachments created by being with people and feeling a connection to others, and offers evidence that this is possible even in a virtual environment.

In their analysis of the alternative festive context, Woodman and Zaunseder (2022) found that the memory of the relationships between people over many years of returning to a specific location at the same time of year was an important component to the experience of place within the gatherings they observed. This raises the question of whether this aspect of place can still occur in the digital and hybrid sphere. Both festivals created a hybrid programme in 2022, having acknowledged in interviews that it would be impossible to entirely recreate a sense of place in a virtual environment. However, they took different approaches to this process. Orkney identified a key aspect of the 'placeness' of the festival as rooted in the landscape of the island and the social connections between people. In its 2020 and 2021 digital iterations this was important to their broadcast. In 2020 it repurposed archival footage to mark the occasion and reach out to its community of artists, visitors and local Orkadians in a national lockdown. The interviewee expressed surprise that this offer was successful with the audience, that the festival was 'so valued by the local community', and that they were able to 'recreate that festival community' even though families and households were apart from each other. One of the reasons identified was that the festival had a captive audience because stay-at-home restrictions were in place. However, by activating the audience's memories through archival footage the festival producers were able to partly evoke the festival feel virtually.

One of the tropes of memory in this form of festive gathering is expressed by Woodman and Zaunseder as follows: 'many, if not most, of the people we encountered had been coming for years, and were not attracted by the line-up of performers, but by the overall ethos of the event, the place where it is held and the friends they encounter there' (2022, p. 113).

This correlates with the feedback the festival received from its 2020 free digital iteration, which highlighted the benefits of collective viewing through 'getting dressed up' and 'texting friends and family' even though audiences were physically separated. It was as much about the experience as it was about the content. This reflects the notion of collective joy articulated by Turner in his work on *communitas*. Turner suggests that 'this relationship is always a "happening", something that arises in instant mutuality, when each person fully experiences the being of the other' (1977, p. 136). This sentiment was expressed in the interviews by both festivals and is theorised by Woodman and Zaunseder, who suggest that: '[t]his ethos evokes several ways these events produced commons: openness to the other, both human and nonhuman beings and nature; practices of care and nurturance; and the formation of collectives that through these orientations produce solidarity and collective joy' (2022, p. 118).

These factors come into play within both festivals and importantly this has been recognised by the organisers themselves. The Orkney interviewee suggested that: 'Because of where we are, people tend to commit before the festival ... the artists are kicking about in the pubs and the clubs, they might have a session on and this is a massive appeal to audiences.' This embodied experience of gathering audiences and artists all in one place in a relatively remote location, which still retains a rural sensibility, is what keeps audiences coming back. It is the spontaneous and unprogrammed happenstances that occur within the festival that evoke this collective joy and create a shared sense of place. Conversely, the popularity of the festival resulted in capacity and accommodation issues on the island and nearby over the last few years, and these were somewhat resolved by its change in presentation. The festival has discovered that digital and hybrid have the potential to help increase capacity by increasing access for audiences who cannot attend in person. Interestingly, in a survey the festival found that over 50 per cent of respondents to the digital festival in 2021 were new audiences, suggesting that adding a permanent hybrid element to the festival can certainly bear fruit in terms of audience development.

Both Big Burns Supper and Orkney Folk Festival produced high-quality live digital broadcast iterations of their festivals in 2021. Learning from their digital work in 2020, these digital festivals were incredibly well attended in 2021 with over 300,000 viewers for Big Burns Supper, owing partly to its free broadcast over YouTube and the fact that Scotland was in another national lockdown at the time. Likewise, Orkney Folk Festival's live broadcast saw over 2,500 weekend passes being purchased and many more views as again collective household viewing came into play. Both festivals reported that these digital iterations democratised access and inclusion to their festivals: because of their rural locations, international audiences that could not travel or are unlikely to attend every year could experience the festival remotely for the first time. They also told stories of disabled audiences with mobility issues being able to experience the festival.

This unprecedented increase in audiences presents a complication to the notion that the memory of embodied experiences of previous iterations of these festivals provides strong emotional attachments. One of the interviewees suggested that instead of discouraging people from actually attending a live in-person event, live-streaming actually 'does the complete opposite … if they can see some of the festival without having to travel for the first visit then they are more likely to come back …certainly for folk from America who can't possibly travel every year but are willing to buy a streaming pass'. Similarly, another interviewee said that: 'we were able to reach audiences around the world …effectively you're giving them a window into Scotland on Burns Night if they are a bit patriotic or if they are from America or Australia'.

This engagement with audiences on a national and international scale reveals the complexity of belonging and particularly the intersections between the two distinct concepts of social location and emotional attachment. Geographically, these audiences were distant but elements of a shared culture and recognisable social practices that they identify with became strong motivating factors for them to attend these virtual festivals. Anderson (1983) argued that interrelationships between concepts of nation, identity and belonging are 'imagined' and that 'in the minds of each lives the image of their communion' (p.6). For Anderson, people cannot know everyone in a nation, and in the festival context audiences cannot know all that attend, especially from multiple geographical locations. The social location of these audiences goes beyond national borders and in this sense becomes attached to histories and to elements of an abstract form of home as conceptualised by Douglas's aesthetic choices and decision-making by the festivals to commit to some forms of regularity and familiarity in the way they presented their broadcasts (Douglas, 1991). However, we cannot verify the extent to which these audiences have links to Scotland or to specific places and locations. The significant increase in attendance across both festivals points to a potential wider dispersed expatriate or ancestral audience where belonging becomes a powerful motivator in attending festivals through virtual means.

Another important finding from our study was that festivals reported an increase of new audiences. An interviewee from Orkney reported that more than 50 per cent of respondents were new to the festival. On the face of it, this is an outlier in the data and contra-dicts some of the findings in Chapter 3 on audiences, which sug-gested that it was the same audiences that were engaging in more online content. Of course, this may have been the case overall at a national scale, but within the festival context and for example at the scale of Burns Supper and Orkney, there was clearly a signifi-cant increase in new audiences.

Turning to the future, the hybrid of live-streaming and the tra-ditional live festival is the key legacy of the pandemic that will play out in the development of Orkney Folk Festival. In 2022 this was implemented for the first time with three live shows streamed nightly on YouTube. In contrast, Big Burns Supper continued with a free online broadcast due to the emergence of the Omicron vari-ant and adapted its programming to host a smaller summer festival with satellite events dispersed throughout the year. These digital and hybrid iterations have resulted in a clear change in production and management with the implementation of different practices delivering positive socio-cultural and economic benefits for these festivals. Understanding notions of belonging through virtual and hybrid offerings will be important as festivals begin to experiment with these technologies.

Conclusion

Belonging is a complex phenomenon that evokes emotive responses but also pragmatic notions and connections between people, places and things. Within the Scottish festival context this complexity was manifest in both collective and individual ways. However, this anal-ysis of the impact of COVID-19 on Scottish festivals highlights how the pandemic brought about rapid changes to festivals, together with a real sense of the need to care and provide for their commu-nities. This interconnectedness of art and life instigated practices that had previously been dismissed or simply remained out of view. This is as much about re-evaluation of festivals' roles within soci-ety as it is about hybrid or digital methods of engagement. This chapter therefore represents a jumping-off point for future research and conversations about festivals' social-cultural, political and eco-nomic dimensions within different places.

In closing, I will now return to the initial questions posed in this chapter, namely: What effect has digital and hybridised programming, performing and gathering had on belonging? Has it changed or shifted how festivals approach future planning? Many festivals embraced digital technologies both within their organisations and to connect with their festivalgoers, communities and audiences. The inability to physically gather appears to have accelerated the creative use of online spaces for forms of collective watching, broadcasting and more participatory cultural practices such as artist-run workshops. Many festivals used these digital spaces to evoke a sense of place that cannot replicate the embodied live experience but which has brought their communities together in surprising ways.

The long-term effectiveness of the integration of digital technologies within hybrid forms of festivals remains to be seen. This was summed up by an interviewee as a multitude of meanings to hybrid: 'I would personally like to see a standing show ...but we would also most likely stream shows from Stromness Hall.' How hybrid manifests really depends on the context and might not even include digital connection. Indeed, jumping to incorporating digital within a live show presents significant challenges for festivals. However, this study suggests that the use of digital within festivals is here to stay, as illustrated by Big Burns Supper and Orkney Folk Festival. The use of digital technologies has in some cases aligned more closely with the social location of belonging by increasing access and removing some disincentives such as the cost and remoteness of some festivals. However, there are already signs of the monetisation of streaming and of weekend passes being replicated in digital spaces, albeit at a reduced cost to attending festivals physically. What is certain is that festivals have changed irrevocably due to the pandemic and that these notions of belonging merit further exploration.

References

Abbing, H. 2002. *Why are artists poor? The exceptional economy of the arts*. [Online]. Amsterdam: Amsterdam University Press. [Accessed 4 October 2022]. Available from: www.jstor.org/stable/j.ctt45kdz4

Anderson, B. 1983. *Imagined communities: reflections on the origin and spread of nationalism*. London: Verso.

Bakhtin, M. 1963. *Problems of Dostoevsky's Poetics*. Minneapolis, MN: University of Minnesota Press.

Big Burns Supper. 2022. *About*. [Online]. [Accessed 4 September 2022]. Available from: https://bigburnssupper.com/about-bigburns-supper/

Bourdieu, P. 1984. *Distinction: a social critique of the judgement of taste*. Cambridge, MA: Harvard University Press.

Condorelli, C. 2014. *In support: a theoretical and practical investigation into forms of display*. PhD thesis, Goldsmiths, University of London.

Douglas, M. 1991. The idea of a home: a kind of space. *Social Research*. 58(1), pp.287–307.

Durkheim, E. 1995. *The elementary forms of religious life*. London: Free Press.

Orkney Folk Festival. 2022. *About*. [Online]. [Accessed 20 August 2022]. Available from: https://orkneyfolkfestival.com/about

Sassatelli, M. 2011. Urban festivals and the cultural public sphere: cosmopolitanism between ethics and aesthetics. In: Delanty, G., Giorgi., L. and Sassatelli, M. eds. *Festivals and the cultural public sphere*. London: Routledge, pp.12–28.

Taylor, J. and Bennett, A. eds. 2014. *The festivalization of culture*. London: Routledge.

Turner, V. 1977. *The ritual process: structure and anti-structure*. New York: Cornell University Press.

Visit Scotland. 2022. *Scotland is calling*. [Online]. [Accessed 12 August 2022]. Available from: www.visitscotland.com/

Woodman, S. and Zaunseder, A. 2022. Exploring 'festive commoning' in radical gatherings in Scotland. *Identities*. 29(1), pp.108–126.

Yuval-Davis, D. 2006. Belonging and the politics of belonging. *Patterns of Prejudice*. 40(3), pp.197–214.

6

Collaborative cultural leadership: Northern Ireland's response to the COVID-19 crisis

John Wright and Ali FitzGibbon

Introduction

This chapter explores how the impact of COVID-19 on arts and cultural activity in Northern Ireland (NI) gave rise to collaborative approaches to leadership across the cultural sector. It draws principally from a series of practitioner interviews, observations and discussions carried out in 2020 and 2021, combining the knowledge of organisational leaders with cultural freelancers and policy-makers (both public body and government department).

Although exacerbated by the crisis of 2020, the tensions surrounding the recognition and definition of cultural leadership predate the pandemic. They are intrinsically linked to concerns of representation and attention in regional, national and devolved (subnational) policy structures and within arts and cultural practices and production systems. Pointing to particular manifestations of leadership equally points to where leadership is absent, excluded or ignored. Here, our focus is on shared and networked leadership and how these forms influence or shape policy relationships over an intense and relatively short period. We examine arts and cultural leadership as a crisis response through collaborative informal networks, and consider how these networked groups engaged in closer working relationships with policy-makers as collaborative policy networks. We then suggest ways in which these collaborative practices could shape future cultural policy-making and speculate about possible inhibitors. Despite many positive dimensions and the power of such collaborations as crisis response, it is apparent that the temporary nature of these alliances, as well as divergent interests and goals, can limit their potential.

While this chapter focuses on networks in NI, we situate this research within existing literature on cultural leadership. This poses questions about how leadership is shaped collaboratively and how it can be mobilised (or not) to address gaps or vacuums in policy and policy knowledge, particularly (as in during the pandemic) when normal systems of policy-making are disrupted and must be rapidly reassessed.

This chapter argues that networked and collaborative leadership are amplified in times of crisis, conditioned by historical precedence and relationships. However, the depth and context of these crises is always specific and their conditions understood differently. As a result, this chapter is presented through multiple perspectives, taking account of the different stakeholders and their relationships to each other.

Understanding collaborative policy/leadership relationships

The study of leadership has moved over time from the pursuit of (what some argue are unachievable) ideals of leadership style manifested by individuals to consideration of multi-faceted, diffuse and shared leadership (Kempster and Jackson, 2021). Increasingly, leadership is explored as a set of behaviours that can be distributed across and beyond individual organisations and systems (Todnem By, 2021). This new ideal of leadership behaviour is arguably better able to negotiate the increasingly complex, uncertain and interdependent nature of society and economy, and the growing attention to concerns of environmental and corporate responsibility (Bardy, 2018).

Cultural leadership by contrast has long been understood as both practice and theory in which shared and collaborative approaches are actually the default (Reynolds, Tonks and MacNeill, 2017). In part, this is explained at an organisational level by cultural organisations' dual artistic and executive logics (Eikhof and Haunschild, 2007). Such studies, however, often focus on the roles of individuals in senior artistic and executive management positions, thus reinforcing leadership as a social construction within organisations (FitzGibbon, 2019; Goodwin, 2020). Embedded practices of cultural production instinctively share or pass on leadership temporarily as part of a creative process (Eikhof and Haunschild, 2007): an artistic director deferring to a choreographer in rehearsal or the transfer of leadership to participants by an artist facilitator in socially engaged practices. These practices of devolved leadership, however, vary widely, with no commonly understood approach across arts and cultural practices. Finally, collaborative approaches to shared leadership and decision-making are consciously adopted from socio-political movements, with political ideologies informing artistic purpose. These are most often manifest in artist-led and community-led programmes, supported by cooperative, collective, 'flatter' and non-hierarchical governance models (Donelli, Fanelli and Zangrandi, 2021; Jeon and Kim, 2021). They prove difficult to study as many players eschew the title of 'leader' (Goodwin, 2020). Many of the members of these groups take on leadership duties depending on their individual skills and experience. The importance for these groups in removing hierarchies is inherent in their political beliefs for communal working practices and has a history rooted in the socialist movements of the late nineteenth and early twentieth centuries (Wright, 2019).

With such a long tradition of collaborative leadership, it might appear easy to form networked sectoral approaches to cultural leadership that can work on a common agenda or address public policy concerns, both in and outside of moments of crisis. Yet cultural leadership studies show us that such networks of leaders and their influence on policy are flawed: victims of benign and malign self-interest, acts of self-justification (FitzGibbon, 2019). Rather than mobilising sector-wide change and policy improvement, such networks often devolve into a 'closed shop' of elite decision-makers tacitly reinforcing inadequate policies while lacking or losing any tangible mandate (Nisbett and Walmsley, 2016). During 2020 and 2021, our research examined what was happening to cultural leadership in a moment of crisis and explored how the informal networks that emerged became a force and contact point for reviewing and prompting rapid policy change. We therefore sought to marry existing (cultural) leadership theory with the study of collaborative policy networks.

Christopher Weare, Paul Lichterman and Nicole Esparza (2014) theorised collaborative policy networks, focusing on the dynamics and cultural forces within interorganisational networks. This work evolved in the study of another quite different crisis: a housing crisis in Los Angeles. Although not focused specifically on an arts or cultural context, its deployment of cultural theories and its effectiveness beyond network theories to capture the dynamics of a crisis moment proved useful here. Through this lens, we focus on how different actors within networks and broader ecosystems can form around 'wicked problems' in crisis situations. We apply this to examine the dynamics between all actors in a system, no matter how 'loose', and to investigate the power dynamics between policy and advocacy. Lastly, we borrow heavily from their work to 'consider the manner in which the interaction between differing cultures may drive the formation and dissolution of collaborative networks' (Wear, Lichterman and Esparza, 2014, p.591).

Methodology

Our methodology is shaped by our positionality. We both arrived to research from practitioner and arts activist backgrounds (working in England, Northern Ireland and Ireland) such that had our lives evolved differently, we might have been interviewees for this research. During 2020 and 2021, we also undertook secondments and advisory roles for policy-makers, including the Department for Communities (NI). As Røyseng and Stavrum (2019, p.3) put it, as policy researchers, 'we are part of relations to both the field of cultural production and the field of policy', additionally embedded in social and emotional relationships within the networks we explore here.

This chapter draws upon empirical data gathered from sixteen semi-structured interviews conducted through the Centre for Cultural Value and carried out between October 2020 and September 2021.The interviewees were selected through both a snowball process and by consultation with various networks. The process was designed to reach a diverse range of interviewees from different localities and art forms/disciplines. Although anonymised for ethical reasons (e.g. as Interviewee, 2021), interviewees' job titles/roles are cited as we felt this was relevant to the analysis. Reflexive thematic analysis was used to analyse interview data and draw out the key aspects of collaborative leadership and networks explored here. We also drew on additional secondary sources pertinent to the Northern Irish context as well as field notes from our observations.

The chapter is structured as follows: firstly, we provide a brief historical context looking at the development of collaborative leadership in NI prior to the pandemic. Secondly, we focus on leadership at the start of the pandemic. This section focuses on the emergency responses and explores how they affected the development of collaborative leadership and policy networks. Then we focus on collaborative leadership outside of organisations and beyond the public sector. This section explores cultural freelancer inclusion at policy level and traces tensions around freelancer inclusion in collaborative leadership at sector level as the pandemic developed. Finally, we analyse the challenges of sustaining collaborative policy networks and leadership by highlighting the uneven process of moving towards 'recovery' and the pressures involved in sustaining these relationships between policy-makers and cultural practitioners.

Collaborative leadership and policy networks in Northern Ireland

To understand 2020 and the networks we describe, we must first understand more about their precedents, either as advocacy movements or as previous attempts and failures at fostering collaborative policy fora. We trace here a small number of networks that arose in NI from the mid-1990s, post-ceasefire and in the wake of NI's first published arts strategy, *To the Millennium* (Deeny, 1995). We concentrate on pan-sectoral networks and engagement with policy-makers. Not only does little record remain of some of these, but we also note that they centre on Belfast, explained in part by the city's position as the seat of the Northern Ireland Assembly and the base of the Arts Council of Northern Ireland (ACNI) and its lead government department, the Department for Culture, Arts and Leisure (DCAL). As the largest urban centre, Belfast also represents the greatest concentration of cultural freelancers and organisations.

The period from 1995 to 2020 witnessed significant strides in arts policy and cultural provision in NI. There was large-scale capital and other investment through National Lottery funds, which led to multiple new arts buildings and boosted cultural provision; NI got its first culture-specific minister and department in 1999 and launched a major interdepartmental strategy on creativity mentored by Sir Ken Robinson (DCAL, 2001); and Derry/Londonderry became the first UK City of Culture (2013). This positive picture was marred by ongoing political instability, a steady diminishing of dedicated arts/culture budgets, and outbreaks of tension between the culture sector and different ministers on the degree of artistic and cultural autonomy that public subsidy should afford.

From 1999, when the first Minister for Culture, Arts and Leisure was appointed, until 2020, when the pandemic hit, there had been seven different culture ministers from three different political parties and three periods of suspension of the NI Assembly (including 2002–2007 and 2017–January 2020). Four 'Direct Rule' ministers had been appointed from the UK Parliament for portions of these suspension periods. By 2016, DCAL had been in part subsumed into a new 'Department for Communities' (DfC) with a new minister (notionally the eighth culture minister). This fragmented the cultural portfolio as NI Screen (film, TV and gaming) moved to the Department for Economy while Arts, Culture, Heritage (and notionally policy responsibility for Creative Industries) remained with DfC. Meanwhile, a restructuring of local authorities from twenty-six to eleven in 2014 had changed the region and its relationships between devolved government, local government and cultural providers. Throughout this period, arts and culture had lacked visibility in successive Programmes for Government. Political and public sector attention was focused elsewhere, while economic and social priorities were heavily shaped by ethnonationalism and political sparring.

Informal mutual support networks (for particular disciplines or in particular regions) formed throughout this period, some disappearing when key people moved on, others becoming resource organisations (for example, the Theatre Producers Group, later NI Theatre Association, and Dance Resource Base, which subsequently became Theatre and Dance NI; or the Arts Managers Group, a network of local authority arts officers). Other networks had formed around common provision or policy agenda as a result of strategic interventions by ACNI and others (Community Arts Partnership formed from Community Arts Forum and New

Belfast Community Arts Initiative; Arts and Disability Forum, now University of Atypical; Voluntary Arts Ireland and Visual Arts NI, both part of networked bodies at UK/all-island levels; Audiences NI, now Thrive). Over time, many of these became the base for targeted and reactive policy advocacy campaigns with pan-sectoral involvement – for example, Professional Arts Lobby (1998–1999), Invest in Inspiration (2007–2008) and Arts Matter NI (launched in January 2015). To varying degrees, these movements assumed cultural sector leadership. They responded to immediate threats (e.g. funding cuts and de-prioritisation within governmental strategies) and sought longer-term shared solutions and presence for culture within governmental priorities.

These campaigns might be described as 'uninvited' contributors to policy development (to borrow from Jane Woddis, 2014). The Professional Arts Lobby openly challenged low spending levels, lack of parity spend and lack of strategy. It was informally welcomed by ACNI officers at the time but could not be openly endorsed by the agency and its council. By contrast, the work of Invest in Inspiration (Northern Visions, 2007), mounted in the consultation period for the 2008 Programme for Government, was described by ACNI as a 'sister' campaign to its own efforts based on per capita spending. The 'Invest' group and ACNI had combined forces under the banner #KeepOurArtsAlive (ACNI, 2007). This alliance of planning and information sharing, however, was not sustained by ACNI following these rallies. In its aftermath, traditional funder–client relationships were reinstated, and tensions became apparent between ACNI and its lead department (DCAL). Departmental reports to a resulting committee inquiry challenged the per capita spend data of its own arts development agency (Bell, 2010).

The next significant mobilisation to arise was Arts Matter NI in 2014, which launched in January 2015. It operated concurrently with, but distinct from, ACNI's No More Cuts to the Arts or #13pforthearts campaign (ACNI, 2014). Arts Matter NI was perhaps the longest running, if intermittent, movement, surging into life to oppose a series of ministerial decisions to ringfence funds and impose in-year cuts (Bluebird Media, 2015). It later encouraged submissions to consultations and lobbied the Secretary of State for NI post-Assembly collapse. Although not initially critical of ACNI, Arts Matter NI eventually called for the resignation of the ministerially appointed ACNI Chair, John Edmond (Shields, 2018). While there were instances of 'invited' policy cooperation (Woddis, 2014) between political/public sector bodies and cultural leadership networks, these were often instigated by public bodies around discrete policy areas such as art forms, youth and disability arts. Commitments to co-design at local authority level produced some interesting collaborative planning (most notably Derry/Strabane District and Belfast City Councils) but the process often exposed disparity in expectations of, and capacity for, visible policy change (Durrer, 2017).

In November 2000, four government departments came together to consult on a new cross-sector strategy for arts and culture with creativity as its main focus.[1] Although widely consulted on, Unlocking Creativity (DCAL, 2001) had been focused on inter-agency and interdepartmental negotiations and did not translate to any overarching cultural or creative strategy for DCAL. In 2015, Minister Caral ní Chuilín established a 'Ministerial Arts Advisory Forum' to consult on the creation of a draft strategy (DCAL, 2015). While this may be seen as an acknowledgement of earlier campaigns, this forum was marred by a lack of clarity over remit, lack of resourcing and buy-in from other departments/agencies, insufficient time and lack of freedom to direct its activities. Forum members publicly distanced themselves from the draft strategy consultation document released in 2016 (Ministerial Arts Advisory Forum, 2016). With the merging of the department into the DfC, a new minister from a different party and the collapse of the NI Assembly by early 2017, no strategy ever emerged.

The Arts Collaboration Network emerged informally into this environment, principally as a quiet and mutual support network, mobilised less by advocacy and campaigning and more by solution finding 'behind the scenes'. The group eschewed any mandate or desire to be 'the voice of the sector'. However, by the time the pandemic struck, successive attempts to influence policy had ended in failure and absence of either strategy or trust, leading many of the cultural leaders to create their own mutual support systems. This was described by one interviewee as follows: 'the inherent fragility [in the sector] has been exposed by Covid …; we have really felt the policy vacuum'. This same interviewee went on to compare NI with other parts of the UK by suggesting that the relationship between

Arts Council England and DCMS at least presents a stronger framework for arts and culture than that in NI.

Reluctant leadership at the start of the pandemic

In autumn 2020, we began to conduct cultural sector interviews in Northern Ireland. Recurrent features of these initial interviews included the wide-ranging emotions of participants combined with a sense of pragmatism. This pragmatism was mobilised by feelings that the status quo had been irrevocably changed. There was a tangible sense of hope in the face of horror, and participants articulated that in this moment they felt that there was room to reimagine leadership and support structures for arts and culture.

One of the most striking themes within these interviews was the invocation of mutual support, with colleagues reaching out to others across the sector. This was echoed in other cohorts throughout our study, especially in the Scottish festivals context (see Chapter 6). Whether through formal networks or through informal connections, these relationships provided places to vent, ask for advice, pool resources and, most importantly, offer mutual support. This sense of collegiality was captured by interviewees: 'it felt like it all happened really quickly .... I am involved in a cross-sectoral network ...; we met very quickly when lockdown happened'. They described the mood of those initial days as trying to overcome the confusion and bewilderment, suggesting that 'the initial conversations were about ... informal exchange of information ...; we had to all react'. However, this was replaced quickly with a realisation that COVID-19 was going to impact the sector on a massive scale and particularly cultural freelancers. This interviewee went on to explain that this informal collaborative network started to move into an 'action phase' in late 2020, talking to funders and policy-makers to 'make the case' and in effect lobby the DfC.

It is vital to understand that although these networks existed pre-pandemic, the crisis itself, and the attendant collapse of the livelihoods of those in the cultural sector and associated sectors, galvanised these relationships into action and produced a shared leadership effort. This is theorised by Weare *et al.* as follows: '[T]he interorganisational dynamics that arise with the shift away from hierarchical and market-based forms of organisation towards more networked forms are shaped by the cultural tensions and affinities that emerge as actors adjust to new patterns of interaction' (Weare, Lichterman and Esparza, 2014, p.591).

Indeed, this interviewee also revealed that they and their colleagues had never before worked so regularly and directly with government departments in such a relatively short space of time. Although it pre-dates the pandemic, the Arts Collaboration Network (ACN) expanded considerably during this action phase. Another interviewee explained this as the rapid development of a network of representative and support organisations coming together with third sector voluntary arts organisations, theatres, galleries, literature groups, venues, performing arts, circus and freelancers/artists. ACN sought discussions with ACNI and DfC, which then identified and started to plug evidence gaps in both agency and department. This was achieved by ACN gathering quantitative and qualitative data from its members. Members pooled knowledge from across the sector and through open online events such as 'the big gathering', producing written documentation which was passed on in meetings with DfC officials. One interviewee who was involved in this process stated that 'it was an attempt to get to the levels where we could really make a difference'.

As this last point implies, many of the interviewees involved in these networks suggested that ACNI and some local authorities had been slow to react in the initial phases of the pandemic and that the galvanised response of this loose network and direct contact with DfC officials (in effect bypassing ACNI) was a direct response to this perceived policy vacuum. Interviewees suggested this vacuum was in effect a leadership vacuum within cultural policy-makers in NI that pre-dated the pandemic and had several important consequences when the pandemic hit. Firstly, interviewees stated that they were thrust into leadership roles within their organisations as they responded to rapid change, uncertainty and rapidly changing restrictions without clear direction. Some were working with skeleton teams with most staff furloughed; others were already in a small team but had to shoulder extra responsibilities. Secondly, they identified that the leadership vacuum in the policy and political landscape had resulted in a plurality of networks – informal groups with different allegiances and varied aims that had formed over the years. At the start of the pandemic, this fragmented cultural voices at policy level (in effect fragmenting strategic decision-making). Additionally, ACNI and DfC meetings with sector representatives were often not advertised or held as open meetings and the rationale of who was invited remained unclear. Nevertheless, common agreement existed within all the fragmented groups and gatherings that rapid policy responses from the government were needed and both short-term and long-term actions were demanded. This led to the development (at least temporarily) of a type of collaborative policy network described by Weare *et al.* as follows: '[C]ollaborative networks should not simply be viewed as instrumental means to achieve fixed ends but rather as particular sets of relationships that are manifestations and support for particular cultural biases' (Weare, Lichterman and Esparza, 2014, p.599).

Within any set of relationships there are tensions which are both essential for action and also potentially fractious. Many of the interviewees described the NI arts and cultural ecology as 'tribal' and at times contentious. This became apparent as ACN's open lobbying and public statements received backlash, according to some interviewees close to the processes. One stated that some individuals questioned: '[w]ho are you anyway and why are you doing this?' Yet the group felt compelled to act and to present evidence to the DfC to back up their recommendations (ACN, 2021). Some of those involved in ACN were also part of other networks and distinct pressure groups lobbying for the commercial entertainment, live events, music or venues sectors, or representing cultural freelancers.

Interviewees that were part of the ACN network made it clear that they were not there to represent 'the cultural sector' in a generalised sense. They resisted formalisation into an official 'voice' of the sector (they did not have an official terms of reference or membership) but had instead mobilised their collective resources to influence policy decisions by the DfC. Therefore, despite displaying traits of shared leadership in acting as advocates and seeking change 'beyond' their own organisations, and identifying a leadership vacuum, many neither espoused the title of cultural leaders nor accepted that responsibility.

One of the characteristics of collaborative policy networks is that they are predicated on both policy-makers and sectors sharing 'information and resources' and engaging in 'joint projects to achieve shared goals' (Weare, Lichterman and Esparza 2014, p.590). Among interviewees, there was a general feeling that at local authority level and at a constituency level (with individual MLAs), trust and some history of cooperation existed. This was emphasised in a press release from the ACN in which the then CEO of Thrive, Margaret Henry (2020), stated: 'We believe local ministers do value the arts, as they have stated in the past, and we acknowledge the pressures they face as they manage the fallout from the Covid-19 crisis.'

However, before the pandemic such cooperation had rarely existed at the level of the NI Executive, not least due to the regular changes in minister, Assembly collapses and political disputes as well as occasional standoffs on cultural freedoms. One interviewee candidly noted the prevailing sense of distrust among many within the cultural sector when it came to the NI Executive, stating 'we don't believe our government'.

The result of this lack of cooperation was that it took a series of channels (pressure through local representation, information sharing with DfC officials and direct approaches to the minister) for the informal group around ACN to achieve progress. Aside from different appeals for support through 2020 and in early 2021, the minister agreed to establish a cultural recovery taskforce, one of the key recommendations made by the network and its collaborators. Our second stage of interviews took place in summer 2021 and interviewees felt that this was a significant moment for the arts and cultural sector in NI. However, they also by that time felt exhausted by the process and expressed concern about the long-term sustainability of such collaborations.

Collaborative leadership

Much has now been documented about the informal radical care networks that came into being among cultural freelancers during the first UK lockdown (e.g. FitzGibbon and Tsioulakis, 2022). However, as seen in the theorising of cultural leadership and discussion of the ACN above, many of the players who formed these freelancer movements were motivated by mutual support and resisted the title of leader, refusing to be made into a sectoral voice. Cultural freelancer networks such as 'NI Freelancers Surviving Corona' and campaigns such as the 'NI Bread & Butter Fund' arose within days of the first closures in March 2020. They too resisted formalisation and showed perhaps a more dramatic reluctance to being made a point of reference for government departments, official bodies or networks. While some of the leading voices of these movements were involved in or attended ACN gatherings, or were invited to departmental and ACNI online meetings, they resisted pressure from both those within the sector and also from policy-makers such as the DfC to become a formal consultation apparatus representing the voice of cultural freelancers. They also refused to be formalised under the umbrella of different resource organisations. These actions, they argued, were in part a refusal to speak on behalf of their peers or have an organisation represent them; but they also highlighted their unsalaried status in the face of evidence searches by salaried officials and organisational heads. Indeed, one interviewee stated that 'it was like a part-time job on top of a full-time job' and that they were working fifteen-hour days, which was not sustainable. This inevitably resulted in many of members of the ACN and their colleagues experiencing fatigue by late 2020 and a degree of disappointment at the slow pace of response.

Where these informal networks intersected with the collaborative policy networks that were emerging, their concerns were focused on how the pandemic had exposed wider and longer-term structural issues within the whole arts and cultural sector. Contributions to sector meetings and a small number of open letters to ministers and officials highlighted concerns of precarity, career sustainability, exploitation, lack of inclusion and lack of accountability, not just at public policy level but also across cultural organisations. While many of these concerns became folded into ACN statements and recommendations, and the recovery taskforce priorities, tensions arose as freelancers perceived organisational players in the networks as lacking reflexivity and failing to execute change in their own structures and processes. Cultural freelancers, particularly artists, also expressed concern at their identity being conflated with their activism, either as 'poster girl' or token representatives for freelancers in a room of organisations with their own interests; or, by contrast, that their creative and professional identity was altered to become the voice and image of complaint, resulting in assumptions that they only wanted to work on issue-driven projects or that they would be 'difficult'.

These cultural freelancer movements brought with them pre-existing tensions and biases, a mistrust of other players and an historic imbalance of power, along with other barriers to their inclusion within collaborative policy networks. They also struggled at different stages to achieve the requisite sharing of information as DfC officials and ACNI offered constructed information-gathering processes and used them for evidence but did not necessarily share the decision-making or indeed discussion of results. As our interviews concluded in summer 2021, it became increasingly clear that there were issues of how sustainable these informal networks could be.

Collaborative leadership and change

Throughout the summer months of 2021, restrictions started to be lifted on NI arts venues and indoor and outdoor gatherings. This included the announcement that on 26 July 2021 theatres could reopen but only with seated events and social distancing of one metre still required (Northern Ireland Executive, 2021). A report to the DfC by the ACN highlighted that this made it financially unviable for many theatres and venues to reopen:

> As long as social-distancing measures allow for only c.20 per cent of capacity – this will render the business economically unviable. In most venues 50 per cent to 70 per cent occupancy is typically needed to break even and means theatres and some venues cannot operate (ACN, 2021).

This situation illustrates the real unevenness in the opening up of society with regard to the cultural sector. In stark contrast to the live arts sector, TV and film had been able to continue production and recover more quickly. This was outlined by an interviewee, who worked in both theatre and TV/film, who explained that they had access to regular PCR testing and full budgets for Covid-safe practices throughout any filming work. However, their theatre work was characterised by uncertainty as they 'were hearing about other productions being stopped a few days in because people were getting Covid'. The interviewee went on to suggest that gearing up for live shows in this way was just not viable because the rehearsal time needed could not be realised in practice.

This correlates with the UK-wide analysis of the impact of COVID-19 on specific art forms, with performing arts (including theatre) and visual arts being affected the most (Walmsley *et al.*, 2022; see also Chapters 2 and 5 of this volume). This was also apparent from data gathered in NI by the ACN, which demonstrated that as theatre productions and performing arts venues' business models are more reliant on freelancers, cultural freelancers and self-employed individuals had been more affected by the pandemic and resulting closures than employed workers (ACN, 2021). This has been supported by numerous studies (e.g. Jones, 2020; FitzGibbon and Tsioulakis, 2022; Walmsley *et al.*, 2022).

Beyond the divergent impacts between art forms there was also notable unevenness between rural and urban contexts in NI, largely as a result of pre-existing disparities. In an interview with a large rural festival, this was discussed in terms of local musicians: 'We're in a rural space, so we will be relying quite heavily on our locality to support that …. I would love to tap into the local [music scene] but from a Northern Irish perspective that would mean more capacity to support local touring' (Interviewee, 2021).

The interviewee went to suggest that there is no infrastructure outside of the big cities (Belfast and Derry) to support touring for live original music and that maybe it was time to discuss this situation, as it had been a recurring issue for many years. Conversely, they also stated that in relative terms at the point of interview in summer 2021, their festival and other live outdoor events were in a better position to open viably with social distancing than indoor smaller live music venues. Indeed, many of our interviewees stated that the effects of social distancing restrictions would take venues time (several years in some cases) to recover from, even when restrictions were completely lifted.

This complexity and unevenness across the arts and cultural ecology in NI led to divergence in the ways the collaborative leadership that had emerged navigated these issues. For example, the festival mentioned above developed a closer working relationship with the Culture, Arts and Heritage Recovery Taskforce thanks to greater levels of networking than they had previously undertaken. This brought the interests of traditional Irish music (their specialism) into the negotiations and the festival was able to 'get music back in the outdoor setting' across Northern Ireland (Interviewee, 2021). The interviewee went on to say that several meetings had taken place with senior figures in government and different parts of the music sector in NI that had not occurred before COVID-19. In their view, this had increased confidence both on a personal level and within the broader music sector.

We draw attention to how each art form carries with it specific socio-cultural relationships that are embedded in the geo-political, historical and economic specificities of place and thus cannot be reduced to generalised or top-down policy decisions. The emergence of these forms of collaborative leadership and broader collaborative policy networks revealed that leadership can arise from and across multiple spaces. Moreover, this collaborative leadership creates its own narratives, which can be less ego-driven and more collective in articulation, both within and beyond cultural settings and activities.

Examples of this collaborative leadership abound throughout the interviews. We interviewed a prominent circus company based near Derry which told us that it began to reach out to videographers and different sector leaders to form collaborative working groups in order to deliver online workshop lessons for schoolchildren and young people. This process changed the content and operational and business models for the company. It shifted its focus towards collaboration with local authorities in order to set up studios under Covid-safe working and worked with experts in videography and technical audio-visual producers. This reflected a wider change in sharing and practice within the NI circus community. This was evident during one of the ACN's Big Gathering events as representatives stated that they had started 'having Zoom meetings about how to recover from this together, sharing risk assessments and conversations about wages too' (ACN, 2021). Another multi-arts and advocacy organisation, which runs a large festival in Belfast, spoke of its movement towards providing creative care boxes, which included food and activities for children (Interviewee, 2021). This became an integral part of its operation in light of cancellations of the festival and the company worked with local community leaders to direct provision where it was needed most. Crucially, these responses were cross-sector, collaborative and responsive to local communities.

Across all the interviews was a sense that the NI Government/ public sector as a whole did not respond quickly enough and that years of underinvestment in arts and culture (including infrastructure) had left NI even more vulnerable than the rest of the UK to the impact of the pandemic. However, this state of play galvanised the rapid response from the sector itself and led to the rise in collaborative and networked leadership. This is nothing new: as we have suggested earlier, patterns of collaborative leadership have responded to previous crises and tended to dissipate once the immediate pressures on the NI cultural sector shifted to another state, which could be characterised as 'less urgent' rather than resolved. The difference in this crisis was in its nature, namely its magnitude and scale, which affected all areas of society. What is certain, though, is that the experience of reopening was fragmented across the cultural sector and in different ways this made sustaining collaborative policy networks especially difficult.

The development of the long-called-for Northern Irish Culture, Arts and Heritage Recovery Taskforce in May 2021 represented an opportunity for a more formal collaborative policy network to develop from the crisis. Throughout summer 2021, the taskforce consulted with a wide range of stakeholders throughout the arts, culture and heritage sectors. Despite the taskforce being a key 'ask' from 'cultural leaders', including ACN, by the time it was up and running the landscape had shifted once again. The taskforce recommendations (which included the rollout of significant highly resourced professional development and capacity building programmes) required momentum and energy. By late 2021, this was no longer present in the sector, which had by then reached the point of chronic burnout. Once the taskforce report was completed, no further plans existed for formalised collaborative policy-making.

Challenges for collaborative policy networks

This chapter has examined pre-pandemic and pandemic activity to explore the mobilisation and potential of collaborative leadership and collaborative policy networks. We have shown that, especially when in crisis, these networks arise through a range of approaches (as 'top-down' taskforces, joint campaigning, and as 'grassroots' informal mutual support networks prompted into advocacy). We also see that many are constructed around traces of pre-existing formal and informal relationships, reinforcing the points of Weare, Lichterman and Esparza (2014) about the social construction of collaborative policy networks. We argue too that these movements were most importantly networks of mutual care and support; sharing emotional and professional difficulties of a challenging practice and policy environment alongside collective acts of change and advocacy.

As we conclude, we articulate the recurring challenges for such collaborations to translate into effective recognised forms of collaborative cultural leadership or collaborative policy networks. As we observed, leadership reluctance (as articulated by Goodwin, 2020) or resistance to 'imposed' leadership (FitzGibbon, 2019), either on individuals or networks, makes discourses of who will be leader, how mandates are formed and what are common goals or defined successes difficult, even when such discourses are collaborative in intent. The second challenge we observed is an imbalance of power, characterised partly by information flows leading to an absence of trust. In order to fully collaborate within policy-making, those with greatest authority and knowledge must find ways to give these away. As we noted, many of the earlier and pandemic-related approaches by public officials to consult and share decision-making were over-defined and operated on pre-determined agenda and timescales. Similarly, where this collaboration arose at a public policy level, it could often be undermined by tensions between and actions from sector, public or political players. This amplified mistrust and generated feelings of tokenism, even when there was pan-sectoral participation.

The third and perhaps most significant challenge is the reliance of such collaborative relationships on interpersonal relationships and sustained personal investment. While the intention and success of a collaborative policy network may be to solve problems through policy action, equally as important is the problem sharing and formation of dialogues based on trust, mutual support and (as above) knowledge sharing. Political uncertainty and the extensive restructuring of the culture portfolio over different levels of government pre-pandemic made it difficult to form sustained dialogues with public officials and politicians. The relationships were coloured by other parallel relationships: between government and its agencies; politicians and staff/sector; funder and client; employer and freelancer; artist/organisation and arts council; funded and unfunded. Inasmuch as these networks thrived through mutual support, they fragmented as interests diverged or other demands encroached. Additionally, they relied heavily on individuals driving momentum and undertaking care. In a sector already characterised by poor working conditions (FitzGibbon, 2019), this human effort eventually became exhausted, demoralised or, as a means of basic human self-protection, key players withdrew or shifted their attention elsewhere.

A feature we explore less in this chapter, but one that certainly merits deeper investigation, is the degree to which the different officials (in public bodies and government departments) as well as political figures (ministers and MLAs) embodied leadership behaviours or saw themselves as taking on a mantle of leadership, particularly cultural leadership. While sector interviewees spoke often about working with government in an unprecedented way, public officials from ACNI and DfC also spoke of a previously unimaginable pace of change in internal processes to enact new policy measures or release funds. DfC especially noted the ramping up of engagement with culture sector individuals and unprecedented levels of consultation on departmental planning. This was, however, not unusual in the pandemic response as all units and departments opened up channels to discuss urgent policy action. While officials made policy recommendations to ministers, we need to understand more about how those politicians understood the role they were playing in encouraging or opening up to such collaborative measures. Further research of this may reveal other understandings or solutions to some of the challenges we describe here.

We conclude our observations by noting that individual commitment and effort and the interpersonal relationships formed are the key drivers of collaborative leadership and policy network success. They are also the principal reasons why such networks rapidly become unsustainable and lose momentum. While a purely theoretical view might articulate this as a failure in leadership behaviour, we would propose that the benefits of collaborative leadership (in crisis and not) can only be realised when the wider environment and relationships are conditioned by mutual support, transparency and trust.

Note

1 The departments were: Department of Culture, Arts and Leisure; Department for Education; Department of Enterprise, Trade and Investment; and finally the Department of Higher and Further Education, Training and Employment.

References

Arts Collaboration Network (ACN). 2021. *Culture beyond Covid.* [Online]. [Accessed 10 January 2024]. Available from: https://crescentarts.org/download/files/Arts%20Collaboration%20Network%20Culture%20Beyond%20Covid%20Jan%202021%20FINAL.pdf

Arts Council of Northern Ireland (ACNI). 2007. *Arts sector rally to save the arts.* [Online]. 10 December 2007. [Accessed 23 August 2022]. Available from: https://web.archive.org/web/20221026043355/http://artscouncil-ni.org/news/arts-sector-rally-to-save-the-arts

Arts Council of Northern Ireland (ACNI). 2014. *Arts Council chief calls for no more cuts.* [Online]. 25 November 2014. [Accessed 23 August 2022]. Available from: https://web.archive.org/web/20221207041811/http://www.artscouncil-ni.org/news/arts-council-chief-calls-for-no-more-cuts

Bardy, R. 2018. *Rethinking leadership.* Abingdon: Routledge.

Bell, K. 2010. *Arts spending per capita in Northern Ireland (Paper 000/00, NIAR 593–10).* Belfast: Research and Library Service, Northern Ireland Assembly.

Bluebird Media. 2015. *Arts Matter NI – Stormont 3/11/15.* [Online]. [Accessed 28 September 2022]. Available from: www.youtube.com/watch?v=2wJs1I7n1AU

Deeny, D. 1995. *To the Millennium: a strategy for the arts in Northern Ireland.* Belfast: Arts Council of Northern Ireland.

Department of Culture, Arts and Leisure (DCAL). 2001. *Unlocking creativity: making it happen.* Belfast: Northern Ireland Assembly.

Department of Culture, Arts and Leisure (DCAL). 2015. *Strategy for Culture & Arts 2016–2026: providing society and outcomes by promoting equality and tackling poverty and social exclusion.* Belfast: Northern Ireland Assembly.

Donelli, C., Fanelli, S. and Zangrandi, A. 2021. Inside and outside the boardroom: collaborative practices in the performing arts sector. *International Journal of Arts Management.* 24(1), pp.48–62.

Durrer, V. 2017. 'Let's see who's being creative out there': lessons from the 'Creative Citizens' programme in Northern Ireland. *Journal of Arts and Communities.* 9(1), pp.15–37.

Eikhof, D.R. and Haunschild, A. 2007. For art's sake! Artistic and economic logics in creative production. *Journal of Organizational Behavior.* 28(5), pp.523–538.

FitzGibbon, A. 2019. Imposed leadership in UK funded theatre and the implications for risk and innovation. *Zeitschrift für Kulturmanagement.* 5(1), pp.15–42.

FitzGibbon, A. and Tsioulakis, I. 2022. Making it up: adaptive approaches to bringing freelance cultural work to a cultural ecologies discourse. *European Urban and Regional Studies.* 29(4), pp.461–478.

Goodwin, K. 2020. Leadership reluctance in the Australian arts and cultural sector. *The Journal of Arts Management, Law, and Society.* 50(3), pp.169–183.

Henry, M. 2020. *NI arts & cultural sector in unique Covid-19 support appeal.* [Online]. 24 June 2020. [Accessed 30 September 2022]. Available from: https://lyrictheatre.co.uk/about-us/news/ni-arts-cultural-sector-in-unique-covid-19-support-appeal

Jeon, J. and Kim, H. 2021. Leading collaborative governance in the cultural sector: the participatory cases of Korean arts organizations. *International Journal of Arts Management.* 24(1), pp.63–74.

Jones, S. 2020. *Support for artists' livelihoods in a Covid-19 world.* [Online]. 15 July 2020. [Accessed 20 October 2022]. Available from: https://padwickjonesarts.co.uk/support-for-artists-livelihoods-in-a-covid-19-world

Kempster, S. and Jackson, B. 2021. Leadership for what, why, for whom and where? A responsibility perspective. *Journal of Change Management.* 21(1), pp.45–65.

Ministerial Arts Advisory Forum. 2016. *Arts strategy consultation: observations by Ministerial Arts Advisory Forum.* Belfast: Arts Council of Northern Ireland.

Nisbett, M. and Walmsley, B. 2016. The romanticization of charismatic leadership in the arts. *The Journal of Arts Management, Law, and Society.* 46(1), pp.2–12.

Northern Ireland Executive Office. 2021. *Statement on Executive decisions – 8 July 2021.* [Online]. [Accessed 8 August 2022]. Available from: www.executiveoffice-ni.gov.uk/news/statement-executive-decisions-8-july-2021

Northern Visions. 2007. *Invest in inspiration.* [Online]. 14 May 2007. [Accessed 12 September 2022]. Available from: https://cathedralquarter.northernvisions.org/portfolio/invest-in-inspiration/

Reynolds, S., Tonks, A. and MacNeill, K. 2017. Collaborative leadership in the arts as a unique form of dual leadership. *The Journal of Arts Management, Law, and Society.* 47(2), pp.89–104.

Røyseng, S. and Stavrum, H. 2019. Fields of gold: reflections on the research relations of the cultural policy researcher. *International Journal of Cultural Policy.* 26(5), pp.697–708.

Shields, C. 2018. The chair of the Arts Council believes the creative sector should wean itself off public subsidy, while seeking it for himself … he must go. *Belfast Telegraph.* [Online]. 8 May. [Accessed 10 October 2022]. Available from: www.belfasttelegraph.co.uk/opinion/

the-chair-of-the-arts-council-believes-the-creative-sector-should-wean-itself-off-public-subsidy-while-seeking-it-for-himself-he-must-go-36883210.html

Todnem By, R. 2021. Leadership: in pursuit of purpose. *Journal of Change Management.* 21(1), pp.30–44.

Walmsley, B., Gilmore, A., O'Brien, D. and Torreggiani, A. eds. 2022. *Culture in crisis: impacts of Covid-19 on the UK cultural sector and where we go from here.* Leeds: Centre for Cultural Value.

Weare, C., Lichterman, P. and Esparza, N. 2014. Collaboration and culture: organizational culture and the dynamics of collaborative policy networks. *Policy Studies Journal.* 42(4), pp.590–619.

Woddis, J. 2014. Arts practitioners in the cultural policy process: spear-carriers or speaking parts? *International Journal of Cultural Policy.* 20(4), pp.496–512.

Wright, J. 2019. *The ecology of cultural space: towards an understanding of the contemporary artist-led collective.* PhD thesis, University of Leeds. [Online]. [Accessed 15 November 2022]. Available from: https://etheses.whiterose.ac.uk/26338/

7

A question of sustainability: the impact of COVID-19 on the screen sector in Wales

Eva Nieto McAvoy and Ania Ostrowska

Introduction

Figures for 2021 indicate that the Welsh screen sector bounced back from COVID-19 relatively better than other sectors, as it increased its turnover by 36 per cent from 2020 with a total of £575m. However, the COVID-19 pandemic impacted the screen sector in Wales profoundly, exposing major shortcomings in how policy-makers understand, recognise and support the industry and its freelance labour. The immediate impact was disruptive and very difficult for freelancers and organisations alike, highlighting pre-existing issues within the sector and can inform future solutions. In this chapter we explore the ways in which COVID-19 brought into focus the challenges and opportunities for change of the Welsh screen sector.

The creative industries represent one of the fastest-growing sectors in Wales. In 2019 it employed over 56,000 people and had an annual turnover of more than £2.2bn, 40 per cent more than ten years ago (Creative Wales, 2020). Central to this creative ecosystem is the screen sector, which holds an international market position based on 'high-end TV production, with strong local supply chains' (Fodor, Komorowski and Lewis, 2021, p.33). It employs more than 40,000 people across Wales, with the majority of the companies concentrated in South Wales and the Cardiff Capital Region (CCR) – a developing film and TV cluster and one of the UK's largest media production centres (Komorowski and Lewis, 2020b).[1]

The screen sector in Wales is a tightly linked ecosystem of commissioning, production and support. Public service broadcasters play an important role in the Welsh media ecosystem as producers and commissioners of content. The majority of small independent companies (indies) and freelancers interviewed for this study work on commissions by Wales-based TV channels: S4C; BBC Cymru; and ITV Wales. Wales is also the most important producer of bilingual factual (news, sport, current affairs and culture) and fictional content in the UK. The presence of strong indigenous media contributes to reflecting and strengthening a sense of citizenship and evolving identities of the Welsh people (McElroy and Noonan, 2022; Fodor, Komorowski and Lewis, 2021).

Wales has become known for its 'hugely popular, widely exported and award-winning productions' (Hannah and McElroy, 2020, p.4), which include *Doctor Who*, *Sherlock*, *Keeping Faith*, *Casualty*, *Hinterland*, and *Sex Education*. This success story is nonetheless overshadowed by high levels of precarity and inequality in a sector characterised by a large number of small and medium enterprises (SMEs), micro-businesses and freelancers (Hannah and McElroy, 2020). The negative impact of the pandemic on creative and cultural freelancers has been the focus of research and advocacy campaigns calling for a recognition of their importance to the sector (Bectu, 2020; ScreenSkills, 2020; Easton and Beckett, 2021; Henry *et al.*, 2021; Ostrowska, 2021). Freelancers make up a large proportion of the screen sector workforce in Wales.[2] Their exact number is difficult to establish and the estimates vary from 50 per cent (or 40,000) of the creative workforce in Wales (Komorowski and Lewis, 2020a) to a more cautious 32 per cent as the UK average of freelance employment in the screen sector (Hannah and McElroy, 2020).[3] Early studies identified that the pandemic 'magnified existing inequalities and laid bare the impact of having a largely freelance sector characterised by high levels of precarity' (Hannah and McElroy, 2020 p.48).

Based on a series of interviews with freelancers, production companies and public service broadcasters, this chapter investigates the effect that the pandemic, lockdown and the subsequent support measures had on the film and high-end TV (HETV) sector in Wales. It does so by focusing on the challenges facing the workforce, including the impact of COVID-19 on creative workers' working practices, financial situations and mental health. The chapter also analyses different organisational approaches to lockdown, the emergency funding made available to film and TV professionals in Wales, and the emerging signs of polarisation in the sector.

This chapter contributes to a body of academic research that challenges what McElroy and Noonan (2019) call the 'the celebratory discourses' of the 'era of abundance' in film and TV production, partly as a result of the entrance of new global media players such as Netflix. It does so by offering a 'situated analysis of the precarity of the current ecology' (McElroy and Noonan, 2019, p.2) that highlights the difficulties faced by those producing the media content that became vital to sustain the public's morale during lockdown, also beyond borders. An emphasis on global markets and players can often obscure the realities of national policies, cultures and markets. This is particularly important here because the media ecologies under analysis operate in the context of a small nation, and often within the logics of minority-language public service broadcasters (PSBs), such as S4C. These are often expected to 'sustain linguistic vitality and cultural diversity ... maintain viewing figures, support indigenous production, and compete in international markets' (McElroy, Noonan and Nielsen, 2018, p.161), all within a context of ever-shrinking budgets. As we found in our study, issues concerning the sustainability of the sector and the quality of the labour market (and not just of the content it produces) need to be at the forefront of the academic debates on the present and future of screen production.

The impact of COVID-19 on the screen sector in Wales and in the UK has been documented in other studies by sector bodies. In this chapter, we complement this activity by focusing on the stories of those who were working at the sharp end of screen work in Wales at the time. Firstly, we argue that the pandemic and the subsequent lockdowns exacerbated inequalities within the workforce, evidencing the fragility and precarity of an industry composed primarily of SMEs and freelancers. Secondly, we investigate the centrality of PSBs in the Welsh audio-visual ecosystem of production and provision, and in particular the crucial role of S4C as a minority-language broadcaster for a 'small nation'. Thirdly, we analyse the implications of the pivot to digital practices for workers, organisations and audiences. Finally, we conclude by indicating some implications for policy.

Methodology

This study focuses on the 'film and TV production and post-production' sub-sector within the screen industries. Depending on the context, various sub-sectors are included under the umbrella term 'screen industry'. In the Welsh context these include film, television, games, animation and VFX, and on occasion online and immersive content production. The choice to focus on film and TV production was based on evidence from early research into the impact of the pandemic on the sector in Wales, which identified it as the sub-sector that was most affected. Sub-sectors such as animation, games and VFX were initially affected positively by the pandemic, leading to 'the acceleration of some workflow processes through technology' (Fodor, Komorowski and Lewis, 2021, p.48). The focus on freelancers was also a result of early evidence from the sector that identified them as most at risk.

Two rounds of qualitative interviews were conducted. The first round of interviews was conducted with freelancers during February 2021.[4] During a second round of interviews in June–October 2021 we broadened the scope to include organisations (small independent production companies and broadcasters).[5] As a follow-up, an interview with a representative of Creative Wales, the Welsh Government's agency for the creative industries, was conducted to gain policy insights in October 2021.[6]

The participants were recruited through an open call publicised by Creative Cardiff and Clwstwr, an innovative R&D programme for the Welsh screen sector; through invitations sent to selected members of the Wales Screen/Sgrin Cymru production staff database; and through snowballing. The sample was mostly self-selecting and therefore non-representative. It consisted of eight men and four women, six of whom were in production roles. However, with ten respondents based in South Wales, the sample is representative of the fact that 80 per cent of creative industries activities in Wales are concentrated in South Wales, with Cardiff Capital Region at its core.

The participants of the second round of interviews to organisations in the Welsh screen sector (six women, nine men) were recruited first through personal email introductions by academics at Cardiff University researching Welsh creative industries and subsequently through snowballing. The interviews included: four directors/managers of small-size indies; eight TV channel employees (4 S4C; 3 BBC Wales; 1 ITV Wales); one person working for Creative Wales; and one person from an industry-facing members organisation – Teledwyr Annibynnol Cymru (TAC).[7] The broadcaster interviews were conducted with commissioners, news producers and operational managers to obtain insights into both the impact of the pandemic on the organisations' work and their collaboration with freelancers and indies.

Data were coded manually to reflect the main research areas of interest to the large COVID-19 project, taking into account the specificity of the Welsh sector and the content of the interviews. The most popular codes were ordered into themes which were then grouped under three headings: (1) characteristics of Welsh screen industry; (2) impact of COVID-19 on the sector; (3) future of the sector, which inform the next sections in this chapter.

Data collected in this study reflect mostly broadcast news and television production (with only a few freelancers and indies in the sample working on feature film production and post-production). The interviews with organisations are dominated by employees of Welsh TV channels (S4C, BBC Wales, ITV Wales), accounting for eight of fourteen interviewees or 57 per cent. This focus led to omitting organisations involved in feature film production and development (like Ffilm Cymru Wales) and exhibitions (like Film Hub Wales), as well as representatives of major international production companies (like Universal) or streamers (like Netflix). Four indies were interviewed (one post-production, three production), none of whom work primarily in film or high-end TV drama. While not comprehensive or representative of the sector as a whole, the findings are illustrative of not only the interviewees' experiences but also speak to findings arising from other reports on the impact of COVID-19 on the screen industry in Wales and across the UK.

In the following sections, we explore (1) the implications of the impact of COVID-19 for the self-employed in the Welsh screen sector; (2) the centrality of PSBs to the audio-visual ecology; and (3) the challenges and opportunities of the 'pivot to digital' in film and TV production and consumption. We finish by highlighting the implications for policy-making to support the recovery of the Welsh screen sector, with a particular focus on the urgency of implementing measures to fill in the skills gap by encouraging and supporting new talent.

Impact of COVID-19 on the Welsh screen workforce

As the whole of the UK went into lockdown in March 2020, film and TV production of certain genres (e.g. drama) stopped. This had different consequences for different parts of the workforce and organisations in the sector. The impact on production companies, for example, varied depending on their profile, main activity, financial model and reserves.

Although post-pandemic film and HETV production in Wales is keeping freelancers and indies busy, COVID-19 exacerbated and exposed the precarity of freelance employment in the sector. It brought into focus the inequalities and fragility of the workforce (see also Burger and Easton, 2020; Comunian and England, 2020; Comunian *et al.*, 2021; Walmsley *et al.*, 2022).

Overall, freelancers and small, independent production companies felt the impact of the pandemic the most. Thanks to the central government's Film and TV Production Restart Scheme, launched in July 2020 and extended until May 2022, many film and HETV productions resumed across the UK, including Wales.[8] However, some of the smaller Welsh indies did not qualify for this support and found the cost of insurance prohibitive. Similarly, the picture for freelancers in this sector was not so straightforward, even in a thriving and tightly linked ecosystem like the screen industry in Wales.

As mentioned in the introduction, freelancers constitute around 30 per cent of the sector's workforce. In the words of one of the interviewees: 'everybody uses freelancers, everybody knows their freelancers, you know some of the freelancers are almost staff except crucially they're not' (umbrella organisation). The sector is small enough for freelancers not to be anonymous; indies often return to the same freelancers, with one company having sixty regular freelancers on the books alongside sixty staff and another hiring up to seventy freelancers on big commissions. During the pandemic, S4C, BBC Wales and indies felt responsible for freelancers and tried to help them by commissioning/hiring. Similarly, Creative Wales has a strong agenda on recognising freelancers' contributions to the sector and improving their working conditions, as discussed below (see also Chapter 2, this volume).

COVID-19 has disproportionately affected freelancers, particularly those with protected characteristics or with caring responsibilities (Donnelly and Komorowski, 2022; Chapter 2, this volume). Different degrees of hardship caused by the pandemic mirrored the polarisation of the screen sector freelancers in general. The immediate impact on the workforce was very uneven, depending on the role(s) performed (e.g. on set or post-production) and the type of employment for tax purposes (e.g. sole trader or limited company). Freelance crew members working on location (one half of our interviewees) had hardly any work between March and September 2020, taking a huge hit on their finances.[9] Live events coverage, including sporting events, was even worse affected. For those who could work on production, the job became almost impossible: 'We did manage to film stuff during the first lockdown. But I think we were the only people I know who could, because my work is filming wildlife. So I could send one guy to sit in a field or on top of a hill in Mid Wales, and it was Covid-safe, but to get that to happen was incredibly stressful' (freelancer in production).

Even for those in employment, we heard of losses of up to 50 per cent in income compared to the previous year, forcing freelancers to survive on very little money and even having to sell equipment. Some questioned whether they would have to quit the industry altogether as they had no means to survive until work picked up again. Some freelancers returned to work in July 2020, but the challenges continued for those in production roles. Crews were required to comply with Covid-safe procedures, but we heard examples of unsafe working conditions, such as freelancers not being tested while those on fixed contracts were.

Being a freelancer in this precarious situation meant that they were vulnerable to the whims of those who employed them. They were left 'in the cold' once work started to dry up, as companies had to make sure their employees had work over and above hiring freelancers. When the phone call came, it was hard for freelancers to refuse to work despite unsafe conditions, such as being asked at short notice to film indoors with no Covid-safe measures. Working in bubbles to shoot was valued by those we spoke to – they felt safe to do their job and emotionally supported once back in their 'on-set families' that they had missed during lockdown.

For those freelancers working in development and post-production, workloads remained the same or diminished only slightly. Editors reported benefits of working from home, from being able to organise their own schedule to avoid long commutes, but during lockdowns had to reckon with working from home and juggling work and childcare. The pandemic impacted those with caring responsibilities the most (Raising Films, 2021): 'And plus, I lost my childcare. So that was tricky as well. And so the double whammy of my job being ten times more difficult plus having to juggle childcare' (freelancer in production).

Some freelancers reported feeling isolated and experiencing adverse mental health effects because of staying at home. They lost their income as well as their in-person support networks with the closing of, for example, co-working spaces like Rabble Studios in Cardiff. Online communities became more important and our interviewees reported a raised awareness of mental health issues in general among professional bodies and agencies, although there were mixed responses about the engagement and usefulness with these organisations during the pandemic.

The support available to freelancers depended on their type of employment for tax purposes. The UK Government had offered the Self-Employed Income Support Scheme (SEISS) in May 2020, but not all those self-employed qualified. Some of the sole traders were lucky to have grants from the SEISS based on a successful tax year, while others received little support because they worked less (in one case because of maternity leave) in that qualifying year. We also learned about the lack of support to those self-employed that were registered at the time as (sole director) limited companies.[10] This 'eligibility gap' is supported by other data (Komorowski and Lewis, 2020a). In the Welsh case an early survey revealed that a fifth of respondents working in the screen sector were excluded from SEISS for that reason. Similarly, some respondents (25 per cent) did not meet the eligibility criteria of 50 per cent of profits coming from their work as self-employed, as many combine freelancing with short-term PAYE contracts. With the rise of the gig economy many workers in the sector had become freelancers shortly before the pandemic hit and therefore also faced eligibility problems (Komorowski and Lewis, 2020a), something that we confirmed through our interviews: 'If you went freelance in January [2020], as thousands of people would have, they can't get any support, because they can't show last year's balance sheets, their accounts for that, because they've only just started. So they get nothing. How are they meant to live? Each pay for rent?' (freelancer in production).

These respondents expressed their disappointment and outrage and two of them had been active in the social media campaigns #ExcludedUK and @ForgottenLtd, calling on the government to rectify the situation.

In October 2020, the Wales Culture Recovery Fund launched the Freelancers Fund, distributed through local authorities.[11] The Freelancers Fund had three rounds of funding – after the second one, data revealed that 3,783 unique freelancers were supported (995 across both rounds), receiving £2,500 per award (a total of £10.39m).[12] Around a third of these had not received income support through SEISS. The fund was opened to freelancers 'whose work has direct creative/cultural outcomes', and therefore had set eligibility criteria that acknowledged the specificities of self-employment in the cultural and creative industries. Our interviewees support this finding as many told us that they had been able to benefit from this support, qualifying as sole directors of limited companies or being able to submit accounts from (better) previous years.

There was general praise for the Welsh Freelancers Fund over the central government's support, although some complained that the grants disappeared too quickly and were not sufficiently advertised: 'I don't know if they [the Freelancers Fund grants] were easier to get because I remember, excuse me, I saw a post to say, the Welsh Government have opened up this grant, at 10 o'clock, for example. And within about half an hour, they closed it, because it just got overrun' (freelancer in production).

Lockdown brought some positives such as having easier access to commissioners, reaching international clients and having opportunities to upskill. Some career opportunities included stepping in for more senior colleagues who needed to self-isolate. More time for relationship building, rethinking strategies and career priorities, editing old material, learning new skills or spending time with family was also reported. On the other hand, interviewees also mentioned colleagues who were forced to take up other jobs or leave the industry altogether. Furthermore, several respondents have already experienced loss of commissions resulting from the UK leaving the European Union and they expect further negative consequences from Brexit for their professional lives.

During the pandemic, TAC (Teledwyr Annibynnol Cymru), an umbrella organisation representing interests of thirty-three Welsh indies, organised regular meetings with broadcasters and Creative Wales to keep everyone updated about the changing situation and work out practical solutions to the crisis. Creative Wales was created in January 2020 as a Welsh Government agency to 'drive growth across the creative industries, build on existing success and develop new talent and skills' (Creative Wales, 2020).[13] The agency's main aim for the screen sector is to support production companies to undertake film and TV production in Wales. It also works closely with broadcasters and it was, at the time of writing, in the process of signing Memoranda of Understanding drafted around different issues with each one.[14] The role of the sector umbrella organisations and agencies (e.g. The Film & TV Charity, Bectu, Creative Cardiff, Ffilm Cymru Wales, Screen Alliance Wales) was important for networking and finding advice and (in some cases) support, but we heard mixed reviews about the engagement with these organisations.

Our interviewees believed that the immediate future of the Welsh screen sector would be bright and prosperous, especially for film and HETV (factual and smaller productions are seen by some interviewees as potentially worse off). By 2020, there was evidence that both demand for freelancers and pay rates were rising, although certain freelancers and indies may have lost momentum because of fewer commissions and some even feared going out of business. There was also a worry that freelancers would be overworked and have to accept more jobs to make up for the income lost during closure. Some spoke about Universal Basic Income as a way forward.

Despite praising the efforts of the Welsh Government, local authorities and other public bodies, interviewees felt that freelancers in the screen sector lacked adequate support and advocated for change. They argued that while in the past trade unions offered some protection from exploitation, they are now seen as 'toothless'. This is being partially redressed by the Freelancers and Public

Service Body Pledge,[15] which will require public bodies in Wales to recognise freelancers' contributions and to pay them fairly for their work, within the framework of the Wellbeing of Future Generations Act.[16]

In the next section, we explore the role of the public service broadcasters during the pandemic, with a particular focus on S4C (Sianel Pedwar Cymru; Channel Four Wales in English), the Welsh-language public service broadcaster. S4C is funded via the licence fee, which played an important role in its response to the pandemic.

Public service broadcasting in times of crisis in small nations

The UK PSBs – BBC, Channel 4, ITV, Channel 5 and the Welsh-language broadcaster S4C – are central to the UK's ecosystem of audio-visual content production and provision, a position that has only been reinforced by COVID-19. The media landscape is rapidly evolving due to the entry of new and well-resourced media players and changes in consumption patterns. The role and value of PSBs in this context has been the focus of recent debate (Chivers and Allan, 2022), and there are ongoing revisions to regulations concerning the current Terms of Trade, online platforms, prominence and funding (for both commercial and publicly funded PSBs), as well as to ensure that PSBs fulfil their commitments to diversity on and off screen (Carey, O'Brien and Gable, 2021). Crucially, PSBs have a statutory requirement to inform, represent and serve diverse communities and to support the creative economy across the UK, delivering significant benefits to the nations and regions.

PSBs based in the nations and regions regularly invest in content that would otherwise not be commissioned, such as children's programming and regional news (including in minority languages) (McElroy and Noonan, 2018). During the pandemic, we saw PSBs across the UK respond by offering audiences support with access to content consistent with its commitment to broadcasting in the public interest, including less commercially viable educational content: for example, *Ysgol Cyw*, 'learning through play', content on the Cyw website,[17] arts and cultural content through 'Culture in Quarantine,[18] religious programming such as *Sunday Morning Stories*,[19] and health and wellbeing programmes such as *Ffit Cymru*.[20]

The COVID-19 crisis highlighted the relevance of the public service value of universality, an essential attribute of public service broadcasting to create a pluralistic, diverse and accessible-to-all service regardless of geography or means. PSBs have the responsibility and burden of delivering both high-quality linear and user-friendly on-demand services, which might help redress a digital divide that has become more apparent with lockdown and in relation to children's access to education (Horrocks, 2020).[21] They operate in a context of market failure but also as market shapers (Mazzucato *et al.*, 2020) by leveraging public funds to fuel innovation, grow new markets and encourage creative ecosystems. This is the rationale behind the BBC's move of their sports and children's departments to MediaCityUK in Salford,[22] the move of Channel 4 National HQ to Leeds (with creative hubs in Bristol and Glasgow), and the recent creation of media.cymru – a collaboration to accelerate growth in the Cardiff Capital Region media sector, where the BBC has expanded and invested over recent years.

S4C (Sianel Pedwar Cymru; Channel Four Wales in English) is the Welsh-language free-to-air TV channel. A broadcaster-publisher, it commissions most of its programmes from indies across Wales, and some from BBC Cymru. COVID-19 has had an impact on the organisation's working practices, but its relative financial security during the pandemic placed the organisation in a position to support their workforce and the sector.

There is ample evidence that supports the claim that public service broadcasting can and does make a significant contribution to democracy by creating informed citizens, more so than market-driven media (Cushion, 2019, p.33). The COVID-19 pandemic highlighted the importance of accurate, reliable and impartial news. PSBs (and the regional news they offer) were among the most used, and trusted, sources of reliable information across all ages (Cushion, 2019, 2020; Carter, 2020; Cushion *et al.*, 2020; Kyriakidou *et al.*, 2020; Sambrook and Cushion, 2020; Ofcom, 2021a, 2021b).

As has been argued elsewhere in this book, lockdown caused an increase of audience numbers and screen time during the pandemic. One of the most demanded types of content was news about the rapidly unfolding situation and changing Covid rules and restrictions. News and current affairs continued throughout, 'covering the biggest news story since World War Two', as one of BBC Wales' interviewees put it. Keeping the public informed became a key priority during the beginning of the pandemic (with news and current affairs kept up throughout in changed formats). They also reported a 'hunger' for hyperlocal news. All broadcast interviewees highlighted the educational role of news in the pandemic and their role in making some audience members aware of devolution and the powers of the Welsh Government for the first time. Broadcasters reported a sense of renewal of their civic mission to keep the public informed. PSBs have the statutory remit to support the public's civic engagement by producing news and current affairs programming.[23]

This was later balanced by moving to 'light relief' as well as programmes bringing people together on air, something that the public appreciated. These were described as a 'lifeline' for people who felt isolated at home. Crucially, these services were also performed in the Welsh language – an important factor in community building of Welsh-speaking audiences. S4C, for example, expressed their mission to support their audience's mental health and wellbeing expressed in the tagline 'Yma i chi' ('Here for you'). We heard that the pandemic reinforced S4C's mission as a PSB to inform, educate and entertain.

For staff working for Welsh public service broadcasters covering the pandemic, the workload increased exponentially. Those that we interviewed reported a negative impact on their mental health, despite the measures put in place by the PSBs to support their workforce. Difficulties for those stuck at home have been widely reported across the board, while the toll on the mental health of broadcast journalists and staff in our sample was due to the long hours and the fact that they could never switch off from the Covid discourse.

There were efforts to diversify the audiences by commissioning and scheduling new content and formats, with some signs of success. New shows covered deprived communities suffering the most from Covid; digital outputs and platforms were updated to engage younger audiences; and there was a push of user-generated content, like the new commission *Fideo Fi yn y Tŷ* produced by Boom Cymru for Stwnsh (the young audience S4C service) with content that children filmed themselves at home during the pandemic. Some of these innovations were creative solutions to producing programmes that, as one interviewee described, were 'designed with a view to ... being Covid safe in [their] DNA'. The S4C panel programme of current

affairs *Pawb a'i Farn* was one of many shows that introduced interviews on Zoom and increased shooting outdoors. Special bubbles
were created to film shows like the sit-com *Rybish*. Some of these
programmes have proved so popular that they were commissioned
again in 2022.

Commissions were also the result of the PSBs' efforts to support
independent companies (indies). The majority of the interviewees for
this study work on commissions by Wales-based broadcasters: S4C;
BBC Cymru; and ITV Wales, unsurprising given that PSBs are the
largest commissioners of content in the UK and quotas for independent producers and the nations and regions ensure substantial investment out of London.

There were consolidated efforts to invest in new work to support
the sector. For example, rather than rely on archive material and
reruns only, S4C honoured all its commissions and commissioned
another £8.7m worth of new programmes during the pandemic
to support the production sector (S4C, 2021). A first round was
announced in April 2020 for ' new content to reflect the current
situation, both on television and digitally' and then another one
in September 2020 for content 'that can be produced within the
Covid-19 restrictions':

> We had a special fund that we have anyway for small independent
> companies to develop ideas, so we put more money towards that just
> to try and support the sector as much as we could because, you know,
> after this is over, we still need a really healthy thriving sector in Wales
> to produce programmes. So I think, for us, it was about delivering pro-
> grammes, but also about thinking of ways we could work with part-
> ners and with the sector to support them, to ensure that they survived
> the crisis, so we worked with partners like National Theatre Wales and
> Arts Council and other partners to try and ensure that we help them
> work differently and create content differently. (PSB manager)

This was a very welcome initiative, but its impact was not always
felt across the board. We still heard of loss of jobs for production companies, the impact depending on the financial model and
reserves, some reporting great losses, while others having savings
and surviving with some form of financial support. The Wales
Culture Recovery Fund and the COVID-19 Bounce Back Loans
were lifelines for some of these indies. Covid-safe production proved

more costly than previous practice and there were widespread skills shortages, from managerial to technical roles. Some of the smaller Welsh indies reported not qualifying for the Restart Scheme and finding the cost of insurance prohibitive. Freelancers' workload was negatively impacted, as there were overall fewer jobs. Needing to prioritise their staff, indie directors were able to offer less work to freelancers and one of them admitted: 'I probably have failed in my duty of care to my freelancers.'

However, there was increasing evidence of sector collegiality, new networks and partnerships within and across sectors. For example, many indies did not charge broadcasters for reusing their programmes, and broadcasters like S4C increased their commissions of new programmes during the pandemic to support the production sector in Wales. Some organisations also had a chance to rethink their strategies. For some, the health and safety of the company became a priority, forcing them to find new ways of filming and editing. Others reported shifting the emphasis to organisational development: 'It bought us some time to take stock and to think and to develop, which is ... which is a bit of a luxury.'

Long-term prognoses are in line with those of the sector in general, and centre on the competition from streamers, both because of the rising cost of drama production and the changes in the audiences' loyalty (with a bigger reliance on subscription services for high-quality entertainment). In a climate of considerable uncertainty and severe budgetary pressures, uncertainty about the future of the licence fee or the possible privatisation of Channel 4 is yet another challenge to the recovery of the sector. Cost-saving measures already have had an impact on the quality and relevance of regional provision, resulting in job cuts in the regions and in news programming being suspended. Even the welcoming news of the funding settlement for S4C (which increases the funding by £7.5m) is tinged by the doubts about the sustainability of the Welsh broadcaster after 2027 (the end of the settlement, and the current BBC Charter), and the impact of the recent two-year freeze to the BBC's licence fee across the UK, including in Wales. The extra funding will in any case help S4C deliver their plans for 2022–2027, including the development of the S4C Clic player – the app for live and on-demand S4C and Cyw (the children's channel) content.

Going digital: skills, networking and the future of screen work

The sector has for the most part gone back to business as usual, but some changes catalysed by the pandemic are here to stay. For freelancers, digital technologies, including remote working, played a significant role, but opinions about their usefulness and future viability are mixed. One the one hand, we heard about more flexibility in organising working days, easier access to commissioners (mentioned by freelancers and broadcasters) and prestigious international clients and partners, and participation in networking events with impressive line-ups of industry figures that could be enjoyed free of charge and from the comfort of the home. Remote parts of Wales felt closer because of online working:

> I think maybe it's a double-edged sword because I'm less likely to travel internationally now on jobs, because they're more likely to hire in their country. But in the same breath, if someone's coming from London to work down in Cardiff, instead of travelling crew up from London, they're more likely to hire someone local. So it's kind of a double-edged sword with that. (Sound recordist)

On the other hand, some lamented the loss of in-person interactions, including in co-working spaces and the demise of local creative networks, often negatively impacting freelancers' mental health by deepening their feelings of isolation. While video meetings were generally seen as more agile, efficient and time saving, some noted a loss of creativity and two respondents complained that online auditions for creative projects fail to do justice to candidates:

> We feel like working remotely works in terms of, you get stuff done. But it doesn't work in terms of having the team job satisfaction working together. And there's always there's always glitches and misunderstandings and stuff with working remotely. And, and if yes, is it, it's like there's this extra parts, that is extra stressful and hurts your head. Don't know how to put it more technically. And yeah, stuff doesn't flow as well. (Freelancer, production)

Editors reported the benefits of working from home, and employees of some independent production companies (indies) and broadcasters also valued remote and hybrid modes of working when this was an option:

> I'm hoping that the remote working, flexible working is here to stay. Because it makes such a difference to kind of work life balance, but also having that creative space away from the office. Like, I write scripts better at home. Or in a coffee shop. I like writing scripts in a coffee shop, that kind of a distraction thing. Works well for me. I can't write scripts in an office, doesn't work for me. And but it still needs that balance of coming together as a team and seeing people. (Freelancer, production)

For organisations, digital and remote modes of working were put in place for non-broadcast critical staff – an easier endeavour for those broadcasters already working in this way before the pandemic. All organisations interviewed, indies and broadcasters, said they are keen to keep hybrid ways of working. S4C, for example, employs around 100 people, the majority of whom were able to remain in their posts throughout. The preparations for remote working had started before the first national lockdown in March 2020, leading to a relatively smooth transition to working from home. S4C commissioners made themselves more available to producers online – viewed favourably by the freelancers we interviewed. These changes were successful enough that the organisation is planning to keep a hybrid working model.

For broadcasters, this was also an opportunity to test new ways of interacting with audiences, some of which proved successful. This acceleration of the digital shift in content production and distribution was seen as extremely successful. Interviews conducted remotely via online platforms such as Zoom allowed for more speakers to participate as fewer resources were needed – this strategy gave journalists more flexibility. S4C, for example, produced new digital news content under the name Newyddion S4C, successfully live-streaming on Facebook, which generated an increase in viewings in 2020–2021 of 388 per cent on the previous year and a 735 per cent increase in hours watched.

Another advantage of the forced 'pivot to digital' was the opportunity to access online training. Echoing the recent analysis of the ONS Labour Force Survey (see Chapter 2 of this book), many of the respondents used the time to upskill, attending online training, including free sessions or taking advantage of the unexpected opportunities for stepping up the professional ladder. Only one respondent was seriously worried about potentially having to quit the sector, having already been selling some of his kit to make ends meet. However, the respondents' friends and colleagues, who were forced to take up low-skilled jobs or leave the industry altogether, emerged spontaneously in their accounts, offering a corrective to the positive picture presented in the interviews: 'The only opportunity was I did my drone pilot's license during lockdown, doing a remote online course, which felt detached and somewhat artificial. But, you know, I've done it, and I have that pilot accreditation now, which, which has been quite useful for the business' (camera production).

Some broadcast interviewees singled out digital skills training and training for Welsh-language speakers as especially urgent and some freelancers asked for transferable (non-craft) skills training, including HR and business skills.[24] Several interviewees mentioned that the National Film and Television School (NFTS) opened its branch in Cardiff, offering training courses for a wide range of roles.[25] In partnership with TAC (Teledwyr Annibynnol Cymru) – the member organisation of the independent TV production sector in Wales – S4C offered tailored training, free of charge for free-lancers. BBC Wales' Factual Fast Track course was mentioned positively several times. However, the robust training schedule should go hand in hand with creating new jobs on all levels. One of the S4C interviewees was concerned that training was not enough to stop young people leave the sector as there were few opportunities for career progression: 'I'm very, very worried about the fact that we can't develop the talent we got within the structure of the companies that we have' (production company). One of the indie directors echoed this sentiment, saying that there are no jobs for the highly skilled people in the Welsh industry.

On the other hand, there is currently a skills gap in the screen sector, the shortage of skilled film and TV workers observed in all roles. At the UK level, the British Film Institute (BFI) has undertaken a major strategic skills review on behalf of the DCMS (BFI, 2022). In Wales, skill gaps in the media industry are identified in two reports, one for the Cardiff Capital Region (Hannah and McElroy, 2020) and another across the whole of Wales (McElroy, Davies and Ware, 2021).[26] The latter report identifies editors, editing assistants, researchers, producers and HGV drivers as specific roles in demand. Our data support the sense that, as one interviewee put it, 'everything from researchers to exec producers there's a massive hole in the sector at the moment, especially Welsh-speaking talent' (broadcaster).

Interviewees advocated for a robust training schedule to support the creation of new jobs at all levels in order to allow for career progression for those employed in the sector and discourage highly skilled workers leaving Wales as their careers develop: 'it has to be an industry for people in Wales and to keep them in Wales, so that they stay here and that they recognise that they can thrive and that they can start' (broadcaster). Interviewees also highlighted the efforts and ongoing need to diversify the workforce and representation in the Welsh screen industry, for example through the creation of specific roles within the broadcasters to establish links with diversity organisations and diverse communities.

Conclusion: what next for the screen sector in Wales?

This chapter has explored how freelancers, indies and broadcasters in the screen sector in Wales were affected by the interruptions in production resulting from the COVID-19 pandemic. They were impacted in different ways, depending on what role they mainly perform in the industry (freelancers), the profile of a company (indies) and the department of the TV channel (drama versus news making). Some of the freelancers, who are the most precarious workers in the sector, complained that the financial support they had access to was insufficient or poorly advertised but in general the interviewees reported that the Welsh Government's response to the pandemic filled the gaps left by the central government's schemes. A negative impact on workers' mental health was reported across the board, whether by freelancers feeling isolated and in financial distress or by overworked broadcast journalists. Some interviewees expressed appreciation for the mental health support put in place by their employers and umbrella organisations.

One of the main consequences of the pandemic has been to uncover the precarity of cultural and creative work, particularly of freelancers (Comunian and England, 2020; OECD, 2020;

Comunian *et al.*, 2021; Easton and Beckett, 2021; Henry *et al.*, 2021; Ostrowska 2021; Walmsley *et al.*, 2022).[27] Many of the concerns expressed by the Welsh respondents working in production roles, like the loss of virtually all pre-booked jobs at the beginning of the pandemic and the ongoing worry about financial security, were shared by freelance theatre and events producers in England and by cultural freelancers in Northern Ireland, which we've read about in other chapters in this book. In contrast, we found that for editors in post-production and, particularly, for journalists at the forefront of reporting on the pandemic, work was not only abundant but too much to handle at times, with workers' mental health also being affected. Finally, the importance of public (emergency) funding has also come to the fore during the pandemic, with governments (central, national and local), agencies and PSBs playing a crucial role for the survival of media ecologies.

The pandemic both affirmed the crucial role that PSBs play in the Welsh screen sector as well as in Welsh society, and created an appetite for Wales-centred and Welsh-language content which they hope to satisfy in the future. Interviewees from broadcasters such as the BBC and S4C said that their channels have felt responsible for helping the sector's survival, which they realised through commissioning new work during the pandemic. Still, freelancers' workload was negatively impacted as indies were not able to offer them as much work as before the pandemic. Looking into the future, the continued work of TAC (bringing together indies, broadcasters and Creative Wales) and the Welsh Government's and local authorities' commitment to the Freelancers and Public Service Body Pledge will hopefully mean that media sector freelancers' working conditions will continue to be improved.

PSBs' contribution to local creative economies is likely to continue being significant over time by providing new jobs, developing workers' skills and building a talent pipeline. Any change to regulations will have to carefully consider the impacts on the range of values – social, economic, industrial, civic, cultural and representational (Chivers and Allan, 2022) – that PSBs deliver to different stakeholders, including audiences and local economies across the UK's regions and nations. We heard about the importance of local supply chains, serving communities and knowing your audiences – broadcasters need to keep up with the audiences' demand for local and Welsh-language content.

Similarly to the rest of the UK (BFC, 2021), film and HETV production in Wales is currently booming, with many big budget productions underway and 'not enough people in the industry to service the demand at the moment' (governmental body). The fact that 'big shiny things' (governmental body) are made in Wales is seen as a positive contribution to the economy by several interviewees, but some participants see it as a threat to smaller companies and to the sustainability of the industry. Despite the narrative of survival and success of film and HETV drama production in Wales, interviewees felt that the Welsh screen sector should aim for sustainability, long-term development and diversity rather than becoming a 'servicing industry' for big (co)productions. These were often described as using Welsh locations and crews but not investing in the region or engaging with above-the-line talent and strategic development plans. While in 2020 the activity of Creative Wales was dominated by managing the Wales Culture Recovery Fund, their long-term goal is to 'have a balanced investment portfolio' (governmental body), both attracting big international players (the most recent productions include Netflix's *Sex Education* Season 3; HBO/BBC/Bad Wolf/Lucasfilm's *Willow*) and supporting smaller Welsh indies.

As one interviewee reflected, big productions should be seen as an 'opportunity rather than a problem' (governmental body). They seem to have positive long-term effects on other parts of the economy beyond the media sector, for example tourism in the wake of productions like *Willow*. However, their presence often creates drawbacks for Welsh producers, including increased costs of infrastructure hire, unavailability of workforce or the difficulty to compete with the quality of high-end drama. A way forward is, for example, to ensure that training and apprenticeship posts for Welsh talent is a contractual obligation for big international productions and co-productions.[28] Creative Wales and Ffilm Cymru will be partners in funding productions, which will be expected (and monitored) to spend part of their budget in Wales and on Welsh talent, crew, facilities and locations as well as to provide paid trainee placements (Welsh Government, 2022). The future of the Welsh media industry depends on striking a balance between attracting external big budget productions and creating a sustainable Welsh media sector.

Notes

1 Film and TV production are 'the region's most dynamic media subsector', the number of enterprises growing by 79 per cent between 2005 and 2018 (Fodor, Komorowski and Lewis, 2021, p. 2). As data for this report was collected before the pandemic, the Clwstwr suggests that the forthcoming studies of the impact of COVID-19 on the sector should use that record of prosperity as a baseline. https://assets.publishing.service. gov.uk/government/uploads/system/uploads/attachment_data/file/ 649980/Independent_Review_of_the_Creative_Industries.pdf

2 The term 'freelancer' is used here as an umbrella term that refers to those who are 'independent workers', whether PAYE freelancers, employed short term or temporarily, sole trader/Schedule D freelancers and those who are sole directors of limited companies (Easton and Beckett, 2021; Henry *et al.*, 2021).

3 Data from a BFI report. The general workforce average is 15 per cent. Using that benchmark, Clwstwr estimates that there are around 2,800 freelancers working in the audio-visual media sector in the Cardiff Capital Region alongside 4,590 full time employees (Fodor, Komorowski and Lewis, 2021).

4 Interviews took place between 12 and 26 February 2021.

5 Interviews took place between 17 June and 8 October 2021.

6 6 October 2021.

7 One of the BBC Wales interviews involved two interviewees (on their request).

8 The 'Working Safely During Covid-19 in Film and High-end TV Drama Production Guidance' was first published by the British Film Commission (BFC) in June 2020 and is continually revised.

9 Other studies suggest that the number might be higher. A survey of freelancers in the Welsh screen sector says that 60 per cent of freelancers lost all work during the pandemic, and 85 per cent reported a significant decrease in business (Komorowski and Lewis, 2020a).

10 Freelancers said they were often forced into this arrangement by some of the companies they work for, while one indie director saw it as a tax avoidance measure.

11 Scotland's Hardship Fund for Creative Freelancers followed at the end of that month. Beyond SEISS, there was no support for creative freelancers in England. Other bodies like Arts Council England and the Film and TV Charity supported cultural freelancers early in the pandemic. DCMS announced emergency funding for freelancers in December 2021.

12 Research into the distribution of the funds allocated through the Culture Recovery Fund, for example, has shown that the maxim 'existing funding attracts future funding' continues to hold true, and that the concentration of support in certain places risks perpetuating structural and place-based inequalities (Gilmore *et al.*, 2021).

13 www.wales.com/creative-wales

14 With S4C: the Welsh language provision; with Channel 4: skills and attracting them to Wales; with BBC Wales: comprehensive agenda; with ITV Wales: news and journalism.

15 Creative Wales has been working with the Wellbeing of Future Generations team (also part of the Welsh Government), Arts Council Wales, trade unions, local authorities and Cultural Freelancers Wales on the Freelancers and Public Service Body Pledge in which local government bodies pledge to recognise freelancers' contributions, hire them and pay them fairly for that work (https://powysw.moderngov. co.uk/documents/s65128/I).

16 When receiving funding from the Welsh government, freelancers were encouraged to sign up to the Freelancers and Public Service Body Pledge, and organisations to the Cultural Contract – the latter aims to ensure that public funds are used for both cultural and social purposes (https:// businesswales.gov.wales/welsh-government-cultural-contract-additional-information).

17 www.s4c.cymru/cy/ysgol-cyw/

18 www.bbc.co.uk/arts

19 www.bbc.co.uk/programmes/m000j4vx

20 www.ffit.cymru/en/

21 www.edt.org/research-and-insights/bridging-the-digital-divide-evidence-and-advice-on-remote-learning-and-digital-equality/

22 www.bbc.com/historyofthebbc/buildings/media-city/

23 The BBC and ITV have the additional requirement to provide regional news.

24 One of the interviewees mentions CULT Cymru, which specialises in providing such training: https://cult.cymru/en/

25 https://nfts.co.uk/nfts-cymru-wales. Another scheme, not mentioned by any of the interviewees, is The Step Across, www.screenalliancewales. com/News/new-step, funded by the BFC with Screen Alliance Wales, Ffilm Cymru Wales, Sgil Cymru and Creative Wales. It aims to support creative sector professionals publicise their transferable skills and meet demands in the various sectors across film, television, theatre and live events. The scheme connects individuals to companies which can utilise their skills and support any retraining needs.

26 A Creative Wales interviewee also mentions creating a central database about available training to avoid schedule clashes.

27 Including all cultural 'independent workers' that fall in this category such as self-employed, sole directors of limited companies, or those employed short term or temporarily. Freelancers is also the term we found in the newspaper items under scrutiny.

28 This is already implemented in England with Netflix-Longcross studios committing £1.2m to the new training programme 'Grow Creative UK' (BFC, 2021). Creative Wales has made training plans a condition to receiving Welsh Government production funding. During 2021/2022, eight productions provided a total of ninety paid work placements for entry level and upskilling roles (BFC, 2021), up to 150 in 2022: www.gov.wales/written-statement-new-approach-film-funding-wales.

References

Bectu. 2020. *Half of creative freelancers borrowing money to survive COVID-19 crisis.* [Online]. [Accessed 25 May 2022]. Available from: https://bectu.org.uk/news/half-of-creative-freelancers-borrowing-money-to-survive-covid-19-crisis/.

British Film Commission (BFC). 2021. Levelling up: UK film and TV sector makes strides in tackling skills shortage. *ScreenDaily.* [Online]. October 13. [Accessed 21 July 2022]. Available from: www.screendaily.com/uk-in-focus/levelling-up-uk-film-and-tv-sector-makes-strides-in-tackling-skills-shortage/5164241.article

British Film Institute (BFI) (2022) *BFI Skills Review.* [Online]. [Accessed 8 January 2024]. Available from: www.bfi.org.uk/industry-data-insights/reports/bfi-skills-review-2022

Burger, C. and Easton, E. 2020. *The impact of COVID-19 on diversity in the creative industries.* London: Creative Industries Policy and Evidence Centre.

Carey, H., O'Brien, D. and Gable, O. 2021. *Screened out: tackling class inequality in the UK screen industries.* London: Creative Industries Policy and Evidence Centre.

Carter, C. 2020. *Children, COVID-19 and the media.* Presentation of UK children's questionnaire results, Prix Jeunesse – global children's media industry festival/awards event, hosted from Munich, 7 June. Unpublished.

Chivers, T. and Allan, S. 2022. *What is the public value of public service broadcasting? Exploring challenges and opportunities in evolving media contexts.* London: Creative Industries Policy and Evidence Centre.

Creative Wales. 2020. *Creative Wales.* [Online]. January 22. [Accessed 21 July 2022]. Available from: www.wales.com/creative-wales

Comunian, R. and England, L. 2020. Creative and cultural work without filters: Covid-19 and exposed precarity in the creative economy. *Cultural Trends.* 29(2), pp.112–128.

Comunian, R., England, L., Faggian, A. and Mellander, C. 2021. *The economics of talent: human capital, precarity and the creative economy.* Cham: Springer.

Culture, Welsh Language and Communications Committee. 2020. *Impact of the COVID-19 outbreak on the creative industries.* Cardiff: National Assembly for Wales.

Cushion, S. 2019. PSM contribution to democracy: news, editorial standards and informed citizenship. In: Połońska, E. and Beckett, C. eds. *Public service broadcasting and media systems in troubled European democracies.* Basingstoke: Palgrave Macmillan, pp.23–39.

Cushion, S. 2020. COVID-19: to counter misinformation, journalists need to embrace a public service mission. *The Conversation.* [Online]. 17 March. [Accessed 7 February 2023]. Available from: http://theconversation. com/covid-19-to-counter-misinformation-journalists-need-to-embrace-a-public-service-mission-133829

Cushion, S., Soo, N., Kyriakidou, M. and Morani, M. 2020. Research suggests UK public can spot fake news about COVID-19, but don't realise the UK's death toll is far higher than in many other countries. *LSE Covid-19* [blog]. [Online]. 28 April. [Accessed 7 February 2023]. Available from: https://blogs.lse.ac.uk/covid19/2020/04/28/research-suggests-uk-public-can-spot-fake-news-about-covid-19-but-dont-realise-the-uks-death-toll-is-far-higher-than-in-many-other-countries/

Donnelly, S. and Komorowski, M. 2022. *Road to recovery? Creative Freelancers Wales Report 2022.* [Online]. [Accessed 8 January 2024]. Cultural Freelancers Wales. Available from: https://cfw.wales/recovery

Easton, E. and Beckett, B. 2021. *Freelancers in the creative industries.* London: Creative Industries Policy and Evidence Centre.

Fodor, M., Komorowski, M. and Lewis, J. 2021. *The media sector in the Cardiff Capital Region: driving economic growth through audiovisual activities.* Cardiff: Clwstwr.

Gilmore, A., Dunn, B., Barker, V. and Taylor, M. 2021. *When policy meets place: 'levelling up' and the culture and creative industries.* London: Creative Industries Policy and Evidence Centre.

Hannah, F. and McElroy, R. 2020. *Future skills and innovation for the screen sector in the Cardiff Capital Region.* Cardiff: Clwstwr.

Henry, N., Barker, V., Sissons, P., Broughton, D.K., Dickinson, P., Lazell, J. and Angus, T. 2021. *Creating value in place: understanding the role, contribution and challenges of creative freelance work.* [Online]. Manchester: University of Manchester. [Accessed 8 January 2024]. Available from: www.research.manchester.ac.uk/portal/en/publications/creating-value-in-place-understanding-the-role-contribution-and-challenges-of-creative-freelance-work(560fdd9d-884e-4a32-831b-0806adc92dd2).html

Horrocks, S. 2020. *Bridging the digital divide: latest evidence and advice on remote learning and digital equality in schools.* [Online]. Education Development Trust. [Accessed 8 January 2024]. Available from: www.edt.org/research-and-insights/bridging-the-digital-divide-evidence-and-advice-on-remote-learning-and-digital-equality/

Komorowski, M. and Lewis, J. 2020a. *The COVID-19 Self-Employment Income Support Scheme: how will it help freelancers in the creative industries in Wales?* Cardiff: Clwstwr.

Komorowski, M. and Lewis, J. 2020b. *The size and composition of the creative industries in Wales.* Cardiff: Clwstwr.

Kyriakidou, M., Morani, M., Soo, N. and Cushion, S. 2020. Government and media misinformation about COVID-19 is confusing the public. *LSE COVID-19* [blog]. [Online]. 7 May. [Accessed 7 February 2023]. Available from: https://blogs.lse.ac.uk/covid19/2020/05/07/government-and-media-misinformation-about-covid-19-is-confusing-the-public/

Mazzucato, M., Conway, R., Mazzoli, E.M., Knoll, E. and Albala, S. 2020. *Creating and measuring dynamic public value at the BBC.* London: UCL Institute for Innovation and Public Purpose.

McElroy, R. and Noonan, C. 2022. 'Rooting' the BBC: an interview with Rhodri Talfan Davies, Director of BBC Nations. *Critical Studies in Television.* 17(1), pp.32–45.

McElroy, R. and Noonan, C. 2019. *Producing British television drama: local production in a global era.* London: Palgrave Macmillan.

McElroy, R. and Noonan, C. 2018. Public service media and digital innovation: the small nation experience. In: Ferrell Lowe, G., Van den Bulck, H. and Donders, K. eds. *Public service media in the networked society.* Gothenburg: Nordicom, pp.159–174.

McElroy, R., Noonan, C. and Nielsen, J.I. 2018. Small is beautiful? The salience of scale and power to three European cultures of TV production. *Critical Studies in Television.* 13(2), pp.169–187.

McElroy, R., Davies, H. and Ware, T. 2021. *Screen Survey Wales 2021.* [Online]. Cardiff: University of South Wales/Creative Wales. [Accessed 8 January 2024]. Available from: https://pure.southwales.ac.uk/en/publications/screen-survey-wales-2021

OECD. 2020. *Culture shock: COVID-19 and the cultural and creative sectors.* [Online]. OECD. [Accessed 8 January 2024]. Available from: https://read.oecd-ilibrary.org/view/?ref=135_135961-nenh9f2w7a&title=Culture-shock-COVID-19-and-the-cultural-and-creative-sectors

Ofcom. 2021a. *Media nations.* London: Ofcom.

Ofcom. 2021b. *News consumption in the UK 2021 – overview of research findings.* London: Ofcom.

Ostrowska, A. 2021. *Impact of Covid-19 on the screen sector workforce in Wales: freelancers.* [Online]. Centre for Cultural Value/Culture Hive. [Accessed 8 January 2024]. Available from: www.culturehive.co.uk/CVIresources/impact-of-covid-19-on-welsh-screen-sector-workforce-freelancers/

Raising Films. 2021. *Back from the brink: a scoping study.* [Online]. Raising Films. [Accessed 8 January 2024]. Available from: www. raisingfilms.com/wp-content/uploads/2021/02/BackFromTheBrink_ ScopingStudy_March2021.pdf

S4C. 2021. *Adroddiad Blynyddol a Datganiad Ariannol Ar Gyfer y Cyfnod 12 Mis Hyd at 31 Mawrth 2021/Annual report and statement of accounts for the 12 month period to 31 March 2021.* Cardiff: Welsh Parliament.

Sambrook, R. and Cushion, S. 2020. Coronavirus: BBC News is uniquely placed to serve the nation – how it does so will define its future. *The Conversation.* [Online]. 1 April. [Accessed 7 February 2023]. Available from: http://theconversation.com/coronavirus-bbc-news-is-uniquely-placed-to-serve-the-nation-how-it-does-so-will-define-its-future-135265

ScreenSkills. 2020. *What can we do to help? Freelancers survey.* [Online]. ScreenSkills. [Accessed 27 January]. Available from:www.screenskills. com/media/3555/2020-04-21-screenskills-freelancer-survey.pdf

Walmsley, B., Gilmore, A., O'Brien, D. and Torreggiani, A. 2022. *Culture in crisis: impacts of Covid-19 on the UK cultural sector and where we go from here.* Leeds: Centre for Cultural Value.

Welsh Government. 2022. *Written statement: a new approach to film funding for Wales.* [Online]. [Accessed 15 June 2022]. Available from: https://gov.wales/written-statement-new-approach-film-funding-wales

8

Civic responsibility in times of crisis: museums and galleries in northern England during the COVID-19 pandemic

Danielle Child, Karen Gray and Harry Weeks

Introduction

As the UK entered lockdown in March 2020, museums and galleries across the country shut their doors. Over the following eighteen months, periods of blanket closure were interspersed with phases of local restrictions. Arts Council England emergency funding, the establishment of the Culture Recovery Fund and the furlough scheme did much to reassure the sector of its immediate safety. However, the long-term closure of gallery spaces, for a sector built around the exhibition form, prompted significant consideration of the role museums and galleries might play during a period of such unprecedented crisis and deviation from norms.

Organisations tended to divert resources towards the more socially oriented, and often unheralded, work that has long been part of the wider remit of much of the museum and gallery sector. Close engagement with local communities became a priority, with existing provision scaled up and new projects established. Exhibition and hospitality spaces were repurposed to social ends, and digital or hybrid technologies used to engage with audiences no longer able to attend in person. Some organisations also contributed considerably to the provision of care and resources to local communities.

This chapter examines these civic functions of museums and galleries in the north-east and north-west of England throughout the COVID-19 pandemic, areas which were disproportionately hit by extended lockdowns and high-tier restrictions for much of 2020 and 2021. Three short case studies serve to illustrate the kind of socially oriented work which took place in the sector during the pandemic. These case studies are then supplemented by insights gleaned from across the thirty-six interviews we conducted with staff from a wide range of institutions, from artist-led spaces and studio/project-space hybrids to major national institutions and regional museums groups. Interviews took place with staff at all levels within these institutions throughout 2020 and 2021. Both case studies and interviewees remain anonymous, given the often-sensitive contexts involved, except when discussion focuses solely on public-facing programming. Based on these interviews, we argue that, far from being a simple by-product of the closure of exhibition spaces, the turn towards civic functions was motivated by a heightened and pervasive sense of civic responsibility on the part of museums and galleries. Here we draw on pre-pandemic discourses surrounding the civic role of arts organisations (Doeser and Vona, 2016) and the idea of the 'useful museum' (Hudson, 2018).

Conceptual framework: civic role and useful museums

Since 2016, the Calouste Gulbenkian Foundation has been leading an 'Inquiry into the Civic Role of Arts Organisations'. In a literature review prepared for the project, James Doeser and Viktoria Vona broadly define civic role as 'the socio-political impact that organisations make on a place and its people through programmes of activity, or simply their existence' (Doeser and Vona 2016, p.9). They note the influence of community art and the rise of socially engaged art practices but highlight that thinking around 'civic role' has tended towards a greater focus on 'arts organisations [as opposed to art practices] as vehicles for delivering instrumental civic and social benefits' (Doeser and Vona, 2016, p.7). This reflects more than two decades of instrumentalising demands placed upon arts organisations by Labour, coalition and Conservative governments alike.

The distinction, often underplayed in the literature, between the civic role of the *arts* on the one hand and of arts *organisations* on the other is important and informs our analysis below. The Calouste Gulbenkian Foundation's Phase 1 Report on the project maintains this distinction, focusing solely on the latter. It is noted that the civic role of arts organisations might be enacted both 'through and aside from the production of artistic work' (Calouste Gulbenkian Foundation, 2017, p.11). While museums and galleries are spaces for the production and consumption of artistic activity, this has been, at least since the 1990s, only part of their broader offer to the civic sphere, with new roles (Head of Learning, Head of Outreach and Engagement, etc.) introduced to reflect the expanded remit of arts and cultural organisations.

It is against this backdrop that discussions of the so-called 'useful museum' have emerged, led by Alistair Hudson, Director of Manchester Art Gallery and the Whitworth Art Gallery until 2022, having joined from the Middlesbrough Institute of Modern Art (MIMA) in 2018. With the appointment of Hudson as its director, the Manchester Art Gallery rebranded itself as 'the original useful museum'. Founded in 1823 as The Royal Manchester Institution for the Promotion of Literature, Science and the Arts, the gallery was 'initiated ... by artists, as an educational institution to ensure that the city and all its people could grow with creativity, imagination, health and productivity' (Manchester Art Gallery, 2023b).

Hudson's thinking on the civic role of the museum is influenced by John Ruskin (Hudson, 2020), whose 1859 lecture on 'The unity of art' is cited on the gallery's website (Manchester Art Gallery, 2023a). As such, the roots of the useful museum or what has sometimes been called 'Museum 3.0' lie in a nineteenth-century conception. Museum 3.0 references the idea of 'usership' (adopting the language of the internet) – meaning that the gallery is co-created by its users. Hudson takes from Ruskin the idea of a museum as distinct from those that are defined by the market and by capital through becoming useful. This use, as Hudson suggested in a talk delivered while still at MIMA, lies in the idea that art should support the 'superstructure' or the state (Hudson, 2015). But, as Larne Abse Gogarty pointed out in her 2017 examination of 'usefulness', this refers to only the 'good' bits of the state (Gogarty, 2017). Gogarty notes that 'presumably MIMA is not interested in supporting police, prisons or borders guards' (2017, p. 122).

Hudson paints the useful museum model as a radical challenge to the orthodoxies of the post-Enlightenment modern museum (the 'Museum 1.0'), particularly what he sees as a belief in the incompatibility of art and use, inherited from the 'software engineer of modernity' Immanuel Kant (Hudson, 2018). He also contrasts the useful museum with the 'Museum 2.0', an institution which foregrounds participation in the wake of post-1990s instrumentalising demands, but which works 'in support of that primary high-art agenda' (Calouste Gulbenkian Foundation, 2023, p.28). Hudson's model of the useful museum on the other hand asks the museum to 'join in with what's happening in the world, and [demonstrate] how art can contribute to some of the main social problems that we have' (Hudson, 2018).

Through Hudson's directorship of both Manchester Art Gallery and the Whitworth Art Gallery between 2017 and 2022, the two institutions operate as part of a network of institutions associated with the Asociación de Arte Útil, led by Hudson and Cuban artist Tania Bruguera. The Whitworth indeed houses an 'Office of Arte Útil', which is 'free for use by local constituents, visitors, students and academics and provides a space to connect with the ideas and processes of "useful art"' (Whitworth Art Gallery, 2021). The Asociación serves as the focal point for a now established but fairly niche discourse around utility in contemporary art practice, theory and museology. Crucially, through the Asociación, the useful museum model is conjoined with Bruguera's advocacy for Arte Útil ('useful art' or 'art as a tool'). That is to say that implicit within the useful museum model is not simply a reconsideration of the role of the museum, but a rethinking of the role of art within society in general. Given the ways in which, as we shall see through our case studies, museums and galleries felt increasingly compelled to be 'useful' to their communities and constituencies, Hudson's model is an instructive precedent to call upon.

Case studies

While our interviews covered a wide range of institutions in terms of geography, scale, scope and funding, it is important to preface our observations by acknowledging that a shift in emphasis towards the civic is not uniformly spread across this range. Organisations that did not pivot significantly to the civic included smaller galleries and museums with more precarious funding situations, in smaller urban and rural contexts, and artist-led project spaces and studios. In the latter case it is worth noting that these institutions still felt significant responsibility to a constituency, but rather than the community-driven focus of the organisations we will be focusing on, this responsibility was largely felt towards the constituency of local artists, who were either studio-holders or regular participants in artist professional development programming. Those organisations that most fully pivoted towards their civic functions tended to almost exclusively represent institutions which conform to three broad 'types'. Our three case studies are representative of each of these 'types'.

1. Large-scale museums and galleries, often primarily associated with exhibiting contemporary art practice, often reliant on Arts Council England (ACE) funding, and always in large and central urban settings. These often had strong pre-existing outreach and engagement programming and/or histories of exhibiting socially engaged artists.
2. Smaller, consciously socially engaged organisations, often rooted in histories of socially engaged art practice and community art, usually in less central urban locations (either in smaller towns, suburbs or inner city areas). These are usually ACE National Portfolio Organisations (NPOs).
3. Urban museums and museums groups (again usually in larger urban centres), with strong ties to city councils and other urban institutions, drawing the bulk of their funding both from ACE and local councils.

Case Study A

The first case study is a major art gallery in an urban centre. Heavily reliant on earned income from events, catering and the shop, lockdowns posed a particular threat to the gallery, and its immediate survival was primarily secured through extensive use of the government's furlough scheme. The gallery has prioritised its social and community functions in recent years, and this was heightened by the pandemic. The director stated that since being in post the gallery has 'been much more focused on a civic impact agenda' and that they have prioritised 'being much more embedded locally', or even 'hyperlocally'. They espouse a model of civic impact built not on outreach, but on 'mutuality'. This profoundly impacted their early response to the pandemic, with one team member asking: '[How can we talk about mutuality] if in an emergency we disappear?' The pandemic also prompted questions as to the identity, value and role of the organisation. In our interview, the gallery's director stated: 'What now is the value, what is the relevance? How are we relevant to the needs of our communities and our constituents right here, right now? So forget about this being a centre for contemporary art. I'm thinking about us as being an anchor organisation within a community.'

Some of its community-facing projects pre-existed the pandemic but have increased in scale and scope. They have also been increasingly enacted in partnership with other civic institutions, the council and local community groups. The director acknowledged that this side of the gallery's work was often 'less visible' pre-pandemic, and other civic institutions struggled to take the gallery's offer to the community seriously. However, during the early months of the pandemic, 'they've finally seen what we're capable of doing and what we are doing, and we've now expanded that provision particularly for the council'. For instance, a creative food provision programme, led by the gallery in partnership with community groups, was delivering to 112 families in November 2021, up from twenty-five pre-pandemic.

This project was emblematic of a common desire to bring the curatorial and learning and engagement activities of the institution into closer contact, with food and care packages that were conceptually tied into the gallery's artistic programming being distributed to local families, and artists who were scheduled to contribute to in-person programming instead being asked to feed into care provision. The gallery's long-term goal is to more fully integrate these two activities, with more exhibitions programming being built upon the gallery's community work. Staff and trustees undertook anti-racism and poverty-proofing training as part of the gallery's drive to a greater prioritisation of its civic responsibilities to the community.

The gallery suffered the withdrawal of its catering contractors early in the pandemic, which led to the closure of their café space. The director then proposed the reuse of this space as a community asset, offering a free-to-access and 'non-commercialised' public space for use by the local community. The gallery used this space, in collaboration with local community groups, for events and activities directed towards marginalised groups, and operated the space the remainder of the time as a 'pay-what-you-like' café. The space has been particularly utilised by local families. The director was keen to stress that this kind of repurposing of space would not get past the board of trustees under normal circumstances. COVID-19 offered the opportunity to bypass the 'economic metrics' which often guide decision-making, and for the director to 'win arguments I never would have done before'.

Case Study B

The second case study is a small embedded local arts organisation with ACE NPO status based in a post-industrial town in a semi-rural location. The institution's mission has always been community focused and, during the pandemic, the pressure to support the local community increased. This was particularly urgent given that, due to financial pressures and furlough, many local voluntary and grassroots organisations had 'gone quiet' at the onset of the first lockdown. Thanks to the relative security afforded by their ACE core founding, they 'felt like [they] had a responsibility to still function in some format and to be useful to the community that [they] were embedded in'. One staff member believed that, in some ways, their organisation had become 'more relevant' than ever before.

Much of their work pivoted to specifically addressing the immediate and real impacts of the pandemic; for example, they organised a Zoom call involving professionals with knowledge and experience of death and dying for those experiencing loss in their communities. The institution hosted a conversation involving an Iman talking about how Muslim burial rituals and practices have been affected by the COVID-19 restrictions. This was one of a number of digitally facilitated projects they ran, largely out of necessity, given the impossibility of enacting the face-to-face work that was at the core of their community-focused programming previously. They found some successes in digital work, but this was predominantly in communities which had strong existing digital access. The organisation 'knew that just using the digital approach would be limiting' as many of the communities they worked with had little desire to engage digitally, let alone in some cases the means or digital literacy to do so. Strategies were developed to mitigate this: many constituents were not keen on joining group Zoom events, so the organisation realised that it needed to offer what the community needed 'right now... if it is just a one-to-one text service that they need, then in my role I can do that'.

This one-to-one digital approach was widely adopted, but put significant and understandable strain on staff members, who, it is important to remember, were also going through the stresses of lockdown. The director commented that 'there was a point, maybe two months in, where you could see that people were still trying to do [their] job but trying to manage their own home life was getting challenging'. Furthermore, the constant need to adapt and rethink strategies proved 'really draining'. Furlough was therefore used as means of relieving pressure on staff, although this did to a degree place even greater strain on those staff members who remained at work. For an organisation built upon an ethos of care for its communities, it was important that this care was also imparted to staff.

The organisation also felt a responsibility to the community of local artists and other cultural freelancers with whom they had been working extensively pre-lockdown. Their work with local artists continued and led to the establishment of a support network of around thirty-forty regular members, which met monthly throughout the pandemic. This commitment to art and artists was a key framing principle in their response to the pandemic. The organisation felt a need to 'respond to some of the things that were happening locally', but in a way 'that still felt true to the organisation' and its focus on art and the value of creativity. The director stated that lockdown had 'refocused our mindset in terms of the importance of how we are working with artists as a part of the work that we do'. They also argued that, although they felt a compulsion to respond pragmatically to the needs of the local community, 'there's a responsibility that we're not becoming an administrative or a management organisation ... that the essence of how we work is not compromised by that'.

Case Study C

The third case study is a local authority museum that sits on the boundary between an affluent area and one of relative deprivation, made up of families, many of whom have experienced third and fourth-generation unemployment. The manager noted the previous difficulties of reaching the latter hyperlocal community, which were made more difficult with the impact of COVID-19. During the pandemic, the museum faced a much longer closure (fifteen months) due to the redeployment of staff to work in frontline provisions such as food and PPE hubs, running helplines and administering business and hardship grants: something that can be identified as 'useful' within the wider society. Preceding difficulties included an ongoing restructure and, as a local authority museum, the lack of financial reserves. Both of these issues were further impacted as the museum had to make savings due to the pandemic, which left gaps in the staffing team including not having a marketeer. Volunteering also stopped.

Prior to the closure, the institution was highly embedded in its local communities and the manager noted that the physical gallery building drove community engagement with regular visitors coming in daily for a coffee. They told us that people missed visiting. However, restrictions placed on visitor numbers during the pandemic and after reopening forced a shift in emphasis to a less locationally defined constituency, driving engagement through innovative (and often digital) use of their collections (daily image posting on social media, for example). The museum is distinct from the other case studies in that it has a collection; as such, the museum benefitted from digitising its collection and 'battered social media' to increase engagement. However, the manager acknowledged the limitations of online engagement: visitors or viewers 'lose something by not having it [the object/collection] in front of them'. From this experience, the museum aspires to make better use of digital technologies around its collections and enhance accessibility, with the goal of creating an online database that has wider relevance for the public.

When the museum doors reopened, it was in a much more limited capacity. The temporary exhibitions did not reopen, visitor numbers were restricted, and they were directed through the museum in a set 'figure of eight' formation rather than having freedom of movement to walk around the institution. Another problem arose with the ventilation of the physical space itself, which was deemed 'not up to standard'. This impacted on how many visitors were allowed in the space at one time. In making these adjustments (i.e. the shift to digital and limited numbers/ movement), it was felt that the museum's community focus had been somewhat lost. It was uncertain whether the 'strong relationships' with specific users that the institution had enjoyed before the pandemic (with foster families, children and carers, for example) would return. The manager referred to the museum as a 'static space', whereas previously the institution had considered itself a community hub. The long-term plan is for the museum to formalise the ad hoc support work that it previously undertook by tendering for services to provide an alternative to day-care within the gallery space.

Rethinking the museum

Localism

The pandemic has placed a renewed focus on the local in the museums and galleries sector, as it has more broadly. Several local authorities in the area covered by this research, for example Oldham and North Tyneside, have recently published cultural strategies identifying the local and 'hyperlocal' as key points of focus over the coming decade. While COVID-19 has, as one museum group director put it, 'sharpened focus' on inequalities generally, this has most viscerally been experienced at the level of the local. They articulated that this had led to an appreciation of the 'importance of what we do in the places that we operate in'.

Accordingly, and as our case studies demonstrate, the vast majority of the socially oriented work undertaken by museums and galleries during the pandemic has been directed at local or even 'hyperlocal' (a term widely used by our interviewees) audiences. A learning and engagement manager at a regional museums group commented that their focus has been 'in particular on this very local offer ... and I would think that is true of all of the cultural organisations, not just ours'. Travel restrictions have dictated that face-to-face encounters be largely limited to communities within easy reach of one another. Even uses of the digital, despite its theoretically international reach, have strived for 'depth rather than breadth of engagement, seeking to build and sustain meaningful relationships with specific and largely local audiences' (Child *et al.*, 2021).

Travel restrictions have also had an impact on audiences for exhibition programmes post-lockdown. The reduction in travel and tourism that accompanied even those periods of relatively relaxed Covid restrictions entailed less focus on enticing national and international visitors. Instead, particular attention has been paid to the visitor experience of local visitors, who have constituted a far greater proportion of pandemic and post-pandemic footfall than they had previously, as reported by many of our interviewees, including Case Study A. Venues that were heavily reliant on tourism pre-pandemic are those that have struggled most post-pandemic.

Local lockdowns have also localised experiences of navigating the pandemic, and a number of organisations reported a feeling of increased camaraderie with other local civic institutions as a result, particularly when experiencing more stringent restrictions than neighbouring regions. This has resulted in the enhancement of local networks, sometimes at the expense of participation in international networks (usually in the case of larger institutions), and an increased commitment to local ecologies, cultural or otherwise. Organisations have widely rallied around freelance artists, and many are reflecting this in their post-pandemic programming. Although also a function of financial pressures and travel restrictions, museums and galleries have prioritised platforming local artists, again often at the expense of international artists.

However, as Case Study C attests, the focus on the local has not been uniform. Here, a highly embedded local institution struggled to maintain its connections with local audiences and communities that they were no longer able to encounter face to face as before. Even in this negative example, the question of localism has profoundly shaped the institution's experience of, and responses to, the pandemic. It is for this reason that we utilise the term 'civic' as opposed to the less locationally specific 'social' in this chapter.

Useful museums?

Museums and galleries' engagements with locality were regularly discussed in our interviews in terms of 'use' and 'necessity'. A director of an urban museums group stated that 'that sense of being useful to the place was vital during the pandemic in terms of that "what are we here for" kind of thing'. A learning and engagement officer told us that 'we are really of use now'. This language recalls Hudson's 'useful museum' model, although there was no sense that this model was being consciously invoked by our interviewees. While Hudson promotes an ideological reconsideration of the mission of museums, our interviewees' references to utility and necessity emerged far more out of pragmatism and their encounter with an unprecedented set of circumstances. A learning and engagement manager at a museums group recounted a particularly successful hybrid digital project with local people with mental health needs. When asked why they thought the project had been such a standout success, they remarked: 'I think there was a real need and I think we were just responding to that need.'

Furthermore, Hudson's model is yoked to a broader belief in the usefulness of art in general, through its ties to the Arte Útil movement. The useful museum, in Hudson's terms, subscribes to a belief in the civic value that art itself might offer, as evidenced in the first exhibition held post-lockdown at the Manchester Art Gallery. This was a show collecting artworks produced as part of the Channel 4 television programme *Grayson's Art Club*, in which the British lockdown public began to make art based on weekly prompts set by artist Grayson Perry and psychotherapist Philippa Perry. This represented a firm statement of the gallery's aspirations and a useful indicator of what the largely theoretical model of the useful museum might look like in practice. Here, art was seen as playing a valuable role in both social wellbeing and community experience in a time of distance and isolation. The accompanying exhibition blurb articulated this as follows:

> Many people sought solace in making art and expressed themselves with humour, pathos and imagination, encapsulating life under lockdown. The programme clearly demonstrates the way people use art as an essential part of their lives. Art Club's ethos chimes with that of Manchester Art Gallery, promoting art for the health of society and as an art school for everyone. (Manchester Art Gallery, 2020)

The use value in this case is deemed to derive from the positive health benefits associated with engagement and participation in art and creative pursuits. This sentiment was echoed in many of our interviews and has been highly discussed in the emerging literature on art and the COVID-19 pandemic (e.g. Bradbury *et al.*, 2021). But while Covid may have amplified the significance of art's value as a means of fostering wellbeing, this already formed the basis of much of the outreach and engagement work of the organisations we studied prior to the pandemic. Crucially, our case studies highlight that this is not the only form of value that institutions have seen themselves as offering through the pandemic. In fact, Case Study A does not articulate a model of value built upon the power of creativity, but one built upon institutions' capacities to offer the basic services and resources essential to the mere survival of communities. If these could be delivered by 'creative' means then all the better, but this was not a priority. Here, it is not art itself which is the source of value, but arts *organisations* as civic institutions acting, as the director of Case Study A put it, as 'anchor organisations' within a broader civic support network. We identify this as the major shift in thinking surrounding value precipitated by the pandemic.

From role to responsibility

We also characterise the changing nature of organisations' conceptions of their civic value in terms of a shift from museums and galleries seeing themselves as having a 'civic role' to play to their feeling a sense of 'civic responsibility'. We are here citing the language associated with the Calouste Gulbenkian Foundation's work on the civic role of arts organisations. While the Foundation's report argues that the 'civic role has to be a choice and not a mandate' (Calouste Gulbenkian, 2017, p.54), this does not reflect the sense of duty and obligation felt by our interviewees. We replace 'role' in the Foundation's research with 'responsibility' to reflect this. We might also frame this shift as a move from a sense of museums and galleries offering a kind of 'additive' civic value – interventions into civic life which might enhance the lives of local residents and communities – to what Larne Abse Gogarty calls 'subsistence models' (Gogarty, 2017, p.129) in which museums and galleries have become increasingly viewed as institutions with a remit to contribute to the survival and maintenance of localities and their communities.

Our interviews demonstrate that this responsibility was generated both internally and externally to the institutions we have studied. On the one hand, we have referenced a number of instances where responsibility seems to emerge from a moral imperative on the part of institutions and their staff to divert resources to helping local communities in the face of the existential threats posed by COVID-19. On the other hand, we must not overlook external pressures placed on museums and galleries to fulfil civic functions. Case Study B highlighted the decimation of the civic ecology in their town during the pandemic. They then felt a pressure to act as an overflow for the civic responsibilities of other (often smaller) organisations.

Funding has also been a crucial factor in the production of this sense of civic responsibility. With many of our case study organisations being reliant on earned income prior to the pandemic (one case study reported that 60 per cent of their income came through these avenues), there was an immediate necessity to seek alternative funding to make up this shortfall. It was noted in an interview with a curator at a mid-size gallery that funding available from charitable organisations had been refocused towards projects that undertake civic work, that is, engage with under-represented and/or local communities. An example of this is the Contemporary Art Society's (CAS) Rapid Response Fund that was launched in spring 2020. While CAS funding typically targets museum and gallery acquisitions, the Rapid Response Fund explicitly stipulates a benefit to the institution's communities in its description:

> The CAS Rapid Response Fund also ensures that when museums reopen, they are able to reach out to their communities through new acquisitions, playing a vital role in civic healing and mental wellbeing. (Contemporary Art Society, 2020)

Challenges

The pivot towards enacting civic responsibility has not been without its challenges. Across our interviews, staff told us of the strain that they had been under throughout the pandemic, and this was often exacerbated by their shifting to work in more community-facing ways. Some who were furloughed felt slighted – 'I felt like I'd got made redundant!' – and worried about their job security. Those in managerial roles found the process of allocating staff to furlough stressful. And those who remained in post throughout were often made to either fill the voids left by furloughed colleagues or diversify their work into new areas. One director commented that within their organisation 'some of those divisions between roles have become more fluid'. This diversification of roles was supported by widespread use of the pandemic as a period for the training, upskilling and reskilling of staff. However, working in unfamiliar roles took its toll on many, and only so much training was possible. Many arts workers had to go in feeling underprepared for new challenges and highlighted to us the kinds of training they felt they were lacking (often around mental health issues and digital technology). Those who were tasked with delivering organisations' community-facing work were also confronted directly with the suffering of those in their immediate localities, This is an emotionally strenuous job to perform, particularly when workers are new to the role and undertrained. A sense of civic responsibility may have driven much of the positive work done by museums and galleries during the pandemic, but this responsibility weighed heavily on the shoulders of staff.

Some, such as in Case Study A, spoke positively of the newfound sense of trust that bodies such as local councils placed in museums and galleries to perform essential civic support work. Others, however, raised concerns about arts organisations serving as an overflow valve for state responsibility or being made to fulfil the civic functions of organisations far more specialised and attuned to these than arts organisations. Although most of our interviewees felt compelled to utilise their resources in any way possible to help in the face of the COVID-19 crisis, there is a widespread sense of unease about the potential long-term sidelining of the cultural functions that define the museums and galleries sector. As one museum director said: 'the days when the sector and museums thought that they could cure all ills I hope are behind them ... that's not what we do'. Partnerships were regularly cited as a means of working through this dilemma, responding to feelings of civic responsibility while maintaining the specificity of arts organisations. As the director of a regional museums group put it: 'who do we work with? We're not social workers. We don't run night shelters, but we work with the people that do that. That's often our route in.' A learning programme manager at large gallery told us that 'cultural organisations don't build the solutions. I think they can be part of a process towards those solutions.' John Byrne's theorisation of the 'constituent museum' as 'one constituency amongst others' (2018, pp.98–99) seems apt here.

Looking forward

The unprecedented and unusual situation brought about by the lockdowns, social distancing, isolation, travel restrictions, sickness and death (this should not be forgotten) of the COVID-19 pandemic demanded that museums and galleries swiftly and pragmatically adjusted in terms of both behind-the-scenes working patterns and their programming. We have identified here four key shifts that these conditions have precipitated with regard to museums' and galleries' civic work. Firstly, that this work became increasingly important, particularly in larger and more secure organisations, and in organisations with a pre-existing commitment to social engagement. Secondly, that the pandemic fostered a heightened focus on localism and hyperlocalism. Thirdly, that this work has been widely framed in terms of utility (although not quite in the sense that Hudson's useful museum dictates). Finally, that the underlying impetus behind this shift lies in institutions feeling a sense of civic *responsibility* (as opposed to a civic role).

In each of these cases, we are only able to identify these as phenomena specific to the particular conditions of the COVID-19 pandemic. It remains to be seen to what extent these shifts constitute a more fundamental turning point in terms of the mission, programming and responsibilities of museums and galleries in the future. The pandemic has, though, clearly offered a moment of reflection regarding these questions, and we encountered almost no desire to 'go back to how things were before', in contrast to other sectors examined by this research (Walmsley *et al.*, 2022, p.32). In fact, the predominance of sentiment concerning the future of the sector was characterised by a desire to utilise the pandemic as a moment to catalyse long-overdue change. An urban museums group director told us:

> There are some things that we've always wanted to change and we weren't able to change so we actually needed to think from where we are now, how do we use this situation to actually do some things differently?

Further austerity since 2021 presents yet more challenges for museums and galleries, but in some ways exacerbates the circumstances which brought about the shifts we have identified in this chapter. Although arts organisations are feeling the pinch in terms of funding, so too are other civic institutions, the duties of which many arts organisations took on during the pandemic. While the pandemic brought about significant shifts in the self-perception of museums and galleries, the navigation of these pressures will no doubt determine the degree to which these shifts endure.

References

Abse Gogarty, L. 2017. 'Usefulness' in contemporary art and politics. *Third Text.* 31(1), pp.117–132.

Bradbury, A., Warran K., Mak, H.W. and Fancourt, D. 2021. *The role of the arts during the COVID-19 pandemic.* [Online]. London: UCL. [Accessed 1 January 2024]. Available from: www.artscouncil.org. uk/sites/default/files/download-file/UCL_Role_of_the_Arts_during_COVID_13012022_0.pdf

Byrne, J., Morgan, E., Paynter, N., Sánchez de Serdio, A. and Adela Zeleznik, A. eds. 2018. *The constituent museum: constellations of knowledge, politics and mediation: a generator of social change.* Amsterdam: Valiz.

Calouste Gulbenkian Foundation. 2017. *Rethinking relationships: Inquiry into the Civic Role of Arts Organisations.* Phase 1 report. [Online]. London: Calouste Gulbenkian Foundation. [Accessed 10 January 2024]. Available from: https://content.gulbenkian.pt/wp-content/uploads/sites/18/2017/10/01175116/Civic-Role-of-Arts-Phase-1-REPORT-lr-.pdf

Child, D., Gray K., Weeks H. and Wright J. 2021. Why digital isn't enough. *Arts Professional.* [Online]. [Accessed 10 January 2024]. Available from: www.artsprofessional.co.uk/magazine/article/why-digital-isnt-enough

Contemporary Art Society. 2023. *Acquisitions & Art Consultancy.* [Online]. London: Contemporary Art Society. [Accessed 11 January 2024]. Available from: https://issuu.com/contemporaryartsociety/docs/2019-2021

Doeser, J. and Vona, V. 2016. [Online]. London: King's College London. [Accessed 10 January 2024]. Available from: www.kcl.ac.uk/cultural/resources/reports/cgf-civic-role-literature-review-final.pdf

Hudson, A. 2015. *What is art for? Part two: the museum 3.0.* Interview by Axis. [Online]. [Accessed 10 January 2024]. Available from: www.youtube.com/watch?v=d9URRUEJ7Tg

Hudson, A. 2018. *The useful museum.* Presented at We Are Museums, Marrakech. [Online]. [Accessed 10 January 2024]. Available from: www.youtube.com/watch?v=AmpCURA9nFw

Hudson, A. 2020. Ruskin unleashed: towards a revised political economy of art. Or, joy for ever: how to use art to change the world (and its price beyond the market). *Journal of Art Historiography.* 22, pp.1–21.

Manchester Art Gallery. 2020. *Grayson's Art Club.* [Online]. [Accessed 3 February 2023]. Available from: https://manchesterartgallery.org/event/graysons-art-club/

Manchester Art Gallery. 2023a. *History of the gallery.* [Online]. [Accessed 3 February 2023]. Available from: https://manchesterartgallery.org/about/history-of-the-gallery/

Manchester Art Gallery. 2023b. *Vision & mission.* [Online]. [Accessed 3 February 2023]. Available from: https://manchesterartgallery.org/about/vision-mission/

Walmsley, B., Gilmore, A., O'Brien, D. and Torreggiani, A. eds. 2022. *Culture in crisis: impacts of Covid-19 on the UK cultural sector and where we go from here.* Leeds: Centre for Cultural Value.

Whitworth Art Gallery. 2021. *Office of Arte Útil.* [Online]. [Accessed 3 February 2023]. Available from: www.whitworth.manchester.ac.uk/whats-on/exhibitions/upcomingexhibitions/officeofarteutil/

9

Epistemic governance and partnerships in place: an ecosystem analysis of Greater Manchester

Ben Dunn and Abigail Gilmore

Introduction

In this chapter, we consider the impact of COVID-19 on the arts and cultural industries from a place-based perspective focusing on a specific geography, the city region of Greater Manchester (GM), and the social and political relationships that comprise its cultural ecology and policy infrastructure. Greater Manchester is a city region of ten district authorities in the north-west of England, with Manchester at its geographical and political centre (see Figure 9.1). Overseen by the Greater Manchester Combined Authority (GMCA) under leadership from a directly elected metro mayor, GM was established as a city region in 2011 and as England's first devolved authority in 2014. Considered a test case for the potential for devolution to help counterbalance 'the powerhouse of London' (Osborne, 2014), the region's history of strategic collaboration and policy development, first under the Association of Greater Manchester Authorities (1986–2011) and now the GMCA, provides an opportunity to examine the role of place and place-based networks, policy and decision-making in the context of the pandemic.

City-regional cultural governance is characterised by a pragmatic, networked approach to cultural policy and development. As one of our interviewees, a local government officer, explained: 'We've got a long track record of working together to try and promote activity across the city region. We don't have to do everything in all ten districts. We do what works.' In the context of the pandemic, this approach catalysed a series of targeted interventions

GREATER MANCHESTER

Figure **9.1** Map of Greater Manchester and its ten districts

that sought to protect the cultural sector and cultural workers from the most extreme impacts of the pandemic. As another interviewee explained: 'Although the pandemic was global and it hit nationally … it also hit *locally*, and while there's similarities – really big similarities – … each area had to take their own approach' (local government officer, our emphasis). Efforts to understand the local impacts of the pandemic and to adapt district and regional authority strategy in response contrast with national policy, which initially sought to stabilise the cultural sector through targeted support for the sector's 'crown jewels' (as discussed in Chapter 1). As Banks and O'Connor observe, this approach established a 'pecking order' (2021, p. 8) with large-scale, building-based organisations at the front of the queue and no direct provision for freelance or independent cultural workers. In comparison, policy-makers and cultural leaders in GM sought to leverage the breadth of the region's cultural infrastructure, and the strong ties between local and combined authorities, to find solutions to the regional and local impacts of the pandemic. The city-regional policy response looked beyond the trickle-down economics of national interventions like the Culture Recovery and Capital Kickstart funds and encouraged an interconnected view, linking policy with place, and the survival of flagship institutions with the livelihoods and wellbeing of cultural workers.

This chapter considers this response by taking an ecosystems approach, examining the ways in which collaboration and innovation from cultural leaders and policy-makers were able to leverage place-based knowledge, networks and resources to nuance national policy and offer targeted support for the local cultural sector. We begin with a short introduction to the policy context that preceded the pandemic and formed the background to responses in the region. We then examine how the pandemic 'hit locally', including how national policy responses, such as the Culture Recovery Fund (CRF), were received, operationalised and challenged by the different localised initiatives that characterise the region's response. Finally, through two case studies, the GM Arts Hub and Salford's *Suprema Lex* cultural strategy, we explore how these two values-driven approaches (Dunn and Gilmore, 2021) were realised in practice. We conclude by exploring the contributions of the GM case study to wider cultural policy discussion and its implications for how we might think and plan culture's relationship to place and policy as the sector adapts to the learning and challenges of COVID-19.

Methodology

The year-long study of Greater Manchester's cultural ecosystem during the pandemic began in November 2020, when we worked closely with our research partners, GMCA, Manchester City Council (MCC), and Salford Culture and Place Partnership (SCPP), to develop a programme of interviews and action research with policy actors, cultural leaders and practitioners across GM's ten districts. Two waves of qualitative semi-structured interviews (n. fifty in total) documented the varied affects and experiences of policymakers, cultural leaders and creative practitioners, capturing their responses in real time, and allowing us to map the impacts of these developments onto the wider cultural sector context. Interviewees were sampled via snowballing, following recommendations from research partners MCC, SCPP and GMCA. Supported by a desk-based policy review and quantitative research from colleagues on this project, including analysis of Labour Force Survey (LFS) data (see Figure 9.2), we draw on an ecosystems perspective (Barker, 2019) to analyse the local cultural ecology and the factors that informed and supported responses in the region.

In the context of GM, an ecosystems perspective highlights the dynamic, interconnected and scalar dimensions that are invoked at the intersection between culture and place, drawing attention to the flows and processes through which policy, leadership and infrastructure inform and regulate cultural production and consumption within the city-region. Our use of this terminology responds to the limitations of the national policy response and recognises the extraordinary efforts of sector stakeholders to acknowledge the layered relationships and interdependencies of the local cultural infrastructure in their responses to the pandemic. It also seeks to highlight this perspective as a strength that supported the region's capacity to resist the worst impacts of the pandemic – work and job loss, skills depletion, permanent closure – to innovate productively,

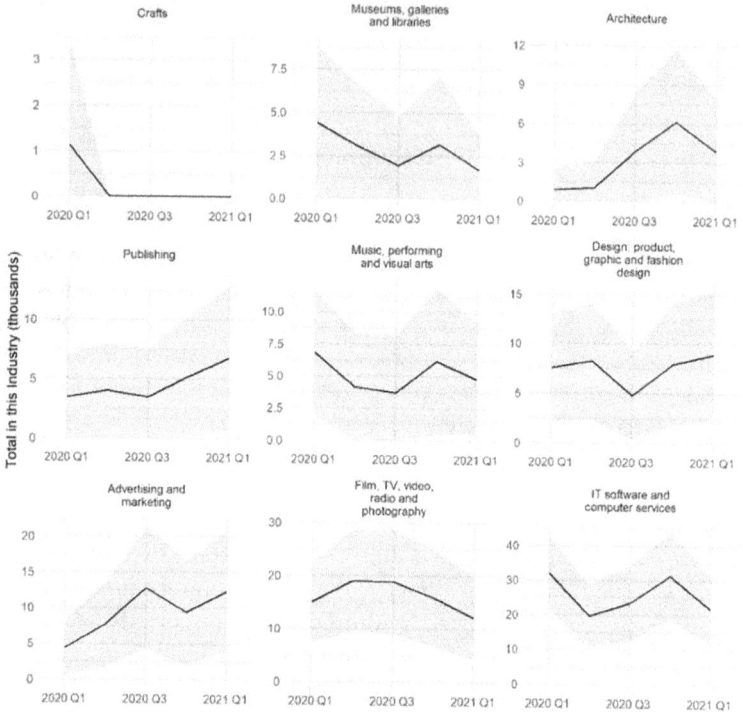

Figure 9.2 Workforce size, Greater Manchester (industries)
Source: ONS, Labour Force Survey

even as business models and conventional principles of cultural strategy collapsed.

The qualitative methodology for ecosystem case study provided access to the narratives and perceptions of our interviewees, presenting insight into the relational forms of cultural governance in the city-region and real-time reflections on the changes to local strategic objectives as these went 'out the window' at the start of the pandemic, leading to an unprecedented period of improvisatory decision-making and policy innovation in the region. Our study is therefore both informed and bounded by the perspectives of our interviewees as research partners and, as such, reflects institutionally informed conceptions of place, context, and the purpose and impacts of policy. This has two main consequences for this research. Firstly, we rely on policy-makers and cultural partners to act as interlocutors for the broader impacts of policy innovation for audiences, communities and other local stakeholders. Secondly, the lens introduced in this study is biased by a political infrastructure that has, historically, privileged Manchester city centre. Though we spoke to policy-makers and cultural partners in each of the region's ten districts, the discussion presented here should be seen as an overview of policy development in the region that would benefit from further place-focused research at a local authority level.

'Everything was on an upward trend': culture before the pandemic

GM has a history of collaborative working across its towns, cities and districts, which paved the way to city-regional devolution. The strength of the relationships within this 'red wall stronghold' of mainly left-wing-led local governments working to create the first combined authority in England has raised the city-region's profile and identity, and has benefitted the strategic negotiation of capital investment related to the Northern Powerhouse, an initiative aimed to rebalance geographic inequalities in productivity and support economic development across the north of England (Gilmore and Bulaitis, 2023). This initiative, choreographed by the former Chancellor of the Exchequer George Osborne and combined with a long-standing advocacy for culture and creative industries, provided visibility for the city-region within Westminster which resulted in £78m of central government investment in The Factory, a new home for Manchester International Festival (MIF), among other component parts of the 2014 devolution deal (Jenkins, 2015).

Manchester itself is an expert in boosterism, with a reputation for strong leadership, place-based working and advocacy at a city-region level (Localis, 2009). City leaders were familiar with the politics and discourse of creative industries and creative clusters, and the technocracy of their extrinsic powers, having come top of Richard Florida's Creative Class Boho Index exercise in 2003, which ranked UK cities by their propensity to host the 'creative class' (Carter, 2003). The city claims a global track record as a cultural capital, particularly in football and music, and has a strong presence of creative industries clusters, concentrated in the city centre and areas of its neighbour city Salford (Siepel *et al.*, 2021; Tether, 2022), including MediaCityUK, the home of BBC North and ITV Granada. The presence of clusters and 'micro-clusters' of creative businesses has long been a lever for targeted investment to underpin strategic development, most recently in a pilot Local Industrial Strategy (BEIS/HCLG, 2019). However, this approach exacerbated long-standing concerns around the uneven distribution of cultural investment and opportunity across the city-region, raising questions for district authorities about the value of their investment into the combined authority's cultural budget. As a representative for Bury observed: 'In GM, the local politicians feel that the outlying boroughs are basically housing estates for Manchester City Centre, and I think it's easier for them to leave all that culture stuff to Manchester City Centre, rather than actually investing in it in local terms.'

Weeks before the first national lockdown, GMCA launched the Culture Fund, an investment of £8.6m over two years, designed to support a 'balanced' (GMCA, 2020a, p.1) portfolio of thirty-five cultural organisations representing each of the region's ten districts. Alongside the inaugural GM town of culture (Bury Council, 2020), the portfolio is a key pillar in the GMCA culture team's efforts to address inequality in the region's cultural offer and to build links between GMCA, district authorities and cultural partners beyond Manchester and Salford. This progress is complemented by efforts from policy-makers across each of the ten districts to develop local cultural strategies at various stages of maturity at the start of 2020. Local cultural strategies 'make the case' for culture, locally and regionally, helping to secure local authority buy-in by identifying opportunities for culture to support local policy ambitions through policy attachments (Gray, 2007) to generate positive outcomes for communities, town centres and the local economy, while providing visibility for local cultural interests and identities as part of region-wide policy discussion. This work is supported by strong lines of communication between the districts and the combined authority, facilitated by bodies like the GM Arts Network, which brings together arts officers from each of the region's districts with a remit for cultural planning and development.

Despite the influence of historical conditions that have tended to privilege the city of Manchester, there was, as a regional policy-maker observed, a strong sense that culture was 'on an upward trend' in the months before the pandemic, both in its legitimacy as part of wider strategy and policy development across the region, and in the inclusion of the diverse districts and communities that make up the region. Though the creative cluster model has undoubtedly helped bolster the case for culture in the region, and continues to receive political and financial support, there are clear efforts at district and combined authority levels to extend thinking about culture's relationship to policy beyond the 'winner-takes-all urbanism' (Florida, 2017, p.6) of Florida's creative class. The GM Culture Fund was led not only by the principle of economic redistribution, but also by the conviction that a healthy cultural ecosystem should transcend the values held by a small number of flagship institutions. Along with region-wide schemes like Great Place GM (2018–2021), a joint funding scheme by Arts Council England and the Heritage Lottery Fund which aimed to capacity build cultural place-making, there have been significant efforts to formalise strategic relationships between culture and substantive outcomes in other policy areas within GM, from municipal cultural strategies to the local industrial strategy for GM, which foregrounded cultural venues and creative industries clusters as economic drivers (Gilmore and Bulaitis, 2023). As a local government officer explained of their district's plans for culture prior to the pandemic: 'it was all about trying to establish a cultural ecology across the borough and to engage stakeholders in what that cultural ecology blueprint could and should look like'. Such initiatives were in progress at the start of 2020 and indicate a direction of travel rather than an established policy environment. Nevertheless, they reflect the approach and ambitions that were in place towards the end of 2019 and the conditions that informed the region's response as the pandemic developed over the following years.

'An overwhelming sense of anxiety and concern': local impacts of a global pandemic

Established relationships between cultural organisations, supported by the region's history of strategic cultural development, allowed for a coordinated response across the city-region, with a number of publicly funded organisations closing their doors on 20 March 2020, in advance of national guidance. Nevertheless, our research found strong similarities between the initial stages of the pandemic within GM and the broader national picture. As interviewees observed, the early weeks of the pandemic were characterised by shock and panic as cultural workers and policy-makers tackled the complete shutdown of venues and in-person activities, and a profoundly uncertain future as they waited for government advice. As the executive director of a Manchester flagship organisation explained: 'The way that the pandemic and the restrictions that came in were handled threw everybody ... into a sort of flat spin because of the lack of guidance or clear direction or structural timing.' Local policy objectives and organisational strategies were quickly rendered untenable and alternatives during these early weeks were described as 'kneejerk' reactions, driven, as a combined authority representative observed, by a 'sense of powerlessness' reflected in testimonies from cultural workers and policy-makers across the four UK nations.

Local efforts attempted to respond to the impacts on work and jobs and the vulnerability of the freelance workforce, effects observed elsewhere which were combined with structural issues that preceded the pandemic (as described in Chapter 2). The exacerbation of already precarious conditions for large parts of the cultural sector was acknowledged by the rapid response of high-profile organisations such as the biennial MIF, which was preparing for its next festival in 2021 and prevented by the pandemic from moving to its new home, the flagship Factory building. By 18 March 2020, five days ahead of the announcement of the first national lockdown, MIF had launched a programme of online drop-in sessions for artists and freelancers offering support and resources (MIF, 2020). This was prompted by the reliance of the festival on freelance labour, but also signalled the collective concerns expressed by the proliferation of cross-organisational, cross-district initiatives that emerged in parallel in GM. As a member of the GMCA culture team explained: 'There was the running around like headless cultural chickens, and then we go: okay, actually, we're all doing this ... Why don't we do this together?'

As Figure 9.2 shows, the pandemic had a significant impact on workforce size for the creative and cultural industries, especially for venue-based activities during the first three quarters of 2020. Results from MCC's annual Cultural Impact Survey suggest a 95 per cent decrease in audiences and an 84 per cent decrease in productions between 2019 and 2020 (Cultural Heritage in Action, 2022) and, as Figure 9.2 shows, sectors such as music, performing arts, visual arts, museums and galleries, where business models are most reliant on in-person participation, were those that showed an overall downward trajectory of workforce across the four quarters of 2020. Additionally, the central government's tiered approach to managing case numbers disproportionately impacted GM as much of the northwest region was placed in 'special measures' with more stringent travel and social distancing restrictions for most of the second half of 2020. These conditions placed particular strain on cultural organisations and on the wider events and hospitality sector, significantly exacerbating the impact on the freelance workforce. As a local authority officer noted, the claimant rate for Universal Credit in the city increased by 100 per cent in 2020, suggesting that 'a lot of that is younger people who might work in the creative industries but are also supplementing their incomes by working in cafés, bars, restaurants, etc.'. Workers in the cultural sector are more likely to hold two or more jobs than those in other sectors (Pasikowska-Schnass, 2019, p.8) and, as our interviewee observed, many creative workers were doubly impacted as additional, often more stable, income streams were cut off as complementary sectors such as hospitality, tourism and the night-time economy also remained closed.

Our qualitative research provides nuance to the impacts of these conditions on the region and on the pressures facing creative and cultural workers. As an executive director of a large-scale cultural organisation in Manchester observed: 'Where we saw the biggest and most immediate impact was just an overwhelming sense of anxiety and concern from artists and the whole arts supply chain in terms of technicians, crew, freelance producers.' These anxieties were exacerbated by the lack of clear leadership or prompt decision-making from central government in the early stages of the pandemic and continued when guidance on social distancing and public events was repeatedly revised throughout 2020 into the first half of 2021. Characterised as an exhausting series of 'false starts', these conditions not only made it impossible for cultural organisations to establish a coherent strategy around reopening, but eroded audience confidence as events had to be cancelled or rescheduled at short notice. Additionally, while centralised policies such as the Culture Recovery Fund (CRF) were universally welcomed, they failed to address the needs of the most vulnerable cultural workers in the region. As one freelance artist explained of the central government's response:

> There was a real lack of care for the way that artists so often sacrifice a stable, singular income in order to make their art and, as a result, piece together an income from different sources. So, for all of the support that was provided, disadvantaged people who were going to be in that position of working multiple jobs .... That disproportionate disadvantage was not met with appropriate support, and I think that was shocking, and I will be angry for a long time.

There were more 'care-full' efforts by local government to find pragmatic solutions tailored to the needs of the region. GMCA, for instance, consulted with cultural sector partners to make an early decision to suspend agreed funding requirements for their Culture Fund portfolio, arranging immediate advance of 2020–2021 funds. MCC took similar action. As a representative explained:

> I remember, my last day in the office, I spent the day drafting a letter to cultural organisations and getting it signed by my executive members to say that we will be suspending the monitoring and conditionality of our funding agreements with immediate effect.

For most organisations that received local funding, these steps allowed them to enter the initial stages of the pandemic with a degree of financial stability. Though anxiety over the potential longevity of the pandemic was high, these provisions clarified the expectations of their local authority partners, signalling their intention to continue support and underlining a flexibility that allowed organisations to think carefully and critically about their resources and how they might be deployed.

Described by a Manchester museum director as an ambition to 'serve the city properly', for most this involved a turn towards place and locality, drawing on relationships with audience groups and stakeholder communities to understand how their surrounding population was experiencing the pandemic and how the cultural sector might mitigate the worst of its impacts, even when they were outside of scope of the organisation's normal business. This values-led response positions the cultural sector as a public service in the context of the pandemic, with unambiguous financial support from government authorities releasing various forms of social and cultural capital in support of the local population. The policy response to COVID-19 often blurred the line between cultural and social provision, including a proliferation of advice sessions for artists and creative workers; creative packs sent out to families, young people and people experiencing social isolation to keep them entertained at home; and a variety of online activities and projects including quiz nights, play readings and community groups for older people and refugees. As the artistic director of a Bolton theatre explained: 'for some people it's a real lifeline .... We felt very keenly the responsibility ... to entertain and connect people remotely during this time.'

These informal strategies were reflected in policy responses within the city-region. GMCA's plan for cultural recovery, published towards the end of 2020, included revised guidelines for its Culture Fund organisations that encouraged them to use their resources to 'support the wider GM Cultural sector' (GMCA, 2020b, p.12) by supporting individual artists and freelancers, emphasising cultural opportunities for hard-hit communities, providing opportunities for young people and reducing structural inequality in the cultural sector. Manchester's Cultural Leader's Group, a de facto steering group of venue and organisation directors and leaders for culture with responsibility for delivering the city's *Cultural Ambition* strategy (MCC, 2016), expanded their membership, reaching beyond the city centre's flagship organisations and subsidised sector to incorporate new members from museums, dance, comedy, marketing and photography. Activities shifted from delivering the pre-pandemic conviction that 'international art and culture brings the greatest local benefit' (MCC, 2016, p.1) towards local communities' concerns and policy attachments to reinforce the relationship between cultural institutions and social goals. As a Manchester-based company director explained: 'it feels like going local is going to be the anthem of our time when we emerge from this'.

This led to some extraordinary coordination across the sector and the city-region, including initiatives like the GM Arts Hub, to be considered shortly. However, the value of the relaxed funding

restrictions for MCC Portfolio and GMCA Culture Fund organisations varied significantly depending on the circumstances of organisations and districts at the start of the pandemic. As a representative
for a Manchester-based theatre explained:

> I think it was the 20th of March that we shut our doors, and for
> our business it was the worst possible moment .... We were at the
> height of producing ... which requires huge sums of sunk cost in
> advance .... We've got a show that was on our stage that didn't make
> its own press night .... We were in pre-production for two other
> plays. The costs associated with that were considerable.

For organisations that fell in the gap between local support and
the introduction of national programmes like the Coronavirus Job
Retention Scheme, Arts Council England's emergency funding and
CRF (see Chapter 1), the organisational impacts were significant,
involving redundancies, scrapped work and high personal and emotional costs.

The picture varied for different local authorities. Not all ten districts had established culture teams at the start of the pandemic,
and, in many cases, already limited teams were reduced further as
officers were redeployed to other duties. As a representative from
Wigan Council explained, 'quite quickly we lost about 60 per cent
of our team to frontline critical service delivery'. While a values-
led approach to managing the pandemic helped establish what
one GMCA representative described as a 'coalition of the willing',
infrastructural issues relating to capacity and resource at organisational level limited the reach of these efforts and their benefits. As
they explained: 'when you don't have people, that's when it trips
up ... because we're all enthusiastically on a joint mission with a
completely shared purpose, and then you'll have a district where
they haven't got staff'. The ambition to 'serve the city' drew on
place-based networks to support understanding of the pandemic's
impacts and the sharing of knowledge, resources and expertise
in ways that made a meaningful difference to organisations and
to those most impacted by the pandemic, within and beyond the
sector. The conditions of place, however, also defined the reach of
these projects and policy interventions, indicating the limit point at
which chains of communication, resource and shared value begin to
break down. In the following section, we consider the relationship

between the pandemic and place in more detail, looking at two projects that sought to establish and extend place-based networks in strategic response to the pandemic, and consider their impacts for cultural sector organisations, workers and audiences.

Place-based partnerships

The examples considered here are the GM Artist Hub, a region-wide network of cultural organisations established to support independent artists in response to the pandemic, and the Salford Culture and Place Partnership (SCPP), a cross-sector steering group for culture in Salford that launched its first major policy initiative, *Suprema Lex* (SCPP, 2020), eleven days before the first national lockdown. Though distinct in their aims, they illustrate common interests associated with place-based thinking, networks and decision-making to highlight the role and potential of an ecosystems perspective in managing sector response during the pandemic.

The GM Artist Hub was established in the early weeks of the pandemic in response to impacts on the livelihoods and wellbeing of independent artists. As a representative explained, the Hub was designed not just to offer financial support, but to provide a point of contact for artists whose relationships with the sector had been cut off: 'they haven't just lost income, they've also lost support .... They've lost their ability to draw on us to understand what the bigger picture might look like.' Led in its initial stages by The Lowry, the Hub relied on partnership work undertaken by their artist development team prior to the pandemic, bringing together fourteen organisations including Manchester-based institutions such as the theatre venues of HOME and Contact, the Manchester International Festival (MIF) along with smaller partners from districts across the city-region.

Initially, the Hub was resourced through the in-kind commitment of its members, relying on contributions of knowledge and time that would adjust as the pandemic developed and in response to the circumstances of individual organisations. Described by one of its members as 'collective responsibility, flexibly delivered', the diversity of scale and art form across the Hub's partners was key to the project's ambitions, facilitating access to a range of artists, networks, resources and expertise that no single organisation would have been able to provide. This approach allowed for the rapid provision of targeted advisory, skills and information sessions, delivered by Hub members over Zoom, and longer-term fundraising initiatives that resulted in a £60,000 grant from the Esmée Fairbairn Foundation. These funds were redistributed through a series of programmes co-designed with the Freelance Task Force and the Disabled Artists Networking Community (DANC). In the eight months between April and November 2020, the Hub was able to support over 500 artists and provide group and one-on-one advisory sessions, hardship bursaries and seed-funding awards targeted at under-represented groups (GM Artist Hub, n.d.).

This was the first time that these organisations had collaborated on this scale or in these numbers; it was noted that previously there had been a tendency for building-based organisations to confine themselves to their 'own little bubble', with little strategic interest or relationship with other organisations in the area. This perspective is emphasised by another Hub member who identified 'competitive barriers between organisations' as obstacles to cross-organisational discussion around programming, development and artist support, highlighting a proprietary relationship between organisations and artists. The innovation behind the Hub was not its interest in freelancers or individual artists per se, but in the reframing of the health and resilience of local cultural ecology as a responsibility in common. As a representative explained: 'We had to ... agree that we were going to collectively work to support the artists in our community, and that that was a shared commitment.' The outcome of this approach was not just the support of artists in need, but a reflexive reconfiguration of the local cultural ecology itself that cut across pre-existing hierarchies and divisions to deliver a collective responsibility to sector sustainability. The Hub's logic was an inversion of Dowden's 'crown jewels' paradigm (Dowden, 2020) (see Chapter 1), which aimed to shore up the cultural sector by channelling money to its most high-profile institutions; the Hub exploited the social and cultural capital of its most prominent organisations to release resource and support for the sector's most vulnerable stakeholders. As a member explained:

> If 70 per cent of our workforce is working on a freelance basis, it's all very well for us to look after the infrastructure, but if the freelancers aren't there to make the work, then we have no way of populating that infrastructure with culture .... Every part of our ecology relies on every other part of our ecology.

By contrast, the SCPP is a network of cultural sector stakeholders established before the pandemic. An attempt to address what was described as a 'fragmented' local cultural sector, the partnership was established in 2019 as a strategic body for culture, linking cultural organisations such as The Lowry and Walk the Plank with corporate partners MediaCityUK and the Peel Group. Led by a dedicated partnership manager and chaired by Salford's elected city mayor, the partnership was described as a 'connective tissue' for the local cultural ecology, linking the diverse interests of its partner organisations through a values-led commitment to people and place. Named after Salford City Council's motto in Latin, 'let the welfare of the people be the highest law', the partnership's cultural strategy, *Suprema Lex*, reflects these ambitions, committing partner organisations to 'a vibrant and sustainable creative ecology in which experimentation, collaboration and culture are the raw materials for change-making with Salford's people and in Salford's places' (SCPP, 2020, p.6).

An important public document signalling collective intent, *Suprema Lex* is the result of careful partnership development between the project's members, articulating a responsibility to the city and its communities that cuts across sector and organisational boundaries. As a partner member explained: 'There were lots of voices, but I think we all listened to each other and realised the power of collaboration. ... It definitely came from the community, I think. There wasn't one person driving it.' It also offers a counterpoint to outcome-driven cultural development: by taking a deliberately broad and open view on what constitutes 'culture', including green and blue space and food heritage, *Suprema Lex* resembles the breadth of New Labour local cultural strategies in the early 2000s (see Gilmore, 2004) without the accompanying performance management framework. Linking the collective ambitions of the project's partners to the production of value(s) for Salford residents, the strategy also recognises inequalities of access and participation in the proposed benefits of creative economies, and the lack of inclusion for Salford communities, some of which neighbour the large creative cluster at MediaCityUK. As an interviewee observed, *Suprema Lex* provides a 'way for everybody to frame their thinking', eroding the 'invisible lines' between sectors, geographies and agendas within the city.

The strategy was launched less than two weeks before the first national lockdown. Intended as a roadmap for cultural programming and investment across the city, it was rapidly reframed as a set of shared principles to guide the emergency decision-making of SCPP members. The success of this adaptability is most visible in the context of Salford Quays. Part-owned by the Peel Group and home to MediaCityUK, the Imperial War Museum North and The Lowry, the Quays has long been an important pillar in local development, implanting culture and creative industries in the place of the Quays' former role as one of the busiest docks in the north of England. First singled out for redevelopment in 1985, the district council's most recent plan for statutory development (Salford City Council, 2017) continues to identify the Quays as a key site for inward investment and an essential component of the city's green infrastructure and recreational offer. Described by a district council economist as a 'place-based sector', the Quays was particularly vulnerable to the layered impacts of the pandemic as the visitor economy faltered and office workers in the large media and creative industries cluster stayed home. Additionally, the site has not always been accessible to city residents. Bordered by areas of high deprivation, social and economic barriers have historically limited access to the site's cultural assets and outdoor space, while, as a representative for a Quays-based cultural organisation explained, funding relationships with GMCA have incentivised collaboration with partners in other districts in ways that have arguably disadvantaged Salford audiences.

Two projects indicate the role of the partnership and *Suprema Lex* in addressing these challenges. *Box on the Docks* sought to offer support for local artists by driving up footfall to the Quays. Led by the commercial partner MediaCityUK, the project commissioned artists to design self-contained outdoor dining spaces for safe, socially distanced use by Quays' hospitality tenants while their premises remained closed. As a representative explained, the relationships established by SCPP were essential to the project, facilitating access to cultural networks that allowed them to work with local artists for the first time, and providing necessary knowledges about how to commission, contract and collaborate with creative workers. As they note: 'I took lots of guidance from them on, like, the correct fee to pay somebody, making sure that the work was paid for, how we contract artists …. I learned a lot through that process.'

A second project, *Mystery Bird*, was a light and sound installation that travelled on the back of a flatbed truck to the streets and estates of Salford neighbourhoods. The project was led by Quays Culture, the organisation responsible for public arts engagement at the Quays, including free-to-access outdoor events such as the annual *Lightwaves* light festival. As the representative noted, the pandemic presented an opportunity to 'kind of blow that all apart', positioning *Suprema Lex* as a framework which looked beyond the geographical boundary of the Quays and found new ways to bring accessible art out to communities, in line with the policy's commitment to putting 'people at the centre' (SCPP, 2020, pp.20–21) of cultural planning and delivery. While Quays Culture had long been concerned with 'audiences that might never have felt that Salford Quays was for them', it took the pandemic to create the impetus to recalibrate audience development and take arts investment out to residents within their neighbourhoods.

Discussion

These examples demonstrate creative local responses to the varied impacts of the pandemic and the ways in which they map onto local and regional characteristics of place, including people, networks, geographies and policies. They also illustrate the ways in which the pandemic made visible otherwise implicit interdependencies that characterise cultural ecologies and point towards the longer-term implications of the pandemic for the regional ecosystem. Following Peter Haas, the networks considered above indicate the significant presence and influence of 'epistemic communities', defined as: 'a network of professionals with recognised expertise and competence in a particular domain and an authoritative claim to policy-relevant knowledge within that domain or issue-area' (Haas, 1992, p.3).

As Haas notes, in contrast to national level policy analysis, the framework of epistemic communities is preoccupied with human agency, 'articulating the cause-and-effect relationships of complex problems' (1992, p.2). The effects of the pandemic galvanised epistemic governance within GM, creating vehicles such as the GM Arts Hub and activating the principles of *Suprema Lex* and the SCPP in bringing local expertise to inform decision-making and create place-based responses which aimed to overcome the increased precarity of creative workers and the entrenched issues of accessibility within the city-region.

The attributes of epistemic communities matter not only in sharing expertise within relational networks (as is described in Chapter 6 in the case of Northern Ireland) but also in attracting further resources, such as the CRF. Analysis of Rounds One and Two of the CRF shows that of the grants distributed up until April 2021, the GM city-region dominated the broader north-west, receiving 60 per cent of all funds awarded to the region (Barker *et al.*, 2021). As interviewees in local and regional government explained, this success was not a coincidence. Rather, significant, coordinated attention was turned towards maximising funding for the region. As a representative for MCC explained: 'ahead of every round of CRF we organised webinars for our cultural organisations in the city to give them advice on how to apply and what to apply for ... they were targeted mainly at small, independent organisations which may have never applied for Arts Council funding before.' We saw these efforts repeated across local authorities, with sector-led bodies such as the GM Arts Hub and the Manchester-based Cultural Leaders Group undertaking similar work. Distributed across 175 organisations, almost 75 per cent of funds awarded to the region went to organisations based in Manchester, of which over 25 per cent comprised capital for building projects, including £21m for the flagship Factory venue alone. Some organisations also accessed public funds for the first time, with 75 per cent of funds to the city centre going to organisations that were not regularly funded by Arts Council England through their NPOs.

More broadly, however, recovery funding followed where funding had gone before, with twenty-nine of forty-one NPOs and twenty-five of thirty-five GM Culture Fund organisations receiving awards from the first two rounds (Walmsley *et al.*, 2022, p.3), with this pattern represented more broadly across England (see Figure 9.3). To some extent, this analysis indicates the presence (or absence) of existing arts and cultural infrastructure, and the efficacy of this national policy in bringing funds to areas and organisations in need. It also highlights the realities of the 'pecking order' identified by Banks and O'Connor (2021), with resources channelled to organisations with the highest levels of cultural, political and

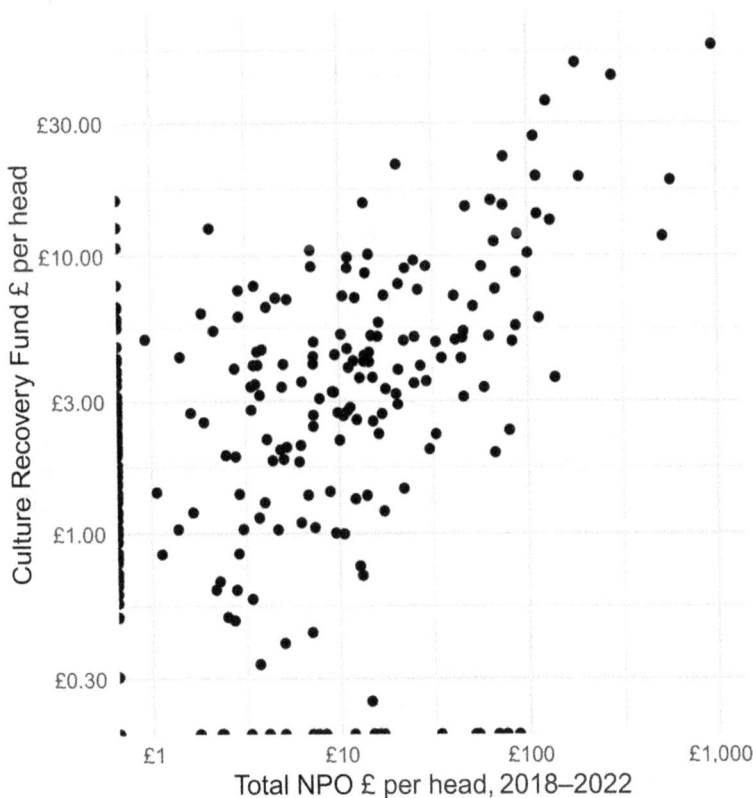

Figure 9.3 Relationship between Arts Council England funding to National Portfolio Organisations (NPOs) and Culture Recovery Fund, in each English local authority

economic capital. The establishment and privileging of knowledge networks within places – in this case Greater Manchester and, particularly, Manchester itself – has been critical in promoting the sector regionally and supporting the local ecosystem during the pandemic. These conditions also indicate a correlation between epistemic communities and the reproduction of structural, place-based inequalities.

Our case studies illustrate the ways in which sector response during the pandemic might be seen to disrupt this equilibrium and the possibility of longer-term change in the epistemic registers that structure and inform cultural policy and ecologies at the regional level. As Zygmunt Bauman notes, community is always a strategic discourse of inclusion and exclusion, offering visibility and agency to its members while making epistemological, if not actual, enemies of those on the outside (2006, p. 14). The projects considered above trouble the long-standing logics, networks and values that have historically determined thresholds of inclusion and exclusion in GM's epistemic communities. Operating as an arm's-length body for culture within its own district, SCPP brings together organisations such as the outdoor arts company Walk the Plank, whose thirty years of practice can be linked to the legacy of the British alternative theatre movement and the counter-cultural ambitions of the 1960s and 1970s, and the Peel Group, one of the region's most prominent property developers. Where contemporary policy contexts can often be characterised by economic priorities that dictate culture's value and significance (Throsby, 2010), SCPP makes explicit the relational and interdependent qualities of cultural policy to bring different value systems together by inviting stakeholders from across the local cultural ecosystem into the same room. This opens up the range of perspectives on how culture is understood and managed in the district, positioning policy as a responsive, dynamic outcome of the partnership itself. As a member noted: 'everyone seems to have a voice at the table … it feels democratic in that way to me … it feels supportive'. The GM Arts Hub, similarly, sought to extend local epistemic boundaries by repositioning cultural workers as stakeholders in the health and survival of the cultural ecosystem. Another member explained that breaking down competitive barriers between organisations was key to increasing the representation of artists within the decision-making processes of the Hub and Hub members:

> By visibly building better collaborative relationships between the organisations in the city-region it created better opportunities for all of the artists … to be supported properly, because they could have honest conversations about what they needed and whether they were getting their needs met or not.

In both cases, these projects extended the practices of inclusion and representation that challenge or complicate the 'normative behaviours' that Haas (1992) suggests are characteristic of epistemic communities and their approach to managing change: while epistemic communities are usually legitimised through the training, prestige and reputation of their members, here the reputations of GM epistemic communities are being used to authorise new discourses in value, decision-making and policy.

The experiences of our interviewees suggest the pandemic facilitated, or perhaps more aptly wrenched, a dynamic reconsideration of values and productivity relationships across the local ecosystem. The GM Artist Hub explicitly promoted an interconnected view of cultural sector activity, positioning a commitment to collective responsibility as a barrier to entry for the project's partners. In contrast to the discrete organisational agendas that were characteristic of the region's cultural ecology prior to the pandemic, the Hub positions the support and welfare of independent artists and freelance workers as a legitimate outcome of organisational activity. More broadly, this shift echoes Holden's framing of the cultural sector as a 'cycle of regeneration' (Holden, 2015, p.27), in which the outcomes of investment are not lost but are recirculated within the wider cultural ecosystem.

SCPP might be allied with similar developments. As a representative for MediaCityUK observed, *Box on the Docks* provided 'proof of concept' to corporate partners that investment in culture could be mutually beneficial. More specifically, it traced these benefits onto place, as a demonstration case which links financial investment from private partners with positive outcomes for city residents. As the interviewee observed: 'There's a realisation from developers – property developers – that actually the days have gone where you can just rent an office without stuff happening in the actual place.' Notably, what this project proposes is a multi-valent interpretation of value that promotes simultaneous benefit for corporate investors, city residents, artists and the wider cultural ecology as a principle of future policy development. Though these developments emerged in specific response to the conditions of the pandemic, the prominence of the cultural sector in the city-region indicates a potential for significant, sustainable change. As an interviewee with responsibility for city-centre development observed: 'the cultural sector very much leads itself and our job is to support it in the way that they want to be supported'. These newly configured communities, then, have the potential to build on the strength of the cultural sector prior to the pandemic to devise a future for local cultural policy that remains attentive to the relationships considered here.

Conclusion

Taking a qualitative ecosystems approach to the exceptional case of GM (Dunn and Gilmore, 2021), this chapter has described how the pandemic lockdown restrictions and the abrupt end they brought to business as normal in GM shifted the balance of power from national policy responses of the central government in England, characterised by indecision and by inadequate consideration of the precarious situation of the freelance creative and cultural workforce, to the local epistemic communities involved in cultural programming, resource allocation and strategic decision-making. Through rich, in-depth qualitative research with policy practitioners, political representatives and arts and cultural leaders which drew on the collaboration of research partners, we have identified the significance of approaches that recognise creative and cultural ecosystems and their complexities as a heuristic framework through which to identify interdependency. Importantly, the relational dynamics of ecosystems revealed by taking this approach, along-side this protracted period of uncertainty, facilitated conditions for experimentation, unlikely new allegiances and collective action. They also foregrounded values-led responses which, given the economic instability created by the pandemic, shifted policy rationales from economic and private interest to the cultural sector's role as a public service, supporting local communities through acts of care and the animation of Covid-safe public spaces and individual creative practitioners with opportunities for employment and subsidy.

The cultural networks and partnerships extant in our case study ecosystem were facilitated by strong political buy-in from a predominantly left-wing complex of local and city-regional government, familiar with narrative discourse on both economic and social returns of arts and cultural investment and mobilised by the challenges of the pandemic to seek collective solutions that could demonstrate further value to both public and private interests. These were represented by local authority policy attachments aimed at addressing not just cultural matters but also economic deprivation, isolation and social exclusion, the strategic aims of national funding bodies such as Arts Council England, whose job it was to effectively distribute public funds to sustain the sector through the crisis, and also the corporate interests of major asset holders and property developers, alongside private companies within the creative industries, events, hospitality and night-time economies.

We argue that the presence of epistemic communities and their connectivity through local partnerships, hubs and networks allowed policy innovations attempting to address existing problems which were surfaced by the pandemic. These included the contingency of creative and cultural production on freelance workers, with their attendant lack of protection for labour and economy, and the inherent problem within arts audience development created by the expectation that audiences should overcome spatial, social and economic barriers by leaving their neighbourhoods to attend dedicated flagship buildings. We also argue that the presence of these networks of expertise and their support by local government aided increased resource development as CRFs were successfully attracted to the city-region, albeit disproportionately favouring Manchester's city centre. Furthermore, we identify how the involvement of corporate partners within some of these partnerships has led to the sharing of new practices and knowledges that may inform future strategic collaboration, overturning the lack of attention historically given by landlords and property owners to the potential of cultural animation and inclusive place-making for mutual benefit to people and place.

There are caveats and limitations to these observations, however. The return to 'normal' operating conditions after the lifting
of restrictions in July 2021 has seen an exhausted and somewhat
traumatised cultural sector attempting to sustain these innovations
alongside the 'digital pivot' and 'pivot to the civic' (Walmsley *et al.*,
2022), amid continued uncertainties over audience return and
retention, turmoil in national government and immanent economic
recession, never mind global concerns of climate change, food
security and international diplomatic relations. Further challenges
remain both locally and national, such as the entrenched structural
inequalities of the creative and cultural sector (Brook, O'Brien and
Taylor, 2020; Comunian and England, 2020), an overreliance on
'trickle down' and the 'gravitational pull' of elite institutions and
their presence (and absence) in cities and towns which continued to
skew arts investment even during the pandemic (Johnson, Gilmore
and Dunn, 2021; see also Chapter 2). Likewise, public–private
partnerships for cultural and high-street recovery require caution as
identified by the critics of cultural policy instrumentalisation (e.g.
Gray, 2007; McGuigan, 2009; Belfiore, 2020), as well as careful
regulation and intervention from local governance to ensure that
social responsibility rather than profit is the primary motivation
for participation and to avoid the pitfalls of gentrification and
social exclusion. These are continuing challenges for cultural policy locally, nationally and internationally as post-pandemic place-
based approaches aim to maximise the benefits of cultural funding
for broader regeneration and economic recovery, and arts and cultural organisations hope to find sustainable ways to plug income
gaps and innovate their business models. Such approaches can, we
argue, learn valuable policy lessons from the exceptional case of
GM and the relations of its creative and cultural ecosystem.

References

Banks, M. and O'Connor, J. 2021. 'A plague upon your howling': art and
    culture in the viral emergency. *Cultural Trends*. 30(1), pp.3–18.
Barker, V. 2019. The democratic development potential of a cultural ecosys-
    tem approach. *Journal of Law, Social Justice and Global Development*.
    Issue 24, pp.86–99.

Barker, V., Gilmore, A., Dunn, B. and Taylor, M. 2021. *When policy meets place: 'Levelling Up' and the creative and cultural industries.* [Online]. London: Creative Industries Policy and Evidence Centre. [Accessed 1 June 2023]. Available from: www.pec.ac.uk/blog/when-policy-meets-place

Bauman, Z. 2006. *Community: seeking safety in an insecure world.* Cambridge: Polity Press.

Belfiore, E. 2020. Whose cultural value? Representation, power and creative industries. *International Journal of Cultural Policy.* 26(3), pp.383–397.

Brook, O., O'Brien, D. and Taylor, M. 2020. *Culture is bad for you.* Manchester: Manchester University Press.

Bury Council. 2020. *Bury Town of Culture 2021.* [Online]. [Accessed 1 June 2023]. Available from: https://web.archive.org/web/20210816100614/https://www.bury.gov.uk/townofculture

Carter, H. 2003. Gritty City wins the boho crown. *The Guardian.* [Online]. 26 May. [Accessed 1 June 2023]. Available from: www.theguardian.com/uk/2003/may/26/communities.arts

Comunian, R. and England, L. 2020. Creative and cultural work without filters: Covid-19 and exposed precarity in the creative economy. *Cultural Trends.* 29(2), pp.112–128.

Cultural Heritage in Action. 2022. *How culture paid for the pandemic.* [Online]. [Accessed 1 June 2023]. Available from: https://culturalheritageinaction.eu/how-culture-paid-for-the-pandemic/

Department for Business, Energy and Industrial Strategy (BEIS) and Ministry for Housing Community and Local Government (HCLG). 2019. *Greater Manchester Local Industrial Strategy, 13 June 2019.* [Online]. [Accessed 1 June 2023]. Available from: www.gov.uk/government/publications/greater-manchester-local-industrial-strategy

Dowden, O. 2020. *Dowden: we will protect 'crown jewels' of UK culture.* [Online]. [Accessed 1 June 2023]. Available from: www.dailymotion.com/video/x7uun4a

Dunn, B. and Gilmore, A. 2021. *Place matters: Greater Manchester, culture and 'levelling up'.* [Online]. Leeds: Centre for Cultural Value. [Accessed 1 June 2023]. Available from: www.culturehive.co.uk/CVIresources/place-matters-greater-manchester-culture-and-levelling-up/

Florida, R. 2017. *The new urban crisis: gentrification, housing bubbles, growing inequality, and what we can do about it.* London: Oneworld Publications.

Gilmore, A. 2004. Local cultural strategies: a strategic review. *Cultural Trends.* 13(3), pp.3–32.

Gilmore, A. and Bulaitis, Z. 2023. Devolved responsibility: English regional creative industries policy and local industrial strategies. In: Durrer, V., Abigail Gilmore, A., Jancovich, L. and Stevenson, D. eds. *Cultural policy is local: understanding cultural policy as situated practice.* London: Palgrave Macmillan, pp. 139–166.

Greater Manchester Artist Hub. n.d. *Welcome to GM Artist Hub.* [Online]. [Accessed 1 June 2023]. Available from: www.gm-artisthub.co.uk/

Greater Manchester Combined Authority (GMCA). 2020a *GMCA culture funding 2020 onwards.* [Online]. [Accessed 1 June 2023]. Available from: https://democracy.greatermanchester-ca.gov.uk/documents/s1771/GMCA

Greater Manchester Combined Authority (GMCA). 2020b. *A recovery plan for culture in Greater Manchester.* [Online]. [Accessed 1 June 2023]. Available from: https://democracy.greatermanchester-ca.gov.uk/documents/s9535/9

Gray, C. 2007. Commodification and instrumentality in cultural policy. *International Journal of Cultural Policy.* 13(2), pp.203–215.

Haas, P.M. 1992. Introduction: epistemic communities and international policy coordination. *International Organization.* 46(1), pp.1–35.

Holden, J. 2015. *The ecology of culture: a report commissioned by the Arts and Humanities Research Council's Cultural Value Project.* [Online]. Swindon: Arts and Humanities Research Council. [Accessed 1 June 2023]. Available from: https://publicartonline.org.uk/downloads/news/AHRC%20Ecology%20of%20Culture.pdf

Jenkins, S. 2015. The secret negotiations to restore Manchester to greatness. *The Guardian.* [Online]. 12 February. [Accessed 30 August 2022]. Available from: www.theguardian.com/uk-news/2015/feb/12/secret-negotiations-restore-manchester-greatness

Johnson, R., Gilmore, A. and Dunn, B. 2021. *Working with and supporting cultural organisations: local cultural policies and Newton's law of cultural funding.* [Online]. Leeds: Centre for Cultural Value. [Accessed 1 June 2023]. Available from: www.culturehive.co.uk/CVIresources/working-with-and-supporting-cultural-organisations-local-cultural-policies-and-newtons-law-of-cultural-funding/

Localis. 2009. *Can localism deliver? Lessons from Manchester.* [Online]. [Accessed 30 August 2022]. Available at: www.localis.org.uk/research/can-localism-deliver/

McGuigan, J. 2009. Doing a Florida thing: the creative class thesis and cultural policy. *International Journal of Cultural Policy.* 15(3), pp.291–300.

Manchester City Council. 2016. *Manchester's cultural ambition 2016–2026.* [Online]. [Accessed 1 June 2023]. Available from: www.manchester.gov.uk/download/downloads/id/25262/manchester_cultural_ambition.pdf

Manchester International Festival. (2020). *MIF drop in for artists and freelance creatives.* [Online]. [Accessed 11 January 2024]. Available from: https://factoryinternational.org/mif-drop-in-artists-freelance-creatives/

Osborne, G. 2014. *Chancellor: 'we need a Northern powerhouse'.* [Online]. London: The Stationery Office. [Accessed 30 August 2022]. Available from: www.gov.uk/government/speeches/chancellor-we-need-a-northern-powerhouse

Pasikowska-Schnass, M. 2019. *Employment in the creative and cultural sectors*. [Online]. [Accessed 30 August 2022]. Available from: www.europarl.europa.eu/RegData/etudes/BRIE/2019/642264/EPRS_BRI(2019)642264_EN.pdf

Salford City Council. 2017. *Draft local plan: economic development*. [Online]. [Accessed 30 August 2022]. Available from: www.salford.gov.uk/planning-building-and-regeneration/planning-policies/local-planning-policy/salfords-development-plan/salford-local-plan/part-one-salford-local-plan/draft-local-plan-2016-17/

Salford Culture and Place Partnership (SCPP). (2020) *Suprema Lex: the Strategy for Culture, Creativity and Place in Salford*. [Online]. [Accessed 30 August 2022]. Available at: www.supremalex.co.uk/download

Siepel, J., Velez-Ospina, J., Camerani, R., Bloom, M., Masucci, M. and Casadei, P. 2021. *Creative Radar 2021: the impact of COVID-19 on the UK's creative industries*. [Online]. London: Creative Industries Policy and Evidence Centre. [Accessed 30 August 2022]. Available from: https://pec.ac.uk/research-reports/creative-radar-2021-the-impact-of-covid-19-on-the-uks-creative-industries

Tether, B. (2022). *Creative clusters and sparse spaces: the geographies of Manchester's creative industries. Discussion paper*. London: Creative Industries Policy and Evidence Centre.

Throsby, D. 2010. *The economics of cultural policy*. Cambridge: Cambridge University Press.

Walmsley, B., Gilmore, A., O'Brien, D. and Torreggiani, A. eds. 2022. *Culture in crisis: impacts of Covid-19 on the UK cultural sector and where we go from here*. Leeds: Centre for Cultural Value.

Conclusion: disruption and continuity in the cultural industries: from pandemic culture to an endemic crisis?

Dave O'Brien, Abigail Gilmore and Ben Walmsley

Introduction

We began this book noting that, even before the pandemic, a series of long-standing problems confronted cultural policy and the cultural sector in the UK. Within national policy, there has been a consistently low level of understanding about how differently individual parts of what are understood as 'creative industries' operate (House of Lords, 2023). This problem is accentuated in the case of the arts and culture; there is a distance between the policy rhetoric about the sector's economic and cultural importance and the reality of precarious workers and undervalued, precarious organisations (Banks and O'Connor, 2017; Comunian and England, 2020).

Audience development and widening participation have equally long-standing issues. Government data shows static levels of engagement with the arts over almost two decades, irrespective of government policy (DCMS, 2020). Academic analysis, of both survey and ticketing data, demonstrates that although there are high levels of engagement and participation in 'everyday' cultural activities (Miles and Gibson, 2016, Taylor, 2016; Gilmore, 2017; Belfiore and Gibson, 2019), audiences for more formal types of culture were both a minority, and unrepresentative, of the wider population (Hanquinet, O'Brien and Taylor, 2019; Brook, O'Brien and Taylor, 2020).

These findings indicate that the conditions for cultural and creative production and consumption can be characterised by structural *continuity* rather than rupture or shift. This is a theme we have stressed throughout this book, and the overarching and dominant theme has been *continuity*. Of course, the pandemic was hugely disruptive and we hope our book has also clearly demonstrated that impact. Yet throughout the range of case studies, national and regional analysis, sub-sectoral and artform-specific discussions, and various methodological approaches, we have consistently foregrounded the ongoing impact of inequalities in the cultural sector. Rather than being products or consequences of 2020, these trends and structures were exacerbated, rather than created, by the pandemic.

Our concluding chapter develops this theme. At the same time, we are also keen to reflect on the impact of our findings for cultural policy researchers. Most notably, we conclude with reflections not only considering the impact of the pandemic on future research subjects, but also on the conditions for cultural policy knowledge production and research itself.

Understanding the pandemic in a global context

There is a clear consensus within research, irrespective of the national context, of the impact of the coronavirus pandemic on creative and cultural production and consumption. The sudden halt to almost all activities, whether international touring or local participation, meant the arts, cultural and creative industries were among the worst-affected sectors. The 2022 UNESCO report on *Culture in times of COVID-19* finds that the global cultural sector's Gross Value Added fell by 25 per cent in 2020. This fall was accompanied by widespread job losses estimated at 10 million, comparable in its severity to sectors such as accommodation and catering (UNESCO, 2022).

The impact of COVID-19 on cultural workers, particularly the freelance and self-employed, cannot be understated. Many saw their income sources disappear rapidly and struggled to access often ill-targeted public wage compensation (Dümcke, 2021; Joffe, 2020; Johnson, 2020; Pacella, Luckman and O'Connor, 2021; Wright, 2020). However, the effects of the pandemic were unevenly distributed. The narrative of absolute market failure does not capture the nuances of impacts that were differentiated by sector, occupational status and socio-economic group (as is discussed in Chapter 2 in this volume with respect to the UK). While some sub-sectors were more exposed than others, they also appear to have received more public support. The sub-sectors of film and television, museums and galleries, performing arts and music appear to have been most targeted by policy interventions both globally and in the UK specifically (IDEA Consult *et al.*, 2021; Siepel *et al.*, 2021).

The state support offered during the crisis, through national and regional policy responses, did protect the cultural and creative sectors. Potentially huge levels of business failure were halted and the capacity for some to continue to invest and employ during the pandemic was protected. The OECD (2022) describes state policy interventions as a 'lifeline' for the sector, with over 85 per cent of creative businesses in the UK receiving governmental support. Globally, most countries offered some measure of intervention for cultural and creative industries, with financial support being the most prevalent form: 82 per cent of all targeted arts and cultural policies were economic (IDEA Consult *et al.*, 2021). The most common among these were emergency relief grants and loans targeting cultural organisations and workers.

The dominance of an *economic* response, the speed and quantity of funding distributed, and the rhetoric accompanying these rescue packages gives some indication that economic impacts are still a dominant way that policy thinks about the sector. Indeed, a European Commission report recommended that the learning from the pandemic for cultural policy should include the introduction of more non-economic measures to balance out the dominance of economic frameworks (IDEA Consult *et al.*, 2021, p.5).

There were however important distinctions, signalling different ideological approaches and policy attachments to culture, and confirming the sense that the COVID-19 crisis illuminates how culture is thought about, valued and advocated for, as well as the grounds on which governments and policy actors are prepared to offer support (Banks and O'Connor, 2021; Comunian and England, 2021). For example, in Germany, the arts, creative and cultural industries were offered immediate and sector-specific support, being publicly described as 'indispensable' and 'fundamental' to democratic societies (Dümcke, 2021, p.20). Argentinian policy addressed culture through notions of care, as 'a caring agent in the midst of a crisis, not just as a sector of the economy or as entertainment' (Serafini and Novosel, 2021, p.60). By contrast, the notion of culture as 'just … entertainment' seemed prevalent in African countries such as Uganda and Kenya, resulting in an imbalance of attention towards the commercial cultural and creative industries (TV, film, advertising, music and fashion) (Joffe, 2020, p.31). Meanwhile, in Australia, sector lobbyists framed arts and culture primarily in economic terms, as an industry requiring investment, an approach that nonetheless 'failed to cut through to the government' when the need was greatest (Pacella, Luckman and O'Connor, 2021, p.42). The early international policy review from this project (Johnson, 2020) similarly uncovered different approaches for compensating artists. These included the application of Universal Basic Income (UBI) and social welfare models that support a need to revisit the UNESCO Recommendation on the Status of the Artist (UNESCO, 2022).

Across the globe, culture's position oscillated between economic and social good during the pandemic. These twin rationalities shaped state policy responses. Arts and culture were helping individuals and communities adapt to public health measures such as lockdowns at the same time as states addressed creative and cultural organisations as businesses.

According to an economic rationalist framing of culture, commonplace in cultural policy discourse but enhanced during the pandemic, we can see four types of relationship. These fit the four types first identified by Potts and Cunningham (2008): welfare, competition, growth and innovation. The first, welfare, assumes these sectors consume more economic resources than they produce and so need subsidy to be properly maintained, justified by the policy rationale of their utility to the welfare of society. The second, the competition model, assumes no cultural exceptionalism for the creative economy and that creative and cultural sectors are like all others. Thus, they require no special policy treatment and must jostle for resources with other activities. In this scenario, we would expect there to be no culture-specific recovery strategies: if the sector shrinks or changes as a result then this is for the market to decide.

The third model sees cultural and creative industries as drivers of growth across the broader economy, stimulating new ideas and growth to other sectors, a spillover of value that also rationalises culture's place in recovery plans and regeneration programmes.

The final, innovation, pitches creative and cultural industries at the heart of industrial strategy. This idea is often used in advocacy for the sector's inclusion in economic policy, for example in the 2017 Independent Sector Review of the Creative Industries and their significance to the UK Industrial Strategy (Gilmore and Bulaitis, 2023). Given the halting of economies-as-usual during the pandemic, it is unsurprising that this final assumption informed few state policy responses to the pandemic.

The *exceptionalism* of culture and its welfare utility were important tools for advocacy within policy discourses. As is articulated above in the empirical chapters of this book, evidence of this utility was increasingly articulated within communities in lockdown, exemplified by small and large organisations through their increased civic missions, and drawn into local government recovery plans and third sector activities.

The welfare utility aspirations of the devolved nations in the UK, such as the Future Wellbeing Commission of Wales, reflects those of supranational bodies like UNESCO and OECD which similarly aspire to protect sectors under threat of exploitation and automation and recognise their social and cultural value (OECD, 2022). However, as a policy instrument for responding to the pandemic, the jury is still out on the value of UBI approaches, both in general and when exceptionally applied for creatives.

Looking at the introduction of UBI in Ireland, Hayes (2022) argues that this approach neglects the endemic precarity and gig economies within the sector, serving instead 'a neoliberal register' (Hayes, 2022, p.14). This obscures the reasons why these inequalities exist in the first place, while emphasising the potential for economic exploitation of cultural production as a sole reason to support it. Likewise, O'Connor (2022) rails against such economic rationalism, which reduces the role of arts and culture only to utility and suggests Covid as the primary lever for state support for the arts. Rather, for O'Connor (2022) it is the precarious and irregular nature of creative work which is the salient fact that needs to be addressed by policy interventions. He warns against the danger that UBI offers a solution of small statism, prompting further reduction in investment more broadly in welfare infrastructure (O'Connor, 2022).

Economic rationality for cultural sector support also fails to provide suitable explanations for distinctions founded in political geography. As this brief review, and previous chapters of the book, make clear, policy responses at national and local levels were distinct and distinctive. Differing types of response reflect nation-states with discrete socio-cultural histories and identities, power relations and discursive practices, which shape the epistemic communities (Haas, 1992) who make decisions about cultural investment and policies.

This point is manifest in the emergence of new networks and partnerships during the crisis, another consistent theme throughout the book. These new allegiances promoted sharing of value frameworks which move beyond economic rationalism and create spaces for new policy formulation that are collaborative and experimental, in the face of adversity and crisis. Thus, we see a story of divergence from the common economic rationales for intervening and supporting the creative industries during the pandemic towards more generative and equitable value creation and exchange.

Divergence and convergence across the cultural sector

The distinctions and commonalities at the international level of policy responses (and the justifications underpinning them) were mirrored also across the UK. Our case studies note the nuances across the constituent nations of the UK, not only in terms of economic rationality but also in terms of longer-standing cultural policy distinctiveness and variation. This divergence and convergence can be explored by thinking critically about the cultural and creative industries paradigm (Casey and O'Brien, 2020) and its attendant flaws and misconceptions as a framework for research in this area. Writing at the end of a hugely successful decade for the UK's creative sector, McRobbie (2011) speculates as to the usefulness of the creative industries concept and its ballooning significance in the New Labour era. Her analysis calls for a 're-differentiated' (2016, p. 937) understanding of specific cultural and creative sectors and sub-sectors.

Our analysis has followed, and reinforced, this theoretical starting point. Siepel *et al.*'s (2021) study of creative businesses in the

UK suggests fewer firms than expected stopped trading between 2020 and 2021, and many were actually able to increase investment in research and development (66 per cent) and hire more employees (18 per cent) (Siepel *et al.*, 2021, p.4). Yet this overall analysis also recognises considerable sub-sectoral distinctiveness. We knew from the outset of the research project that the performing arts, for example, would be impacted in a fundamentally different way from museums and galleries; that festivals would have to pivot in a very different way from the screen industries; that freelancers working across different sub-sectors would have markedly different experiences in each one and possibly need to migrate from one to the other. Indeed, we saw these themes richly illustrated in the divergent findings across Chapters 5 to 9. While the screen industries bounced back very quickly, indeed within several months, theatre and the wider performing arts sector struggled to recover its production rhythms and audiences well into 2022. Performing arts were then hit with the cost-of-living crisis, as well as the ongoing complications of the Conservative Government's approach to leaving the European Union (particularly for touring performers).

Inevitably, this divergent impact culminated in a significant number of freelance technical and production workers migrating from the performing arts to TV and film, leading to desperate outcries from theatre leaders such as Rufus Norris at the National Theatre who warned of a 'huge craft drain' in the sector (Hemley, 2022). The apparent 'boom' in the film and TV sector was not only in contrast to the struggles of performing arts; it also had direct consequences for the accelerating problems in the latter's labour market. For festivals, museums and galleries our analysis has discussed rapidly developing hybrid models that often led to slower modes of production and distribution; to 'glocal' models of audience development; and to deeper and even more activist modes of engagement. As we reflect back on these times, there is evidence of a divergence between differing parts of the cultural and creative sector. As many festivals, museums, galleries and libraries seek to embed hybrid modes of production into their long-term planning and business models, performing arts and media companies resolutely continue their struggle to re-establish the pre-pandemic status quo, particularly in terms of relationships with audiences and, in person, modes of consumption. The 're-differentiation' discussed by McRobbie (2016) is not only an issue for analysis: it has consequences for the politics of the arts and cultural policy itself.

Alongside this divergence, there were a number of further trends across the sector. The most notable of these was a renewed sense of collegiality and collaboration. This is twofold. In the first instance were the practices of collaboration between freelancers and organisations, between organisations themselves (both on a regional and artform level), between cultural leaders, between cultural funders, and between policy-makers and academics. The examples here are best illustrated by the early weeks of the pandemic, where a palpable sense of collective endeavour and of collegial care and support drove much of the rhetoric and some of the activities constituting the sector's response to the impact of lockdowns.

Secondly, we have charted the *recognition* of collegiality and collaboration as vital to the sector. This recognition in some ways reflects failures of those early responses, as freelance workers were marginalised and smaller organisations struggled with both new business models, appeals for funding and state support schemes such as furlough. Much of our fieldwork, conducted in 2020–2021, showed evidence of the high prominence given to the need for future collaborative practice. However, by 2023, there were more signs of 'business as usual' in the arts, exacerbated by the increased competition for more sustained resources, such as the membership of the national Arts Council England portfolio. This quest for a return to pre-pandemic norms represents a missed opportunity to establish a healthier ecology based on mutual support, fair pay, more regenerative modes of production engagement and greater diversity of cultural workers and audiences.

The pivot to civic and the need for leadership

Regarding this last point, we have repeatedly discussed in this book what we've called the 'pivot to civic'. This has been another point of convergence across the sector. Although the civic role of arts organisations had been a subject for cultural policy before the pandemic (e.g. Calouste Gulbenkian Foundation, 2017), 2020 brought it to the centre of thinking. Recognition and reinforcement of culture as a social good; the responsibilities of publicly funded institutions;

and the need for organisations to be relevant to their local, regional, national and even international communities (e.g. Lane, 2022) were all part of this discursive and practical shift.

These organisational realisations were perhaps long overdue, providing a wake-up call for radical change and for many in the sector, including academics and boards of trustees, to reconceptualise their notions of resilience, which our study reveals became associated more with collaborative networks than to the diversification of income streams. This in turn led many to question (or re-question) the growing future directions for the sector and the increasingly tense interrelationship between the arts and the wider cultural and creative industries.

Yet despite these moments of rethinking, our analysis has shown the wickedness of the problems facing culture in the UK. Here, even with the examples of new forms of best practice, the sector still needed, and continues to need, leaders willing not only to share and collaborate but to make substantive changes. Commentators have been mulling over the apparent crisis in cultural leadership since the beginning of the century (Hewison, 2004), acknowledging skills gaps and structural barriers to entry and progression, which combined with the #MeToo and Black Lives Matter movements highlighted a prevalence of white, male and all too often abusive leadership in the sector. Progress remains slow and cultural leadership and governance remains alarmingly 'male, pale and stale' (Clare, 2009, p.34).

Cultural leadership is too often overlooked in analysis of organisational success. It remains a topic that, given its significance to the strategic development of the sector and its research prevalence in other sectors, remains woefully under-explored and under-theorised for culture. Although many scholars have justifiably argued that we need to move beyond the sector's quasi cultish romanticisation of charismatic leaders and shift our focus from leaders to leader*ship*, leaders themselves are still key agents or blockers of change (Walmsley, 2019b). If the positive changes that the pandemic inspired, required and/or foreshadowed are to endure or be adequately addressed, then capable, strategic and representative leaders will be vital.

Collaborative models of leadership emerged to be particularly effective in a time of crisis. This was set against a more general context of calls for a shift away from charismatic and transformational leadership towards a more distributed and relational approach (Jancovich, 2015; Nisbett and Walmsley, 2016). Chapter 6 offers excellent examples, where collaborative models drove change in Northern Ireland's cultural sector at an unprecedented pace. The learning from the Northern Irish case is that change needs principles of mutual support, transparency and trust. These values are difficult to nurture and sustain in the much more demanding context for workers and audiences that the analysis in Chapters 2 and 3 has demonstrated.

Future audiences

The findings regarding audiences are especially crucial. Prior to the pandemic audience researchers had been calling for a more sustained focus on processes of audience engagement (Walmsley, 2019a) and for greater understanding of marginalised audience groups, such as working-class audiences (Barrett, 2022), d/Deaf, blind and neurodiverse audiences (Hadley, 2022) and audiences of colour (Conner, 2022; Novak-Leonard, 2022). The physical disappearance of audiences from arts and cultural venues during the pandemic focused minds and forced producers and organisations to radically rethink their relationships with audiences. As questions of relevance and community or civic engagement rose to the fore, processes of participation, co-production and co-creation were actively realised and pernicious barriers to access (especially for disabled audiences) were temporarily removed as production shifted online.

As we emerge from the pandemic, and as highlighted in Chapter 3, we are possibly witnessing a radical shift in audience behaviour and demographics. Families and younger audiences appear keen to attend cultural venues and older audiences remain more hesitant. This inevitably begs questions about cultural programming (and the poor theorisation of such) and about the sustainability of art forms such as classical ballet and opera that have long relied on older audiences.

Thanks to insights provided from our Cultural Participation Monitor, the pandemic taught us that audiences equate arts and culture with solace and wellbeing – especially outdoor arts and heritage activities. The Monitor also highlighted positive public perceptions about public funding for arts and culture and a growing propensity to donate. These findings have three important implications.

Firstly, they suggest that cultural policy and funding should prioritise investment in outdoor arts and heritage, especially since previous research has demonstrated that more representative audiences are attracted to these activities. This could offer a much-needed breakthrough for the apparent deadlock in the flagging audience development project that has failed to diversify UK audiences for over fifty years.

Secondly, our findings signal the need for cultural venues, producers and marketers to engage with audiences as artistic partners rather than transactional ticket-buyers. Audiences are hungry for high-quality cultural content and we would all benefit from them having a much greater voice and stake in our public cultural institutions. This observation has implications not only for cultural policy but also, and more urgently perhaps, for arts management and marketing.

Thirdly, the nuanced, timely and representative insights offered by a regular population survey proved the benefits of empirical audience research conducted by a team of specialists and integrated into a comprehensive mixed-methods analysis of the cultural sector. As we witness our national audience data being tendered out to commercial management consultants (Puffett, 2022), the urgency of open-source cultural sector data has never been more acute. This should serve as a rallying call to cultural funders and policy-makers as well as to the sector itself.

Where next for cultural policy scholarship?

The writing of history, and arguably all social science and humanities, has been one of debate on the explanations and the tools and epistemologies that provide them: what causes change, what mitigates it? In the context of crisis, this is even more fundamental but complicated by an urgent need for speedy answers to provide the rationale for mitigation. In our study, we have identified various longer-term trends that help to explain the severity of the impact of the pandemic on specific parts of the cultural sector and its workers. However, we leave open the exact balance between the specific decisions of individuals and organisations and longer-term structural trends.

To give a clear example, we know that inequalities in the workforce were present for decades before the pandemic (Brook *et al.*, 2023). We also know that audiences for state-funded art forms and institutions are drawn disproportionately from the older, professional middle-class segments of society (Bennett *et al.*, 2009; Hanquinet, O'Brien and Taylor, 2019). These structural characteristics of the arts workforce and of audiences were also identifiable in the demographics of those more likely to leave cultural jobs and more likely to be cautious about returning to in-person performances. In turn, these impacts of the pandemic have knock-on effects for a further lack of diversity for the arts and cultural workforce and question the sustainability of revenues generated from ticket sales and related conceptions of organisational resilience.

Teasing out the degree of impact to offer precise causal explanations is complex; this may be a key challenge for further cultural policy studies. What we *can* say with certainty is that the structural problems confronting arts and cultural organisations have certainly not been ameliorated by the pandemic, nor have any of the supposed new ways of working and innovative forms of delivery adopted during 2020 been particularly effective in addressing these wicked problems (Feder *et al.*, 2022), with the notable exception of greater accessibility offered by digital performances for disabled audiences.

This question of challenges for cultural policy leads to the concluding discussion of this collection and our research project. It is not, of course, the conclusion of research on the impact of the pandemic. COVID-19, as of 2023, has become endemic across the world. At the risk of an insensitive analogy, the issues our analysis has highlighted are seemingly endemic to the cultural sector.

Where does this leave cultural policy research? This question is twofold. In the first instance there is the question of academic labour and the sorts of partnerships needed to conduct responsive research at speed. In the UK, as universities face funding constraints and academics face worsening labour conditions, particularly at the early-career and entry stages to the profession, there are acute challenges for undertaking the sorts of cultural policy research discussed in this book. As academic workers are made more precarious, the sorts of skills and rich subject and field-specific knowledges required are increasingly under threat. Reinforcing capacity is a crucial task for both institutions and those who set the policy framework under which they work.

The question of the future for academics and their institutions is mirrored when we think of partnerships with organisations and practitioners in the cultural sector. A significant part of the success of our project, and the breadth of research approaches and perspectives in this book, was the positive and productive working relationships with the cultural sector. This included sector organisations, practitioners and consultants who act as researchers themselves. The impact of the pandemic will not only impact the sector's ability to deliver on its aims; it will also constrain the sector's capacity to know itself, and thus be responsive to long-term trends and immediate shocks. Research capacity here is essential, not only for the sorts of R&D required to deliver successful 'hits' (House of Lords, 2023) but also for the longer-term strategies of the organisations, practitioners and policy-makers complicit in such an exercise.

Secondly, there are the specific questions for cultural policy researchers. There are many obvious ones: international comparisons are crucial to thinking through the social, economic and cultural impacts of the pandemic on local, national and international cultural policies, as are mixed-methods and interdisciplinary approaches providing conceptual challenge to questions of rationalism, evidence and care. We have referenced some of the initial work here already in this conclusion. More generally, there is the problem of *innovation* in cultural policy research. As the question of explanations that opened this conclusion illustrates, cultural policy research may be trapped in a too-narrow focus on identifying the pandemic's role in changes to longer-term inequalities. Rather, the challenge for cultural policy research is to connect the pandemic to more existential questions, such as the role of policy in supporting the rights for all to access culture and creativity for a fairer and more just cultural sector, and indeed a better global society.

References

Banks, M. and O'Connor, J. 2021. 'A plague upon your howling': art and culture in the viral emergency. *Cultural Trends*. 30(1), pp.3–18.

Banks, M. and O'Connor, J. 2017. Inside the whale (and how to get out of there): moving on from two decades of creative industries research. *European Journal of Cultural Studies*. 20(6), pp.637–654.

Barrett, M. 2022. At what cost? Working class audiences and the price of culture. In: Reason, M., Conner, L., Johanson, K. and Walmsley, B. eds. *The Routledge companion to audiences and the performing arts.* London: Routledge, pp.159–176.

Belfiore, E. and Gibson, L. eds. 2019. *Histories of cultural participation, values and governance.* London: Palgrave Macmillan.

Bennett, T., Savage, M., Silva, E.B., Warde, A., Gayo-Cal, M. and Wright, D. 2009. *Culture, class, distinction.* London: Taylor and Francis.

Brook, O., O'Brien, D. and Taylor, M. 2020. *Culture is bad for you.* Manchester: Manchester University Press.

Brook, O., Miles, A., O'Brien, D. and Taylor, M., 2023. Social mobility and 'openness' in creative occupations since the 1970s. *Sociology.* 57(4), pp.789–810.

Calouste Gulbenkian Foundation. 2017. *Rethinking relationships: Inquiry into the Civic Role of Arts Organisations, Phase 1 report.* [Online]. London: Calouste Gulbenkian Foundation. Available from: https:// gulbenkian.pt/uk-branch/wp-content/uploads/sites/18/2017/08/Civic-Role-of-Arts-Phase-1-REPORT-lr-.pdf

Casey, E. and O'Brien, D. 2020. Sociology, sociology and the cultural and creative industries. *Sociology.* 54(3), pp.443–459.

Clare, R. 2009. Male, pale and stale: time to work for change. In: Cultural Leadership Programme, *Governance now: the hidden challenge of leadership.* London: Cultural Leadership Programme, pp.34–36.

Comunian, R. and England, L. 2021. Creative and cultural work without filters: Covid-19 and exposed precarity in the creative economy. *Cultural Trends.* 29(2), pp.112–128.

Conner, L. 2022. Disrupting the audience as monolith. In: Reason, M., Conner, L., Johanson, K. and Walmsley, B. eds. *The Routledge companion to audiences and the performing arts.* London: Routledge, pp.53–67.

Department for Digital, Culture, Media and Sport (DCMS). 2020. *Arts – Taking Part Survey 2019/20.* [Online]. [Accessed 27 January 2023]. Available from: www.gov.uk/government/statistics/taking-part-201920-arts/arts-taking-part-survey-201920

Dümcke, C. 2021. Five months under COVID-19 in the cultural sector: a German perspective. *Cultural Trends.* 30(1), pp.19–27.

Feder, T., McAndrew, S., O'Brien, D. and Taylor, M. 2022. Cultural consumption and Covid-19: evidence from the Taking Part and COVID-19 Cultural Participation Monitor surveys. *Leisure Studies.* 42(1), pp.1–18.

Gilmore, A. 2017. The park and the commons: vernacular spaces for everyday participation and cultural value. *Cultural Trends.* 26(1), pp.34–46.

Gilmore, A. and Bulaitis, Z. 2023. Devolved responsibility: English regional creative industries policy and local industrial strategies. In Gilmore, A., Stevenson, D., Durrer, V. and Jancovich, L. eds. *Cultural policy is local: understanding cultural policy as situated practice.* London: Palgrave Macmillan Ltd., pp.139–166.

Haas, P. 1992. Introduction: epistemic communities and international policy coordination. *International Organization*. 46(1), pp.1–35.

Hadley, B. 2022. A 'Universal Design' for audiences with disabilities? In: Reason, M., Conner, L., Johanson, K. and Walmsley, B. eds. *The Routledge companion to audiences and the performing arts*. London: Routledge, pp.177–189.

Hanquinet, L., O'Brien, D. and Taylor, M. 2019. The coming crisis of cultural engagement? Measurement, methods, and the nuances of niche activities. *Cultural Trends*. 28(2–3), pp.198–219.

Hayes, C. 2022. To BI or not to BI: against Artists' basic income. *Art Monthly* no. 457. [Online]. June. [Accessed 27 January 2023] Available from: www.artmonthly.co.uk/magazine/site/issue/june-2022

Hemley, M. 2022. Rufus Norris defends Netflix remarks as he warns of 'craft drain'. *The Stage*. 16 March. [no pagination].

Hewison, R. 2004. The crisis of cultural leadership in Britain. *International Journal of Cultural Policy*. 10, pp.157–166.

House of Lords. 2023. *At risk: our creative future. Communications and Digital Committee, 2nd report of session 2022–23*. [Online]. London: House of Lords. [Accessed 10 January 2024]. Available from: https://publications.parliament.uk/pa/ld5803/ldselect/ldcomm/125/125.pdf

IDEA Consult, Goethe-Institut, Amann, S. and Heinsius, J. 2021. *Research for CULT Committee – cultural and creative sectors in post-COVID-19 Europe: crisis effects and policy recommendations*. Brussels: European Parliament, Policy Department for Structural and Cohesion Policies.

Jancovich, L. 2015. Breaking down the fourth wall in arts management: the implications of engaging users in decision-making. *International Journal of Arts Management*. 18(1), pp.14–28.

Joffe, A. 2021. Covid-19 and the African cultural economy: an opportunity to reimagine and reinvigorate? *Cultural Trends*. 30(1), pp.28–39.

Johnson, R. 2020. *Policy report: social security for cultural practitioners*. Version 1, October 2020. Leeds: Centre for Cultural Value.

Lane, A. 2022. *The club on the edge of town: a pandemic memoir*. Bristol: Salamander Street Ltd.

McRobbie, A. 2011. Re-thinking creative economy as radical social enterprise. *Variant*. 41(Spring), pp.32–33.

McRobbie, A. 2016. Towards a sociology of fashion micro-enterprises: methods for creative economy research. *Sociology*. 50(5), pp.934–948.

Miles, A. and Gibson, L. 2016. Everyday participation and cultural value. *Cultural Trends*. 25(3), pp.151–157.

Novak-Leonard, J.L. 2022. The future of audiences and audiencing. In: Reason, M., Conner, L., Johanson, K. and Walmsley, B. eds. *The Routledge Companion to audiences and the performing arts*. London: Routledge, pp.83–95.

Nisbett, M. and Walmsley, B. 2016. The romanticization of charismatic leadership in the arts. *The Journal of Arts Management, Law, and Society*. 46(1), pp.2–12.

O'Connor, J. 2022. *Art, culture and the foundational economy*. Working Paper 2, Creative People, Products and Places. Adelaide: University of South Australia.

OECD. 2022. *The culture fix: creative people, places and industries, Local Economic and Employment Development (LEED)*. Paris: OECD Publishing. https://doi.org/10.1787/991bb520-en

Pacella, J., Luckman, S. and O'Connor, J. 2021. Fire, pestilence and the extractive economy: cultural policy after cultural policy. *Cultural Trends*. 30(1), pp.40–51.

Puffett, N. 2022. Controversial PWC contract has 'commercial exploitation' clause. *Arts Professional*. [Online]. 18 November. [Accessed 31 January 2023]. Available from: www.artsprofessional.co.uk/news/controversial-pwc-contract-has-commercial-exploitation-clause

Potts, J. and Cunningham, S. 2008. Four models of the creative industries. *International Journal of Cultural Policy*. 14(3), pp.233–247.

Serafini, P. and Novosel, N. 2021. Culture as care: Argentina's cultural policy response to Covid-19. *Cultural Trends*. 30(1), pp.52–62.

Siepel, J., Velez Ospina, J., Camerani, R., Bloom, M., Masucci, M. and Casadei, P. 2021. *Creative Radar 2021: the impact of COVID-19 on the UK's Creative industries*. [Online]. Creative Industries Policy and Evidence Centre. 13 July 2021. [Accessed 7 February 2023]. Available from: https://pec.ac.uk/research-reports/creative-radar-2021-the-impact-of-covid-19-on-the-uks-creative-industries

Taylor, M. 2016. Nonparticipation or different styles of participation? Alternative interpretations from Taking Part. *Cultural Trends*. 25(3), pp.169–181.

UNESCO. 2022. *Culture in times of COVID-19: resilience, recovery and revival*. Paris: UNESCO.

Walmsley, B. 2019a. *Audience engagement in the performing arts: a critical analysis*. London: Palgrave Macmillan.

Walmsley, B. 2019b. Managing change and the implications for leadership. In: Byrnes, W. and Brkić, A. eds. *The Routledge companion to arts management*. London: Routledge, pp.121–137.

Wright, J. 2020. *Policy review: cultural policy responses to COVID-19 in the UK*. Leeds: Centre for Cultural Value.

Index

EU authorised representative for GPSR:
Easy Access System Europe, Mustamäe tee 50,
10621 Tallinn, Estonia
gpsr.requests@easproject.com

www.ingramcontent.com/pod-product-compliance
Lightning Source LLC
Chambersburg PA
CBHW071015280326
41935CB00011B/1363